CUTTING EDGE: A LIFE DEDICATED TO TRANSFORMING CANCER TREATMENT

Jack A. Roth, M.D.
Cutting Edge: A Life Dedicated to Transforming Cancer Treatment

The Science, Personalities, and Politics of Cancer Treatment and Research

How I contributed to successes in helping cancer patients live longer and better, and what needs to be done to get to the next level.

Published by Spines
ISBN 979-8-89691-153-1

CUTTING EDGE: A LIFE DEDICATED TO TRANSFORMING CANCER TREATMENT

THE SCIENCE, PERSONALITIES, AND POLITICS OF CANCER TREATMENT AND RESEARCH

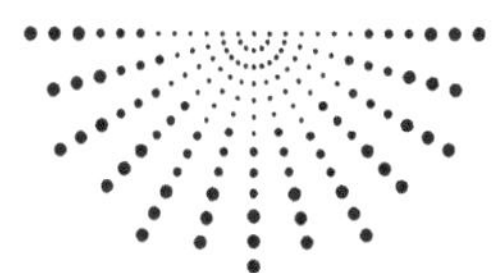

JACK A. ROTH, M.D.

Dedicated to my loving and supportive family; my colleagues, without whose tireless efforts this work would not have been possible; and the courageous patients who participated in clinical trials. I am indebted to Elizabeth Grimm, whose advice and meticulous editing were invaluable.

CONTENTS

PROLOGUE

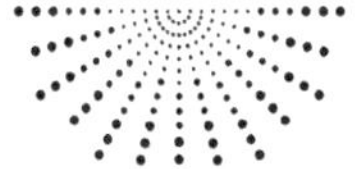

> It is not the critic who counts, not the man who points out how the strong man stumbles or where the doer of deeds could have done better. The credit belongs to the man who is in the arena.
>
> —Theodore Roosevelt

> Biographical subjects are like snakes; they are best handled dead.
>
> —Joseph Epstein

Research into the causes and treatment of cancer has made extraordinary progress over the past twenty years. This research has not only benefited cancer patients but has also fostered progress in many other medical fields, with the most recent example being the development of COVID-19 vaccines. For over forty years, my laboratory and clinical research have been dedicated to improving treatments for lung cancer and cancers arising in the chest. Discoveries made in my laboratory were focused on understanding the vulnerabilities of cancer and developing new treatments to target those vulnerabilities that can rapidly be brought to patients.

Why have I written a memoir? My primary purpose is to share those discoveries with all who are interested, address the challenges facing cancer research, and rapidly facilitate the data availability of new discoveries to the scientific community. I have described the events in this book factually and objectively, without judgment. Writing a memoir is not an exercise in modesty. My life experience has involved working with the medical-industrial complex, as well as navigating the National Cancer Institute grant-funding process, the Food and Drug Administration regulatory process, scientific journal publishing, cancer politics, and scientific awards. Thus, I feel I am qualified to comment on all these subjects and institutions and how they can be improved for the betterment of science and, ultimately, patients.

Memoirs are sometimes considered intrinsically opportunistic and self-aggrandizing. However, these faults are justified if the reader finds the story interesting or if my experience and views result in useful reforms. Every reader should make their own judgment. But do not take my word alone that the science in this book is important, has been highly cited by other scientists, and has led to significant changes in medical practice. There are objective measurements of scientific impact and value that supersede the subjectivity and politics of scientific prizes and academies. One of the important topics I discuss in this book is how the money and effort put into prize endeavors can have a negative effect on research and could be more effectively used to support early-career scientists (Chapter 7). My work, which includes over 700 peer-reviewed scientific publications, was cited over 80,000 times by other scientists (with 10 papers cited over 1,000 times each) and has been published in the highest-impact journals, including Nature and the New England Journal of Medicine. I have an h-index of 142, which is over twice as high as 12 recent Nobel laureates in three disciplines, three times that of National Academy of Science members,[1,2] and seven times greater than the median for medical researchers overall[2] [the h-index is achieved by calculating the number of publications for which an author has been cited at least that same number of times; an h-index of 10 means the author has 10 papers cited at least 10 times].[3] ResearchGate, an academic research social media site with 25,000,000 members, calculates a research interest score primarily based on citations, which places my research in the top 1 percent compared to my peers. Four days after submission, my latest publication in 2024 on BioRxiv was in the top 5 percent of research outputs and the 99th percentile of high attention scores.[4] My publications include many research firsts and practice-changing clinical trials described in detail in this memoir. My research has attracted over $100,000,000 in external research funding, with $71,000,000 awarded to me as the principal or coprincipal investigator, including continuous peer-reviewed funding from the National Cancer Institute for over 40 years. The reader can rest assured that, based on objective and reproducible measures, the science discussed herein represents progress in cancer treatment research and cancer care. However, all the views and opinions expressed in this book are entirely my own.

All this aside, I hope that reading about these adventures in surgery, cancer research, drug development, and my family life is interesting and enjoyable. I am certainly having a great time both living this life and writing about it.

1
BREAKTHROUGH

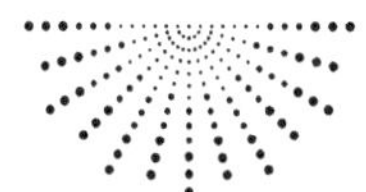

> Nothing in life is to be feared; it is only to be understood. Now is the time to understand more, so that we may fear less.
>
> —Marie Curie

"Do not bring that virus in here!" His voice increasing in intensity, one of my thoracic surgery colleagues at MD Anderson was agitated. "I am operating in the next room, and I do not want to risk infection." However, this virus was inactivated, not contagious, and posed no risk to other patients. The protocol had undergone exhaustive review by local institutional and federal regulatory committees. In addition, my operating room was sealed. This was one more obstacle to overcome, and it turned out to be the last. I finally convinced my colleague that there was no danger to his patient, and, mollified, he left the room.

These events took place in 1995, twenty-nine years prior to writing this. The patient, Joseph, and his family were desperate—a situation that, as a cancer surgeon, I had unfortunately experienced many times before. On Friday afternoon, Dr. John Nesbitt, my thoracic surgical colleague, and Dr. Randi Shea, a radiation oncologist, came into my office to talk about Joseph. Joseph had been diagnosed with left lung cancer one year ago. It could not be removed with surgery and was treated with radiation therapy. Now, narrowing of the main airway to the left lung was noted on a chest X-ray, and a cancer recurrence was suspected. I had just opened a new investigational gene therapy clinical trial. We agreed that the patient might be a candidate for the protocol and decided to bronchoscope him on Monday, which involved putting a fiberoptic tube in his airway to biopsy the suspected tumor recurrence.

What was this new clinical trial? For the past four years, our research laboratory had been developing ways of transferring genes into cancer cells. A gene is the basic unit of heredity made of the chemical DNA and located on the chromosomes in the nucleus of every cell. For many years, a controversy swirled around the cause of cancer: Are most cancers caused by viruses, or is there a central genetic mechanism responsible for cancer development? As happens frequently in science, both hypotheses were correct, and both mechanisms have now been confirmed. However, one of the major discoveries in cancer research was that the process of malignant transformation is caused by a genetic paradigm, for which Michael Bishop and Harold Varmus were awarded the Nobel Prize in 1989. The major mutations detected in cancer cells occur in dominant oncogenes and tumor suppressor genes present in normal cells, not caused by infecting viruses. Dominant oncogenes have alterations in a class of genes called proto-oncogenes, which participate in critical normal cell functions, including signaling and making proteins. Mutations in the dominant oncogenes can cause a cell to go into hyperdrive and become cancerous. There is a set of genes that opposes oncogene functions. These are called tumor suppressor genes and require the loss of function of both copies of the gene—by mutation, deletion, or a combination of these—for transformation to cancer to occur. It is possible that the modification of the expression of dominant oncogenes and tumor suppressor genes may influence certain characteristics of cells that contribute to the development, growth, and spread of cancer.

One of the most frequent findings in lung cancer is the inactivation of the tumor suppressor gene p53 by a mutation, effectively disabling the brakes that slow down cell growth. One of our earliest laboratory findings was that if we restored a normal p53 gene to a cancer cell that had a mutant p53 protein, the cancer cell would die. However, putting extra p53 genes in a normal cell had no effect on that cell. This is the holy grail of cancer drugs—a drug that selectively kills only cancer cells with no effect on normal cells, thus having no side effects. Even as I write this, I feel incredulous that our group was able to develop a gene delivery system using an inactivated type of virus called a retrovirus to deliver the p53, carry out experiments that showed the gene killed cancer cells in the test tube and in mice, and establish a process to produce a clinical-grade drug, all of which was sufficiently convincing to multiple regulatory bodies, including our institutional review board and bio-safety committee, the National Institutes of Health Recombinant DNA Advisory Committee, and the FDA, to allow us to go ahead with the clinical trial—and all the while, I was operating on patients, running and funding a research laboratory, training surgical fellows, and administering a large department.

As for Joseph, the bronchoscopy showed a tumor in the left main bronchus as well as the lower lobe. He was in good shape medically. We biopsied the tumor for p53 analysis. On Friday, a mutation was found by sequencing in regions of the DNA called exon 5, codon 130. I checked the database and found that the mutation had previously been described in lung cancer. I was elated. The patient could receive the experimental treatment. But first, my whole family, my wife, and our two daughters traveled from Houston to Leisure World, California, near Laguna Beach, to celebrate my fiftieth birthday. We had a great time with my parents and returned on Sunday. Meanwhile, a flurry of activity had resulted, and everyone was calling at the last minute. The pharmacy wanted to know how to prepare the drug. The OR was concerned about safety issues. The nurses on the floor wanted to know how to handle the isolation procedures. The anesthesiologists were in an uproar too. My research nurses were preparing all the forms and getting all the specimens. I saw Joseph in the clinic on

Friday, and he was calm. He was a tough individual who tended to complain only about minor things (in one hospital, they sold him a razor that did not work well). He refinished antique furniture in New Mexico. We were prepared for Monday.

On February 6, excitement was palpable throughout the hospital. Before going down to the operating room, I received yet another telephone call. There were eighteen people in the room. The patient had a rigid bronchoscopy done by Dr. Nesbitt. Two lesions were apparent: one in the carina between the upper and lower lobes and one in the lower lobe. The most tedious part of the procedure was debulking the two tumors. The p53 drug arrived from the pharmacy. The injection went very smoothly. The patient was extubated, but upon returning to his room, he had difficulty breathing and had to be reintubated. This was due to oversedation. I followed the patient carefully and was awake most of the night. The patient also had a fever, probably secondary to the bronchoscopy and laser treatment of the blockage. We decided to proceed with the procedure the next day.

Over the ensuing days, it was clear that the tumor was regressing. Biopsies on the fifth day showed fibrosis and inflammation but no evidence of a tumor. The patient was discharged on Monday, feeling well. There was no toxicity associated with the treatment. For the first time ever, a mutated cancer gene responsible for the patient's cancer was replaced with its normal counterpart. Eventually this would lead to treatments helping thousands of cancer patients and to the development of a drug that would go beyond directly injecting only the tumor but would be given intravenously to target all cancer cells in the body and insert a gene that directly kills cancer cells, turns off growth-signaling pathways, and stimulates an anticancer immune response—but I am getting ahead of myself.

Joseph was not cured by our gene therapy treatment. However, he lived an additional four months, and the tumor that we injected did not come back. After he died, I met with his daughter, who was very appreciative of the efforts we made. She brought me two of his handmade wooden toys, a yo-yo and a small duck on wheels, which I displayed on my bookshelf. These were exciting moments in my life that represented the culmination of years of intense study and research. But I should now go back and begin at the beginning.

2
THE BEGINNING

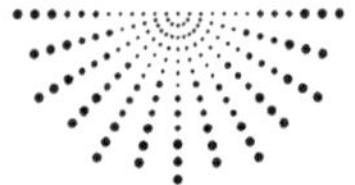

> For my part, I consider that it will be found much better by all parties to leave the past to history, especially as I propose to write that history myself.
>
> —Winston Churchill

Snow was swirling, and the temperature was frigid on January 29, 1945, when I was born in the Holy Family Hospital in La Porte, Indiana, at 7:40 a.m. I started life as an early riser. The Holy Family Hospital was a Catholic hospital run by nuns, so my birth there to two Jewish parents was auspicious. La Porte, located in the northwest corner of Indiana, had a population of about twenty thousand. Although La Porte had a Jewish cemetery, there were only a handful of live Jews in the town, mostly related to me. My birth, according to my mother, who should know, was very difficult. After the beginnings of a painful labor, a caesarean section was performed. The whole process was so traumatic for my mother that she and my father swore not to have any more children. Neither Germany nor Japan had surrendered by that date. My father, Richard Roth, was a lieutenant in the U.S. Army who spent the war as an ordnance instructor in Aberdeen, Maryland, and would not be discharged until 1946. He was a first-generation American.

The original family name of my paternal great-grandfather was Rudolselski. I am grateful to my first cousin, Allison Roth, for uncovering much of the following information. Richard (possibly Ralph) Rudolselski and his wife lived in the vicinity of Kiev (now Kyiv, Ukraine). He supervised the care of animals on a farm owned by a Russian farmer. They had a daughter and three sons, one of whom was my paternal grandfather, Joe (Josel), born on September 19, 1881. Joe landed in New York around 1904–05. The details are not clear. There is family lore, likely apocryphal, that Joe was conscripted into the Russian army to fight in the Russo-Japanese War but managed to desert and eventually disembark in New York. He lived in Cleveland briefly and then moved to Indianapolis, Indiana. The first record of this is a newspaper clipping from the Indianapolis Star documenting his arrest by sanitary officers for allegedly selling melons unfit for food at the Market House on August 30, 1912.

Indianapolis is the state capital and has been a transportation hub since the 1850s. Indianapolis became the center of the Jewish population in the state. The first Jews to the city came in 1849. The evolution of the Jewish community in Indianapolis was typical of what was happening throughout the state, with the first wave of immigrants being German Jews. By the late 1860s, Eastern Europeans began moving into the city. Indianapolis was unique because of its ethnic diversity, which allowed many of the ethnic communities to establish their own synagogues. Most Jews were peddlers (which led to dry goods stores), tailors (which led to department stores and clothing stores), grocers, or scrap dealers. The South Side Hebrew Ladies' Charity Organization established a shelter house at 907 Maple Street, which was very close to my grandfather's dwelling.

My paternal great-grandfather on my grandmother's side, Noah (Noach) Lass, was born on September 2, 1856, in Wilma, Russia, now Vilnius, Lithuania. In about 1890, he married Minnie (Menna) Feinberg (Ppfiers) in Wilma, and on October 15, 1891, a daughter, Dora, my paternal grandmother, was born. Forty percent of the population in

Wilma was Jewish. Jewish culture and population were so dominant that some Jewish national revival leaders argued for a new Jewish state to be founded in the region, with Wilma as its capital. I do not know the reason Noah left, but likely it was not due to persecution. Tragically, of my relatives remaining during World War II, over 90 percent of them were killed during the Holocaust.

On November 11, 1898, forty-two-year-old Noah arrived in New York after sailing from Hamburg, Germany, on the SS Pretoria of the Hamburg-Amerika Line. Noah found his way to Indianapolis as well. He became employed as a janitor at the county courthouse. In 1902–03, his wife, Minnie, and their daughter, Dora, joined him in Indianapolis. On Minnie's passport, which I still have, her daughter is shown accompanying her. Noah had several different jobs, including peddling and working as a janitor at the county courthouse. In 1909, Minnie filed for divorce, although she is listed as being a widow, probably because divorce was uncommon at that time, and fewer questions would be asked. Now, Minnie and her eighteen-year-old daughter were on their own in a country where they had lived for only six years. In 1911, Dora graduated high school and became employed as a bookkeeper and stenographer. Her mother, Minnie, died in 1914, and Dora went to live with her father. On the one-year anniversary of her mother's death, Dora posted this touching tribute in the Indianapolis News:

A shadow o'er my life is cast,
A precious one from me is gone.
A sad and lonely year has just passed.
Time brings no relief.
I miss her more and more each day.
Yet in memory's love, I see her
While in sorrow I weep alone.
Friends may think the wound healed.
But they little know the sorrow in my heart concealed.
YOUR SAD AND LONELY DAUGHTER, DORA LASS

However, her loneliness was, happily, short-lived, as she married Joe Roth on January 28, 1917, in Indianapolis. How they met and the details of their courtship are unknown to me. They then moved to New Castle, Indiana, because Joe was told of good opportunities there to open a store. This was around the time New Castle was struck by a tornado, killing 21 people and destroying 350 buildings. Jewish immigrants in the nineteenth century often relocated to smaller cities such as La Porte and Michigan City, where my maternal grandmother's family settled. The low startup price for businesses in smaller Indiana towns and cities was often attractive to the new Jewish immigrants compared to larger, more expensive cities.

My paternal grandparents, Joe and Dora Roth, celebrated their 50th wedding anniversary in 1967.

On December 26, 1917, their first child, my father, Richard Roth, was born. Between then and 1932, they had three more sons and two daughters. They were not latchkey kids because the doors to their home were never locked, even though Joe and Dora were working in the store. To feed all those mouths, they operated a store selling fruit and produce up to the time of the Depression and then opened a bar in the back of the store after the repeal of Prohibition in 1933. My father, aged sixteen at that time, purchased the first cases of beer for the store and began delivering it around New Castle to celebrate the end of Prohibition. Joe then received a license to open a bar in the back of their grocery store. Eventually, they booked acts in the bar, including singers and jugglers. Later that year, a deadly bar fight caused Joe to lose his license. One of the men entering the bar made a remark about another man's wife, causing a fight to erupt. One man stabbed the other with a pocketknife, resulting in a fatal injury. The man wielding the knife was convicted of second-degree murder and sentenced to prison. However, six months later, after Joe filed a lawsuit, his bar license was restored. The case was so highly publicized that an ordinance mandating midnight closing for bars was enacted. Four months later, another brawl occurred, but without fatalities. The licensing board did mandate that music and floor shows be discontinued and that the establishment operate only as a restaurant and not as a nightclub.

Despite these many setbacks, the Roth family was finally able to achieve some financial stability. One of their indelible family values was education. Dora Roth was committed to having all six of her children receive a college diploma. To this end, she was successful, with three of her children earning advanced degrees leading to careers in ophthalmology (Nate), neurosurgery (David), and law (Ruth). One daughter became a teacher (Toby). Manny Roth, the second oldest, established the Cafe Wha? in New York's Greenwich Village, which is still in business. Manny had been a B-17 navigator during World War II and had flown many missions over Europe. Many famous singers and comedians began their careers at his club, including Bob Dylan, Woody Allen, Joan Rivers, Jimi Hendrix, Richard Pryor, and Lenny Bruce. At Manny's wedding in Greenwich Village, Peter, Paul, and Mary were the entertainment. Manny later opened the Cock and Bull Club in Greenwich Village, which became the Bitter End. There is a bronze plaque memorializing him at the entrance to Cafe Wha?. Nate Roth, an ophthalmologist, was the father of David Lee Roth of Van Halen fame.

The older children took care of the younger ones. This tradition continued in my family as my father supported his siblings financially so they could complete their graduate education. My father, Richard, as the oldest, was the first to enroll in college and attended Indiana University in Bloomington, graduating in 1940. He majored in government and economics. While there, he met my mother, Bernice Saperstein, an English major and music minor. Bernice was a second-generation American, and her ancestors had followed a path like that taken by my father's parents.

Bernice's grandfather, Morris Levine (my great-grandfather) delivered milk from the family cow to nearby shtetls (small towns with predominantly Ashkenazi Jewish populations that existed in Eastern Europe before the Holocaust) in Poland. One summer day, as Morris was driving his milk cart, he noticed Dora Wortell on the front step of her home. He stopped and threw a bunch of cherries in her lap. It may have been love at first sight, or it may have been an arranged marriage, but they were married on November 10, 1874, when he was sixteen and she was fifteen. After the wedding, the ambitious Morris went to London to learn the tailoring trade, and shortly thereafter, Dora joined him. They had ten children, of whom six survived to adulthood (two sons and four daughters). Their first surviving daughter, Rachel, was born in London in 1878. They moved to Boston, where Morris opened his own tailoring shop, now employing several tailors.

My maternal great-grandparents, Morris and Dora Levine, circa the early 1900s.

In 1890, Jacob Lowenstine, Morris's cousin who had opened a clothing store in Valparaiso, Indiana, in 1885, wrote to Morris, saying that his business was prospering and that Morris should move west. This again highlights the economic advantages of opening a business in a small Midwestern town. Morris and Dora moved to Michigan City, Indiana, where he set up his tailoring business. Soon, their journey led to a calamity and possible financial ruin. A fire burned down his business, and he was without insurance. He borrowed money to open another store, which did not survive. A second store, called The Boston Store, survived, prospered, and was the heart of the business supporting my parents. Why was it named The Boston Store? There were likely several reasons. Its founder came from Boston, and at that time, Boston was the center of the clothing industry. There were several large Boston Stores in the Midwest at that time, and vendors might just assume it was a branch of the larger stores, which would help increase its credit rating.

Levine's Boston Store in La Porte 1913-1975 from the Herald Argus

My grandmother, Julia, was born in 1894, and another son, Isadore (Izzy), was born in 1897. Izzy was the first of their children to attend college at the University of Michigan, graduating from law school in 1921. He practiced law in La Porte and, in 1954, was appointed to the Supreme Court of Indiana, the first Jew to be appointed to the court.

In 1905, the La Porte Boston Store was opened and eventually renamed Levine's Boston Store to distinguish it from other Boston Stores in the Midwest. It began as a general store selling everything from tires to linoleum to groceries. This retail business ultimately flourished under the management of my father and his partner, Maurice Levine, son of Izzy. At its peak in the 1980s, Levine's Boston Store was composed of two of Morris's original department stores, eight women's and men's specialty shops, and four leased shoe departments in other stores in northern Indiana, plus sixty leased accessories and lingerie departments in ladies' apparel stretching from Youngstown, Ohio, to Grand Island, Nebraska.

Morris also took an interest in the emerging motion picture business. He organized a consortium to build a complex with stores, apartments, a hotel, and a 1,700-seat theater. This was still functioning during my childhood. Because my family were owners, I could enter to see movies for free! I loved motion pictures and would sometimes see the same movie two or three times. One thing I have in common with Steven Spielberg is a love for The Greatest Show on Earth (1952). Morris died in 1925, while Dora died in 1929.

My maternal grandparents, Jack and Julia Saperstein, with their daughter Bernice (far right), circa the early 1930s.

Morris and Dora had friends from their Boston days, Hannah and Isaac Saperstein. Hannah and Isaac were married in Boston after immigrating from Lithuania. They had a son, Jack, who was then introduced to my grandmother, Julia Levine. They were married, and my mother, Bernice, their only child, was born on January 17, 1918. They lived in La Porte, and Jack became the manager of the La Porte Boston Store. Tragically, Jack Saperstein died in 1938 from bacterial endocarditis, a condition that could be cured today with antibiotics. My grandmother and mother were both devastated by this loss, which I believe haunted them for the rest of their lives. The courage, sacrifice, resilience, and ingenuity of my ancestors are remarkable. As I sit here writing this in comfort, with protected freedom of expression and the guarantees of a lawful society, none of which they had in their countries of origin, I can only feel profound respect, love, and gratitude.

Richard was an active brother in the Sigma Alpha Mu fraternity at Indiana University. Through social events with the Sigma Delta Tau sorority, he met Bernice. Bernice said she was not only attracted to Richard but also noted the benefit of taking on his short surname should they be married, at a time when assuming the husband's surname was traditional.

My parents, June 13, 1942.

Richard Roth married Bernice Saperstein in La Porte, Indiana, on June 13, 1942. Immediately after they were married, Richard was called to serve as an officer in the Army, fighting in World War II. Richard was inducted into the service at Camp Benjamin Harrison, Indianapolis, in 1942 and was immediately put on KP. He then shipped to Aberdeen, Maryland, for ordnance training. His next assignment was in Cincinnati, inspecting an ordnance plant, checking the hardness of shells and tank parts. He rose to the rank of lieutenant and was honorably discharged in 1946.

And all this led to my birth on that frigid January day in La Porte.

3

THE FORMATIVE YEARS

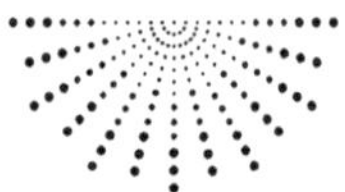

Any sufficiently advanced technology is indistinguishable from magic.
—Isaac Asimov

La Porte is a city in the northwestern corner of Indiana. French fur traders, possibly dating from the seventeenth century La Salle, called the land in what is now La Porte county la porte (meaning the door in French) because it was an opening for Indigenous trails to the prairie beyond.[5] There are four beautiful lakes in the region, and in the 1850s, numerous maple trees were planted, and La Porte became known as the Maple City. The first settlement by non-Indigenous people was in 1832. The United States extinguished land claims by the Potawatomi and other historic tribes of the area by treaty and removal to Indian Territory, and in 1833, a federal land office was established in La Porte. In 1894, the current La Porte County Courthouse was opened. It is a classic Midwestern building of red sandstone that dominates the town, standing in the center square. In 1950, the population of La Porte was 17,882, and in 2020, it was 22,471. There is a single main street called Lincoln way, and Levine's Boston Store and the movie theater were located there. In the 1950s, manufacturing was thriving in La Porte. Allis Chalmers assembled farm machinery. Whirlpool had an appliance center there. Bendix and Studebaker automobiles were nearby in South Bend. La Porte was surrounded by farms that used the city as a distribution hub.

After my father returned from military service in 1946, he, my mother, and my maternal grandmother, Julia, lived together in a small white bungalow in La Porte. My grandmother became a major caregiver for me and her brother, Jae, who was disabled from a stroke, a role that expanded when my mother started working full-time at the store. La Porte was a tranquil town to grow up in during the 1950s, and it seemed that most families there valued education and a system that provided a diversity of activities for children. The town was not diverse in terms of ethnicity. I recall only one Black student and no Hispanic students. I was the only student of Jewish descent in my class, although there were a handful in other classes. There was no systematic antisemitism, and by then, the visible Ku Klux Klan had disappeared from our region of Indiana. However, since I did not participate in the church groups, which were a focus of social activity, I was aware that I was an outsider. This was not necessarily detrimental because it forced one to develop independence of thought and purpose. Nevertheless, I always felt I was striving to be accepted.

My earliest memories are from around age five when I started kindergarten. Preschools did not exist in La Porte, or if they did, my parents did not consider them. The school system consisted of several elementary schools for kindergarten through sixth grade, a middle school for seventh and eighth grades, and a single high school for grades 9–12. I went to the school nearest my home, Lincoln Elementary. The curriculum was relatively easy for me, and I received top grades. This absence of intellectual challenge likely fostered risk-taking, a characteristic I credit with being responsible for much of my success in clinical and laboratory research. If you are focused on the safety of incremental experiments and clinical trials, you will not make the big breakthroughs. Neither my elementary nor middle school had any type of gifted program, so I instead developed a wide range of interests and read voraciously. This chapter will appeal to anyone with a love of 1950s nostalgia.

My parents were able to provide many interesting activities early on. One of the first was an Erector Set, which had various-sized metal beams with regularly spaced holes, sheet metal in various sizes, rods, screw clamps, gears, and motors. I was always building. By fifth grade, I was able to construct a self-propelled robot with swinging arms that I proudly showed to my class. Of course, microchips and robotics did not exist then, so the movement and control were limited. I had multiple chemistry sets and remember doing various mixing experiments. Fortunately, none of these sets contained explosives, but the chemicals did stain clothing, to the consternation of my grandmother. My microscope set was fascinating, allowing a detailed view of the minutiae surrounding me. I also used it to examine clues when I played detective. I received a model train set as a gift, and this was the impetus for my father and me to construct a city and landscape in our basement for the train. I must have played alone often as an only child, but this helped me develop imagination and creativity. Much of what I learned was self-taught, which served me well during my career as I ventured into fields where I had little or no formal education.

The retail business was going well for my family, and a decision was made to build a new house. My grandmother Saperstein's brother, Jae, had land behind his home that fronted on a major street in one of the nicest neighborhoods in La Porte, which he generously provided. My father took a major interest in the design and construction, which included innovations such as radiant wall heating and concrete block walls (perhaps they were anticipating tornadoes or nuclear war). Our new house had two rooms where I spent much time: a library and a finished basement with a stage for students of my mother's speech lessons and a record player.

I had an aggressive streak as a child. The Korean War was on, and toy soldiers were everywhere in stores. I persuaded my parents and grandmother to purchase these whenever I could. I was also given a treasure trove of metal soldiers likely dating back to World Wars I and II. Merging these provided large enough companies to engage in battles with my friends and cousins, which I did at every opportunity. The stage in our basement provided the perfect battlefield. However, the sine qua non for make-believe military games was genuine U.S. Army and Navy gear, which I obtained from my grandparents' army/navy surplus store in New Castle. This included helmets, backpacks, spades for digging foxholes, canteens, ammunition belts (no live bullets), and pea jackets. I loved to browse that store, and, of course, my grandparents did not make me pay. The only guns I had as a child were toys, such as cap pistols into which you insert a roll of tape with small nodules of a low-level explosive that pops when the pistol is fired. Guns and hunting were not part of my family's culture.

My mother majored in English literature in college. She loved Shakespeare's plays and directed plays for the La Porte Little Theater Club. My father and I were recruited for various roles in these plays. I remember roles in Cheaper by the Dozen and I Remember Mama. During the latter, there was a grandfatherly character who sang me a song before bedtime:

10,000 Swedes ran through the weeds
At the Battle of Copenhagen,
10,000 Swedes ran through the weeds
Chasing one Norwegian.

I loved that song, and during every rehearsal, I would ask him to sing it over and over.

The stage in the basement of our house was built for a purpose. My mother taught public speaking and speech recitals to La Porte's children. She called them elocution lessons. These occurred after school, and I was able to sit in on many of them. Here, I learned some of the most important lessons in communication: Speak to the last person in the back of the room. Slow down. Pronounce each word distinctly. Her directions and my further experience in debate in high school honed my public-speaking skills, enabling me to clearly communicate scientific findings and present scientific papers at national and international meetings to frequent acclaim.

I loved magic tricks. I purchased them from stores and by mail. A large pitcher of water was poured into a cone made of rolled-up newspaper. The water disappeared! A vase could be continually emptied of water and would mysteriously fill up again. Silk scarves were rolled up in your hand and would disappear. There was a neat device that looked like a small guillotine. You placed your finger through one opening and a cigarette in another smaller opening. Then you would lower the blade. The cigarette was cut in half, but amazingly, your finger remained intact! I put together a thirty-minute magic show, which I began performing for family, friends, and at school. My stage training helped me develop a compelling presentation. I even had a female assistant. The word got out, and I began receiving invitations to perform at church meetings, such as the Methodist Men's Club Father-Son banquet and other events. Although I loved magic and read extensively about famous magicians, I fortunately avoided developing magical thinking, which would have been highly detrimental in my subsequent medical and research careers.

The 1950s were a golden age for both motion pictures and television. At the time, television was thought to be the death knell for the movies, but both media upped their games. I will mention some of my favorite entertainments growing up in case there are still a few readers who enjoy 1950s nostalgia. I Love Lucy, the situation comedy with Lucille Ball and Desi Arnaz, was a family favorite. Many old movies and serials appeared regularly on television. The Flash Gordon serials from the 1930s starring Buster Crabbe were my favorite. Each episode always ended with a cliffhanger enticing you to watch the next episode. Westerns were another favorite. The Lone Ranger with his horse, Silver, and sidekick, Tonto (played by the Indigenous Canadian Jay Silverheels), and Hopalong Cassidy and his horse, Topper, were the best. The music at the beginning of each Lone Ranger episode is a section of the "William Tell Overture" by Gioachino Rossini. Only the last section of the overture was played with the famous trumpet fanfare. This was another introduction to classical music, but for years, I thought this was the entire overture. There are three other sections that precede it! Of course, I had to have all the associated gear. Today, I still have my Hopalong Cassidy cookie jar displayed proudly in our kitchen. Movies were shown on TV, and I loved the old horror movies. It was a thrill to stay up late with my dad to watch the original Frankenstein and Dracula.

The Hopalong Cassidy cookie jar

Disney was entering television during this time. The Mickey Mouse Club was good after-school entertainment. I did not care much for the singing and dancing. However, there was a serial called Spin and Marty taking place at a dude ranch. Spin was the popular kid with horse-riding and roping skills. Marty was a rich orphan who arrives at the ranch in a limo and is contemptuous but finally overcomes his fear of horses and wins acceptance, becoming a close friend of Spin's. I could see myself as the outsider and was very emotionally involved in the series.

There were fine dramatic performances. Playhouse 90 stands out with productions such as Days of Wine and Roses and Requiem for a Heavyweight. Although I was quite young at the time, I was enthralled by the drama, even though I did not understand all the implications and plot twists. And then there were the quiz shows, including

What's My Line, the $64,000 Question, and 21. These were fascinating not only because of the drama of watching the contestants sweat but also because of the challenge of answering the questions. It was disheartening to eventually learn this was all a fraud, with the contestants given the questions and answers beforehand. When contestants lost in the early rounds, ratings dropped, and so the producers wanted to ensure dramatic success. The exposure of this charade was a good lesson to me about the sanctity of personal integrity. I also recall the drama of many current events, including the McCarthy congressional hearings and televised nuclear bomb tests. Although the 1950s are often remembered as a peaceful, golden age for America, there were strong, anxiety-provoking undercurrents stoked by fear-mongering McCarthyites and the specter of nuclear confrontation with the Soviet Union.

My family owned a movie theater in La Porte, built during the earliest days of the motion picture but recently renovated with a wide CinemaScope screen. The 1950s were a golden age, producing many of the greatest motion pictures. On the Waterfront (1954) was a riveting drama, and I saw great acting on the screen for the first time. I was unaware of the behind-the-scenes drama related to the House Committee on Un-American Activities when the director, Elia Kazan, named individuals in Hollywood as possible communists. Marty(1955) was a touching love story about two lonely people who find each other. There were the sand and sandals films like Land of the Pharaohs with spectacle that enthralled my ten-year-old self. And then there were the westerns, many of them written with a psychological twist that revolved around a hero much different from those of the gunslingers on white horses of the 1920s and 1930s. My favorite was Shane (1953), which I must have seen three or four times. It is about a loner who saves homesteaders harassed by cattle barons. There is an iconic scene at the end where Shane, wounded in a gunfight, rides away while the young boy who has befriended him calls for him to come back. The concept of the outsider who would take on risks was inspiring to me. And then there was the excitement of the new technology of three-dimensional (3D) cinema. I would put on cardboard spectacles with polarizing filters before viewing the movie. The first 3D movie of my generation was Bwana Devil. The story and acting were forgettable, but I remember one of the first scenes when a spear is hurled directly at the audience, accompanied by audible gasps and screams.

One of my favorite rooms in our new house was the library. The room had built-in bookshelves, a fireplace, and was home to our new stereo record player. My parents read extensively, and the shelves were filled with classics and new bestsellers. I read voraciously. One fascinating book was The Egyptian, which stimulated my interest in ancient Egypt. It is a historical novel by Mika Waltari that tells the story through the eyes of Sinuhe, a physician, of the reign of Pharaoh Akhenaten of the Eighteenth Dynasty, whom some have claimed to be the first monotheistic ruler in the world. Another fascinating book was Kon-Tiki by Thor Heyerdahl. Heyerdahl believed that people from South America could have reached Polynesia during pre-Columbian times. He mounted the Kon-Tiki expedition by building a raft with only the materials and techniques from that time to show that there were no technical reasons to prevent this migration. Both books highlighted extraordinary individuals who were brave enough to challenge existing dogma.

My parents had a collection of shellac 78 rpm records, which was the technology that preceded the long-playing 33 rpm vinyl records. We had a Victrola, and the turntable had an arm with a metal stylus. If you dropped a record, it shattered. The playing time was twelve minutes per side, and the sound was distorted but still music to my young ears. I loved to listen to everything in their collection, which was eclectic. There was the Anvil Chorus from Verdi's Il Trovatore, probably my first introduction to opera as well as music from films and operetta. Also, this engendered a lifelong love of music that would lead to developing musical skills and ultimately playing a role in major music professional performance companies. It also began a campaign to get my parents' approval for upgrading to a high-fidelity playback system that was compatible with the new LP discs. I was exposed to music in other ways. My parents awoke every morning to a clock radio set to the local radio station playing the top hits. I am not sure how many times I heard the Shirelles' "Will You Still Love Me Tomorrow" at 7:00 a.m., but it made a big impression on my middle school psyche. Frankie Valli and the Four Seasons was another group that made an impression, and seeing Jersey Boys on Broadway many years later was a nostalgic trip. Leonard Bernstein initiated a wonderful series of Young People's Concerts on the CBS television network from 1958 to 1972. I tuned in to all of them. The concert that really inspired me was the 1960 "Who Is Gustav Mahler?" This was the first I had heard of Mahler and his music. The performances, combined with Bernstein's musical and personal insights into the composer and his music, were spellbinding. He created for me a musical experience that has lasted a lifetime. At this time, our new hi-fi was in place, and Mahler's symphonies were being recorded in the LP format. I eventually acquired the entire Solti symphony cycle as well as many other recordings. Mahler remains, for me to this day, a composer who captured and expressed all of life's experiences in the most beautiful, expressive, and emotionally affecting music. I still tear up when I hear any one of his works.

Fortunately for me, the La Porte school system at that time had a large, active, and high-quality music program. It began in the fourth grade with the introduction of the flutophone, a pre-band instrument very similar to the recorder. Using this, we learned to read and play music with very elementary treble clef fingerings. This rapidly led to a major decision about which instrument to play in the band. I decided to play the trumpet because I liked brass music, and the instrument seemed very cool, not realizing ultimately how difficult it would be to play it well and continue to play over a lifetime. There was, in La Porte, a store, the Roxie Music Shop, that specialized in everything musical, including instruments, sheet music, and records. I started on the cornet, a somewhat abbreviated version of the trumpet, but later moved up to a trumpet in high school. There was a private music teacher in La Porte for trumpet, Robert McQuaig, who lived only a few blocks from us. He played professionally and was responsible for all my progress on the instrument. He had two sons who, of course, played instruments not usually chosen but greatly needed by our school band and orchestra—oboe and bassoon. I must have progressed rapidly because, by age twelve, I was in the middle school band, sitting fourth chair out of twenty-two, many of whom were older. By 1961, I was the second trumpet and, in the following years, the principal trumpet in the band, jazz band, and orchestra. I was disciplined enough to practice at least an hour each day. I was also the student conductor in both junior high and high school.

Every year, there were regional and state competitions for both individuals and ensembles. The director of our high school instrumental groups was Guy Foreman, who was a master at preparing the band and orchestra for these competitions. The competition involved playing three prepared pieces and sight-reading two pieces not previously published. In my senior year, the three pieces were the Dunedin March by Alford, the Phedre Overture by Massenet, and the first movement of "Symphony No. 2" by Borodin. Sight reading included a march and excerpts from Rienzi by Wagner. Throughout my time in high school, our band and orchestra won first place every year, and by my senior year, 1963, that was extended to eight consecutive years. The solo competitions were a real challenge. My private teacher would select a solo piece that was always above my current level. I would memorize it and play with piano accompaniment. I began competing in sixth grade and continued through high school. I remember some very difficult solos, such as the Grand Russian Fantasia with lots of triple tonguing. The most difficult of all was a solo played by the Mexican trumpet player Rafael Mendez—often called the greatest trumpet player of all time—called La Virgen de la Macarena, or Bullfighters Song. It is fiendishly difficult and ends with a high C, which you need to hit with very tired lips. Here is a link to Mendez playing it: https://www.youtube.com/watch?v=Dk6kmnnzCfI. I worked it up, memorized it, and performed it without a mistake at the competition. Afterward, the judge came up to me, glared, and said, "I am going to give you second place because I did not like your tone. It sounded pinched." My bandmates heard about this from my piano accompanist and classmate, Kathy Link, and consoled me. It was an important lesson: you can work hard, do your best, and still fail. If you are going to achieve your goals, you need to continue to improve your abilities. Overall, I received eighteen medals in these competitions, with eleven of them being gold in both the solo and ensemble categories. A group of us formed a dance band to play for money at various school dances and other functions. This was an instrumental group with trumpet, alto and baritone saxes, bass, and drums. Rock and roll was still in its infancy in La Porte, so there were no electric guitars. After the band formed, the drummer pulled me aside and said, "If we are getting paid to play, you need to be a member of the union." This was clearly an offer I could not refuse. The union was the American Federation of Musicians, of which I was a card-carrying member for two years. I continued to play in college, and in medical school, there was an odd annual event called the Turtle Derby, culminating in a turtle race, that had a band in which I played. I continued to play from time to time, mostly at holiday events at the National Cancer Institute or MD Anderson. However, the lack of practice and an aging embouchure took their toll, and I am no longer able to play.

Music became a great avocation and a significant part of my life early on in middle school and up to the present. I remember very infrequent performances by live orchestras touring through La Porte and playing in the Civic Center auditorium, but most of my exposure to music was via recordings. Fortunately, this was the golden age of the long-playing vinyl record. I subscribed to High Fidelity magazine to learn about the newest recordings. It seemed like every month recordings of works never before available were released. The greatest orchestras, New York Philharmonic, Vienna Philharmonic, Boston Symphony, Chicago Symphony, with the greatest conductors, Solti, Bernstein, Reiner, Karajan, and Walter, would appear. My favorite recordings were conducted by the legendary Arturo Toscanini. Most were with the NBC Symphony, the orchestra that was formed specifically for him after he left the New York Philharmonic. However, there was a remastered recording of the Beethoven Seventh Symphony with the New York Philharmonic that remains one of the greatest symphonic recordings. I acquired a complete set of the Beethoven symphonies. Works such as the Berlioz and Verdi requiems appeared and were artistic and sonic masterpieces. After the Bernstein television program on Mahler, I began accumulating various versions of his symphonies and lieder.

The band and orchestra played transcriptions of difficult works by great composers. The orchestra played works by Mozart, Dvorak, Wagner, and Boccherini. Works by Massenet, Rimsky-Korsakov, Borodin, and Johann Strauss were on my senior-year band program. Exposure to these composers whetted my appetite for more classical music. My parents traveled to New York every year to place merchandise orders for the stores. There was a large record store in New York called Sam Goody, which had a huge selection of classical, jazz, and popular LPs. I would give a wish list to my parents, and they graciously returned bearing the albums. They returned one year with an album entitled Toscanini Conducts Wagner. This was only the orchestral music, but after listening, I was hooked. The prelude to the third act of Lohengrin, the prelude to Die Meistersinger, and Siegfried's funeral music were spellbinding. Thus began a lifelong love of Wagner's music. I knew little of the controversy surrounding Wagner's personal life and had never heard his complete operas performed live or recorded. However, I read about the new release of the first complete stereophonic recording of Wagners Der Ring des Nibelungen, conducted by Georg Solti with Birgit Nilsson in the role of Brunnhilde. I listened raptly to each opera of the Ring cycle as they were released. It was only much later, after reading multiple books on Wagner's life and works, that I became aware of the depth of his antisemitism in his personal beliefs and writings. This cannot be excused or rationalized as simply a manifestation of the time and culture in which he lived; it forever reflects poorly on his character. However, Wagner has not been canceled. His works continue to be performed worldwide, and there are 147 Wagner societies with 26,000 members. His music has been compartmentalized. Wagner's artistic integrity was such that his operas reflected life and art as opposed to being political or social statements (although there are infrequent exceptions, e.g., Hans Sachs praising German art at the conclusion of Die

Meistersinger). Wagner portrays an ambiguous moral universe that, in the end, favors justice, love, forgiveness, and compassion. As Patrick Summers, artistic and music director of Houston Grand Opera, said to me, "Someone who can compose the third act of Siegfried cannot be all evil." Wagner's operas are populated with loners and outsiders, such as the Dutchman, Lohengrin, Parsifal, and Siegfried, who overcome personal hardships to eventually triumph. These themes inspired me in what has become an underlying theme in this narrative.

Classical music was not my only interest. I played in a dance band in high school and became interested in jazz. Of course, I listened most to the jazz trumpet. Dizzy Gillespie was incredible technically, and his improvisations were amazing. I was able to find remastered early recordings with Charlie Parker, who changed the concept of jazz with his saxophone. Miles Davis, Maynard Ferguson (who could hit the highest of high notes), and Doc Severinsen were other favorites. Dave Brubeck and Cannonball Adderley were cool, and our band used riffs from their pieces. I listened to popular music as well, including the Beatles, the Rolling Stones, the Beach Boys, Tina Turner, and the Temptations, all of whom I have heard in live concerts. I had eclectic tastes. Music that was creative, innovative, and technically well played could appeal to me irrespective of the genre. Liz and I still enjoy going to jukebox musicals on Broadway that celebrate the life stories of these groups.

Middle school, grades 7 and 8, was held in a separate building on the block adjacent to my elementary school and next to the high school. Academics were very straightforward, and once again, I received top grades. I was in the band, and we formed a trumpet trio. The Daughters of the American Revolution sponsored a history test and award for seventh-grade students, which I won for both semesters. I had no inkling at the time that I would marry a Daughter of the American Revolution with historic links on both sides of her family, but that story begins twenty years later. I attended my uncle David's medical school graduation from the Johns Hopkins School of Medicine in 1959. Little did I realize that eight years later, I would be enrolling in the same medical school.

Entering high school was a big deal, with a new building and a potential new group of friends transferring from the local Catholic school. Of course, you entered at the bottom of the ladder as a freshman. It was an exciting time. I realized I needed the highest academic achievement possible, along with meaningful extracurricular service activities, if I was to be accepted by one of the top universities. Fortunately, my high school provided all the opportunities; I just needed to take advantage of them. I was focused on music. I really enjoyed playing in the various ensembles. I had tried out for some athletic teams, but it was clear, because of my size and mediocre ability, that I would spend most of my time on the bench. I was a member of the bowling club, but I cannot remember attending many competitions. There was a new bowling center just on the outskirts of town. It also had pinball machines, and I think I spent more time with those than bowling. However, there was a new interest developing relating to my past exposure to public speaking and acting—debate. I was always an argumentative sort, which sometimes got me into trouble and certainly caused some to dislike me. Nevertheless, I could not tolerate fools, and I let them know if I disagreed and why. Thus, I was naturally drawn to the debate team.

The debate format at that time was straightforward. A statement was presented, such as "Resolved, That all United States Ambassadors should be career diplomats." Each team consisted of two debaters, one of whom argued the positive case, while the other argued the negative case. The first presented their case, positive or negative, and the second was charged with rebutting the opposing team's arguments. I got off to a great start as a sophomore. Our team of first-time debaters competed in a tournament at Jefferson High School in Lafayette with sixteen other schools. We came in first. In the Indiana High School Forensic Association district tournament, our team again came in first. The following year, our team was invited to appear on the television show Rebuttal, broadcast on Chicago's WBBM-TV, to do a televised debate.

All was not smooth sailing. Our nemesis was a team from Hammond Morton High School. Hammond is a suburb of Chicago near the Indiana-Illinois border. The Hammond team was extremely smooth and looked like they had just walked out of a motion picture studio. The male debater bore an uncanny resemblance to Robert Redford, and his female teammate, who handled the rebuttals, was drop-dead gorgeous and whip-smart. The first time we competed against them, we were annihilated. Afterward, my teammate, Kathy Jacomb, and I strategized extensively for the next debate. We knew we would meet the Hammond team again. We had a new and very challenging topic: "Resolved, War between the United States and the Soviet Union Is Inevitable." I spent hours in the library going over current event speeches and documents by U.S. and Soviet government officials. Kathy and I were assigned the negative side. Hammond's opening arguments were contained in a pre-prepared speech, and of course, Kathy and I had heard it before. Her arguments were on point and delivered forcefully. I was the last speaker and was charged with the negative rebuttal. I was able to destroy the Hammond team's arguments point by point. Finally, I was positioned for the coup de grace. I had found a direct quote from the then-current Soviet leader Nikita Khrushchev, where he states unambiguously, "War is not inevitable." The looks of disgust on our opponents' faces were priceless when our team was announced as the winner. That was a sweet victory.

The pinnacle of my brief debating career was the Purdue Legislative Assembly, which I attended for three consecutive years. The assembly was modeled on the state legislature based on parliamentary procedure, with ninety students in the House of Representatives and seventy in the Senate, all elected from across the state. For example, in my senior year, I was in the Senate and introduced a bill putting Indiana schools on a year-round trimester plan. Surprisingly, the bill passed with no amendments and was the sole bill passed by the Senate that year. I was elected a Top 10 Legislator for all three years, which was a first for La Porte High School.

The debate and legislative experience propelled me into politics. I decided to run for student council president, the highest office in our high school. I recognized that, not being a jock or a super-popular guy, I would need a strategy. There were three other officers (vice president, secretary, treasurer), and I convinced a prominent three-sport letterman, a cheerleader, and a very intelligent female student with a great personality to run with me so the ticket was balanced. Then I appointed a good friend from one of La Porte's most prominent families, who was also universally well-liked, to be my campaign manager, promising him that I would support him for senior class president. We named our party the Privilege Party with the motto "More student privileges through better student government." We were running against two other parties. One party with two jocks was named the Launch Party with the slogan "While others are out to lunch, we'll be out to launch," clearly too much of a negative vibe. The presidential candidates made speeches to the student assembly. After mine, one of the candidates for president, who had always been a frenemy, came up to me, visibly upset, and said, "You didn't need to give an oration!" When the votes were counted, we won.

It appeared that I was headed toward a career in law or public service, like my great-uncle Izzy, who became a justice on the Indiana Supreme Court. But I also had a passion for science. In my junior year, I was selected as one of sixty applicants out of four hundred for the High School Science Institute held during the summer at Indiana University in Bloomington, the same campus my parents attended. The program was funded by the National Science Foundation. One disappointment was that I would miss Boys State as a delegate because of the conflicting dates. I had previously attended the Junior Engineers and Scientists Summer Institute at DePauw University in 1961. The IU program consisted of lectures, Russian language lessons, and hands-on experience with graduate students in the sciences. We lived in the university dormitories. I was paired with a chemistry grad student who was studying the chemical bonds of the trace element boron. By the end of the program, I was doing experiments independently.

I really was not prepared for the unique experiences of my senior year. After four years of planning and three million in 1962 dollars (almost twenty-seven million in today's dollars), the new La Porte High School was opening its doors. It was state-of-the-art and the first centrally air-conditioned school in La Porte. The classrooms and laboratories were modular. There was a large cafeteria, which could be repurposed as a study hall or meeting room, and excellent athletic facilities. As incoming student body president, I had a long to-do list.

Graduation from La Porte High School with my parents and the high school building, 1963, from the Herald Argus.

The first order of business was the new high school dedication ceremony. On Sunday, October 14, 1962, at 3:00 p.m., the dedication ceremony began with the high school symphony playing Berlioz's Rakoczy March. George Boklund, the president of the school board, made a presentation, and I, as student council president, was called to respond. The text of my response that day has long since vanished, but I did find a letter from the school superintendent and high school principal stating, "You carried your part of the program in a superb manner," so I must have said the right stuff.

One of our campaign promises was to establish a student paperback bookstore that would be affordable and stock a wide range of books beyond our high school curriculum. We located a room for this and identified the funding. Student council members would staff the store, which became very popular. However, it also stoked a major controversy. One of the young new English teachers was interested in discussing the ideas of the John Birch Society, which was a right-wing political advocacy group supporting social conservatism. It was staunchly anticommunist and promoted some very far-out conspiracy theories. The founder, Robert W. Welch Jr., authored the Blue Book of the John Birch Society, which somehow made its way into the bookstore and into the hands of several students. Parents found out about this and demanded that all copies of the book be removed and that no discussion of these ideas be permitted in classes. The English teacher defended the book using arguments based on freedom of speech and expression. He lost, and the book was removed. His tenure at the high school was relatively brief. Despite all the controversy, the bookstore not only survived but continued to be used frequently by many students.

I completed my time in high school with other awards, including Honor Society president, National Merit Scholar, United Nations essay contest winner, and the Elks Lodge Leadership Award. A couple of weeks before the end of the year, I was told that I would be valedictorian, and this was described in a ceremony published in the local paper. However, a week later, I was called into my college counselor's office and told there had been an error. Apparently, the mother of one of the female students thought her daughter had perfect grades. This triggered a review, which showed that, as a freshman, I received a C in my only physical education class. The instructor did not think much of my athleticism. Whenever I performed an exercise or competed, the instructor, who was also an assistant coach, would sneer at me or make some derogatory comment. There was no attempt to help or provide a program for increased fitness. The female student in question had been excused from all physical education classes for "health reasons." I knew this student, and although she was well enough to never miss class, she was not a fit athlete. When my PE grade was averaged in, I was lower compared to her all-academic average. I did not protest because it was a meaningless and insignificant issue. I had been accepted at Cornell, and nothing would change. Now high schools look exclusively at academics and award multiple valedictory titles to placate highly competitive students and parents. It emphasized to me the lack of importance of the grading system. The real reward for education is learning how to learn and developing critical thinking. Much later in my professional life, I met colleagues from La Porte. Three other La Porte High School students from the three years preceding my graduation became cardiothoracic surgeons. Was there something in the drinking water?

4
THE EDUCATION OF JACK ROTH

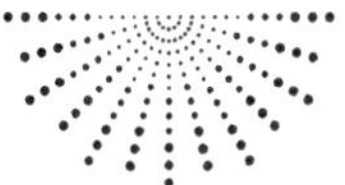

We do not learn from experience... we learn from reflecting on experience.
—John Dewey

College applications were a big part of my senior year. My priority was to be accepted at a university or college with top academic credentials. I did not have a specific career in mind but knew I would probably need additional postgraduate education. Cornell University seemed to be a good fit. It had world-class departments in economics, physics, history, and government, all of which were strong interests of mine. The structure of the university was unique in that it had a combination of privately funded arts and sciences, architecture, and engineering colleges coexisting with state-funded programs, including industrial and labor relations, business, and public policy, which added to the diversity of the student body. All this was present on one of the most beautiful campuses in North America, with hills, lakes, and gorges. An added benefit was that the campus was about as far away as possible from La Porte, as I was eager to leave home. I was accepted and decided to start immediately with summer school.

Cornell required one year of foreign language credits. Languages were difficult for me, so I wanted to take courses that would not be counted toward my GPA to fulfill the requirement. I had taken several years of French in high school; thus, that was the logical choice. However, I could never convincingly imitate a French accent. This caused my instructor, who was a native Frenchman, to conclude that I was not a serious student of the language. Fortunately, the grade, while satisfying the requirement, would not appear on my transcript. I had three roommates, including two from the Bronx High School of Science, who were entering Dartmouth in the fall and spent most of their time trying to solve calculus problems. The third fellow was failing his summer course, this being the first time he was on his own and away from his parents, and he never entered the freshman class at Cornell.

I returned in the fall with housing in a brick-façade contemporary-design dormitory and a roommate from Colorado who seemed more interested in social rather than academic activities. The dormitory had a cafeteria euphemistically named the Barf Bar. I was enrolled in the College of Arts and Sciences. I was still unsure about the direction of my postgraduate education, with law and medicine being the primary choices. So I decided to fulfill the premed requirements along with a major that would be interesting and acceptable to law schools. My courses included chemistry, economics, a final French course, and calculus.

The one indelible memory from that year was the assassination of President John F. Kennedy. I was in my dorm room on November 22, 1963, when I heard a loud discussion in the hall. I was told that the president had been shot but thought it could not be true. I made my way down to the common room, which had a television, and watched the story unfold. I was engulfed by this feeling of sadness and loss. Kennedy was an idol to most of us and represented the future direction of the country. The previous year, we were spellbound by the Cuban missile crisis and thought that Kennedy's handling of it was courageous. Now he was gone, and I was unsure what the future would bring. I had a college deferment for the Vietnam War, but the future was an unknown abyss. The rest of the year was overshadowed by this one event.

During this year, I was presented with a decision —should I join a fraternity? It was coincidental that the first chapter of Sigma Delta Tau, my mother's sorority, and the second chapter of Sigma Alpha Mu, my father's fraternity, were established at Cornell University. All the Ivy League schools have student-run organizations that are selective; some would say elitist in their choice of members. At Cornell, there were many fraternities and sororities, although these played no role in my decision to go there. In the spring, formal rush began. I decided to participate, primarily out of curiosity. My roommate was determined to join the highest socially rated fraternity. Fraternity brothers would enter your room for an interview. If you passed that, you would be invited to the fraternity house to meet all the brothers. During one of the visits, the fraternity man went to my closet to look at the labels on my clothes. They were obviously not from the right stores, as I was not invited to visit that fraternity. This was a great lesson in fraternity values. But the major issue for me was the constant distractions and pressure for social events, which could interfere with studying. I was invited to become a pledge in the Sigma Alpha Mu fraternity, my father's fraternity at Indiana University, which I declined. My parents thought my college career was ruined. However, on the contrary, this was one of the best decisions of my early life, as it eliminated many distractions that derailed some of my classmates. My freshman college roommate proudly joined the most socially prominent fraternity on campus, Chi Psi. A week before graduation, we saw each other for the first time since freshman year. When I told him I was entering the Johns Hopkins School of Medicine, his jaw visibly dropped. He did not have any postgraduate plans. When I looked up the Cornell chapter today, I found that it is on probation for hazing. The year passed quickly. The grading scale at Cornell was numerical, and there was no grade inflation. A grade of 85 or higher was considered excellent. Despite a heavy class schedule, I made the dean's list, which I would then do again for the following three years.

For the summer, I decided to take a break from academics and work in a book warehouse that opened on the outskirts of La Porte. This went well for a while, with the manager bragging to anyone who would listen that he had a college student from Cornell working for him. The way it worked was that you would get a list of books in the shipment and then find them on the warehouse shelves, stacking them on a cart to take to the shipping dock. One day, I had a large order, which I stacked carefully so I would make only one trip. On my way to the shipping dock, the stack became unbalanced and collapsed, strewing books everywhere. Just as this happened, the manager was walking by. I was fired the following week.

Returning to Cornell in the fall for my sophomore year, I needed living arrangements. At the end of the previous year, I found three others who wanted to share an off-campus apartment. It needed some painting and fixing up, and my dad helped. One roommate, Arnie, was from Westchester County, New York. He had gone to summer camps in the Catskills and would strum his guitar and sing "This Little Light of Mine" until we pleaded with him to stop. He had not been accepted by the fraternity of his choice and still tried to hang out with the fraternity brothers at every opportunity, such as joining their table in the student union; although, sadly, he was never fully accepted. Another roommate, Don, was his polar opposite from Hazleton, Pennsylvania, which had prospered as a center for coal mining but now faced hard times. Neither Arnie nor Don could hide their contempt for each other due to their disparate origins and backgrounds. This made for some uncomfortable confrontations and the occasional need to physically restrain them, though Arnie would have come out on the short end of any fight with the much bigger Don. I would just go to class and spend my evenings studying in the library.

I needed to choose a major. One of the highlights of my time at Cornell was an economics class in my sophomore year taught by Alfred E. Kahn. The course was divided into two semesters for micro- and macroeconomic theories. Microeconomics focuses on the behavior of the individual and the economic forces that can modify that behavior. Macroeconomics focuses on general, large-scale economic forces, such as interest rates and productivity, that influence national and international economies. Kahn was a dynamic and humorous lecturer who could make the most arcane concepts interesting and vital. He was an advocate of deregulating industries, making the point that market forces could do a much better job of maximizing value and benefiting the consumer with lower prices and higher quality than regulators. Kahn was able to put his theories into practice when he was appointed chair of the Civil Aeronautics Board (CAB) in 1977. Up until that time, airlines had been tightly regulated in terms of routes and fares. The Airline Deregulation Act was passed in 1978, and the CAB closed in 1985.[6] Kahn and his course inspired me to major in economics, although subsequent courses were less consistently interesting. Claudia Goldin was a classmate who was also inspired by Kahn's course to major in economics.[7] We were both on the Student Government Finance Committee. My honors thesis was entitled Supply and Demand Conditions in the Market for Physicians. Markets in medicine are often distorted because of a lack of information, monopolistic and oligopolistic conditions, and difficulties with rapidly changing supply to meet demand. I used a tool that was relatively new at the time called cost-benefit analysis, which attempts to determine the sum of the potential rewards minus the total costs of an action to determine which changes could optimize the market for physicians. This concept is now commonly applied in economic analysis. It was a valuable lesson for me. I found cost-benefit analysis very useful in medicine when determining the best course of treatment for a patient. When alternative treatment regimens are compared using this strategy, it becomes much clearer which one is preferable. I observed that colleagues would look only at potential benefits or would be biased by experience, thus advocating over- or undertreatment. The cost-benefit strategy most often leads to the best treatment strategy. My thesis was awarded the prestigious Frank H. Vedder Prize in Economics for 1966. I do not know if Claudia was disappointed at not receiving this recognition as an undergraduate, but she was compensated with the Nobel Prize in Economics in 2023 for her studies identifying causes of gender earnings differences in the labor market.

One hears currently about the demise of liberal arts education.

This would be tragic and have major social consequences. Exposure to a broad spectrum of knowledge and the fine arts imparts knowledge and perspective that are invaluable in any career. I took several philosophy courses, which I found enthralling. The philosophy faculty at Cornell was heavily influenced by the twentieth-century philosopher Ludwig Wittgenstein. Wittgenstein wrote relatively little and in an arcane style. Much effort was expended by the faculty trying to figure out what he was saying. Much of earlier philosophical thought attempting to understand existence and consciousness ultimately ended in conclusions that defied common sense. For example, Descartes argued that only in our own mind can we be certain we exist. But such an explanation requires additional beliefs to account for the external world and defies common sense. Wittgenstein emphasized the critical role of language in thought and took a very commonsense approach. Language mirrors reality without the need for additional concepts outside our experience or postulates that defy what we see, hear, and feel every day. If we can see, think, and speak of propositions, then they exist. Or the reverse, as he put it: "Whereof one cannot speak, thereof one must be silent."[8]

Courses in the government department were considered some of the best. One highlight was a course on the American presidency taught by Clinton Rossiter, a world-renowned expert who had authored a widely read book on the subject. A course on the works of William Shakespeare was another highlight. At the same time, I was fulfilling the premed requirements in case I decided to go in that direction. The killer course was organic chemistry, which included a lab. I recall one experiment of mine that exploded, but luckily no one was hurt. Fortunately, I got high grades. During the summer after my sophomore year, I took additional courses in economics at Harvard. The summer in Boston was enjoyable. I was able to spend some time with my uncle, David Roth, who was a neurosurgeon on the faculty of Harvard Medical School. He was only twelve years older than I and a bachelor at that time. His mentorship would become invaluable the following summer when he was able to secure a position for me as a scrub technician in his neurosurgery operating room on the Harvard

Service of Boston City Hospital. I was still undecided on a career path. I felt that the opportunity to experience medical practice could be a deciding factor. Working in the operating room turned out to be fascinating and exciting, unlike anything I had experienced before. The most striking observation was the ability to get immediate results that would help patients. If a blood clot was compressing the brain, removing it solved the problem. This contrasted with my older impression of chronic illnesses in my family, which slowly progressed but could never be cured. This aspect of surgery greatly attracted me. The operating room rituals appealed to my sense of order and control. There were also scientific studies being done in the clinic and laboratory, which had the potential to transform the care of some patients.

That summer was not all work. Uncle David had a sailboat, and we sailed to Bar Harbor, Maine, spending the night on board, rewarded with a fresh steamed lobster dinner. I also managed to get tickets to see the Beatles perform live at the Suffolk Downs racetrack. The highlight of the summer was performing part of a neurosurgical case. In today's highly litigious and risk-averse medical climate, as a college student, I would likely not be allowed near an operating room, let alone perform a procedure on a patient. I was in the OR alone with the chief resident in neurosurgery. We had become friends over the summer. He was supportive of my career and impressed that I had learned to handle the instruments and understand the operations. The procedure was perhaps the simplest in neurosurgery. The patient had a subdural hematoma (blood clot) that was causing pressure on the brain and needed to be evacuated. In this case, it was an old clot that had liquefied, so it would be easy to drain. First, a small incision is made in the shaved scalp and carried down to the skull. An instrument resembling a hand drill was used to drill through the skull to expose the tissues covering the brain, of which the dura is the outermost. The dura is incised, and the fluid is drained. I was guided through this by the chief resident and felt a real sense of accomplishment after the procedure was completed. Fortunately, the patient recovered quickly and did very well. However, I also experienced some very tragic outcomes, including a patient who had a seizure in the hallway and other patients with untreatable brain tumors.

It was clear to me after my summer at Boston City Hospital that a career in medicine was the right personal choice. I had taken the Medical College Admissions Test earlier on a hunch that I might apply to medical school, and all my premed science course requirements were completed. I began the application process. Late that summer, Uncle David informed me that he had arranged for an admissions interview with Harvard Medical School (HMS). We went to the main building and, walking up the steps, met a short, rotund man wearing wire-rim glasses and a bowtie, which I later observed was the uniform de rigueur for HMS faculty. He was Perry Culver, the dean of admissions for HMS. As we walked up the steps of the administration building, he exchanged some professional banter with David, and then we entered a small office. I introduced myself. After a brief review of my qualifications, Culver squinted at me and said, "Well, you're a big fish in a small pond, aren't you?" I was taken aback and was not sure what his frame of reference was, thinking that if he meant my origins in La Porte, this was not relevant. So I countered by informing him that Cornell and Harvard Universities were about the same size and were both very large ponds. I could tell from his deepening squint that this comment did not sit well with him. After the interview, I felt my chances were close to nil for admission. However, if Culver's attitude and arrogance were typical of HMS professors, this was not an environment I wanted to enter. Forty-three years later, I was reading The Art and Politics of Science, a memoir written by Harold Varmus (W. W. Norton and Company, 2009). I was astonished to read that he had a similar experience: "I was soon granted an interview with the notoriously confrontational dean of admissions, Perry Culver, who quickly made it clear, in a parental tone, that he found me too inconstant and immature in judgment to be admitted to his school. He then recommended something my parents would never have suggested: a maturing experience in the armed services." Varmus was not admitted to HMS but developed the consistency and maturity to win a Nobel Prize, along with Michael Bishop, discovering that genes in human cells, called oncogenes, cause human cancer; but more on that to follow. I have met several HMS graduates during my career, and it is obvious to me that Culver's attitude and approach had a pervasive influence on the admissions process, attracting students with similar personality traits. One of the residential halls at HMS has a small student lounge named after him, unsurprisingly, as the Perry Culver Lounge. There appears to be a pool table in the background. I doubt he would approve.

My next interview was at the Johns Hopkins School of Medicine (JHSOM). This was a totally different experience. JHSOM admitted its first class in 1893. Several daughters of Baltimore's wealthiest business families provided financial support contingent on the medical school being equally open to both sexes, thus becoming one of the first coeducational medical schools.[9] Four physicians, The Big Four, played major roles in establishing Hopkins as the top medical school in the country. William Welch was the first professor of pathology, established the first school of public health, and became the school's first dean. William Halstead, the first chief of surgery, established the modern principles of surgery and the surgical residency program. William Osler, the first physician in chief, was the most respected physician of his day and established the medical residency program. Howard Kelly established gynecology as a specialty. This was a period of major change in medical education in the United States. In 1904, the American Medical Association created the Council on Medical Education, whose purpose was to reform medical education, increase standards, and eliminate substandard medical schools. Abraham Flexner, chosen to conduct a survey of medical education, visited all 155 North American medical schools. Many schools were harshly criticized. The new Johns Hopkins School of Medicine was described as the "model for medical education," and its curriculum and standards of excellence were the model for the recommendations of the Flexner report.[10] At the time I interviewed, Hopkins was still considered the best medical school and hospital in the United States. The first two years were structured around courses in the medical sciences, including anatomy, physiology, pathology, and physiological chemistry.

The final two years involved direct participation in clinics and rotations on various clinical services rather than the lectures used in other medical schools.

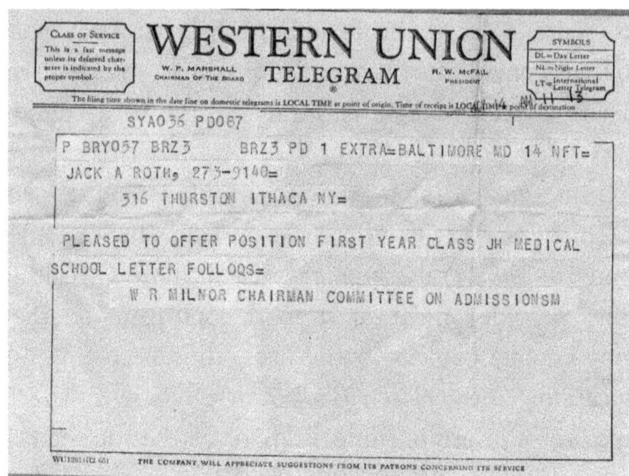

CLASS OF SERVICE
This is a fast message unless its deferred character is indicated by the proper symbol.

WESTERN UNION
TELEGRAM
W. P. MARSHALL CHAIRMAN OF THE BOARD
R. W. McFALL PRESIDENT

SYMBOLS
DL=Day Letter
NL=Night Letter
LT=International Letter Telegram

The filing time shown in the date line on domestic telegrams is LOCAL TIME at point of origin. Time of receipt is LOCAL TIME at point of destination

SYA036 PD087

P BRY057 BRZ3 BRZ3 PD 1 EXTRA=BALTIMORE MD 14 NFT=
JACK A ROTH, 273-9140=
516 THURSTON ITHACA NY=

PLEASED TO OFFER POSITION FIRST YEAR CLASS JH MEDICAL SCHOOL LETTER FOLLOQS=
W R MILNOR CHAIRMAN COMMITTEE ON ADMISSIONSM

THE COMPANY WILL APPRECIATE SUGGESTIONS FROM ITS PATRONS CONCERNING ITS SERVICE

Telegram from Johns Hopkins School of Medicine informing me of admission, November 14, 1966.

The first thing you see when you arrive is the dome, which sits atop the original hospital building. The term rounds were derived from the circular wards inside the dome where bedside teaching occurred. The first part of the interview process was a tour of the hospital and medical school. I was then directed to a room in an administration building for my interview. The door opened, and I was greeted by a long conference table surrounded by faculty, all wearing their pressed white coats. Despite the intimidating vista, the faces were smiling, and I was warmly greeted. They were very interested in hearing about my experience at Boston City Hospital and seemed impressed. I had a good feeling after the interview ended. On November 14, 1966, I received a telegram (the form of rapid communication prior to email and text message) offering me a place in the first-year class. The rest of my senior year passed rapidly. I was inducted into the Phi Beta Kappa academic honor society and graduated magna cum laude.

5
CONTINUING MEDICAL EDUCATION

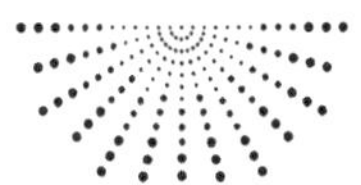

There are more things in Heaven and Earth, Horatio, than are dreamt of in your philosophy.

—Hamlet, William Shakespeare

Now it was time, following graduation in the spring of 1967, for some recreation and relaxation. I had wanted to travel, and Europe, with its cultural and historical sites, was the destination. A friend of one of my Cornell roommates, Richard (Richie) Prager, was also planning a European trip, so we decided to go together. We had a general plan for the countries and destinations we wanted to visit, but otherwise improvised for lodgings and tours. We traveled around using a Eurail pass. I found my handwritten journal I wrote during the trip, in addition to photos from my Nikon single-lens reflex camera, so I do not need to rely on memory in writing this. I landed in London on June 25 and met up with Richie and another friend, Steve. We toured London and saw The Prime of Miss Jean Brodie in the theater. The British Museum was astonishing, with documents signed by Shakespeare, the Magna Carta, the Gutenberg Bible, and scores signed by Brahms, Mozart, and Wagner. The evening was topped off with an open-air performance of A

Midsummer Night's Dream. A visit to the Tate Gallery was my first exposure to the paintings of Turner, which made a profound impression. The next day, we were off to Oxford and Stratford for a performance of As You Like It. Richie was a tennis player and taught me the game, for which I am forever grateful as it became a lifelong pursuit. Wimbledon was in progress, and of course, we had to see a match. We stood in line for an hour and finally got seats on Court 1, where John Newcombe defeated the U.S. player Clark Graebner. We saw the classic sights, including Windsor Castle, the Tower of London, and Westminster Abbey, and then took a train to Penshurst to begin a tour of the Kent countryside with its stately manors and castles. We were constantly improvising, and during a hike to Chiddingstone Castle, we had to scale a barbed-wire fence. We returned to London and, from there, flew to Paris. After viewing the great art and architecture of Paris and celebrating Bastille Day, we made side trips to the Normandy coast, Cannes, and Monaco. Amazingly, I left Monaco three hundred francs wealthier after some lucky spins at the roulette table in the Le Sporting d'Ete casino.

Riding a Velo motorbike on the Normandy coast, July 1967

The next day, our luck ran out, and we found out that French railway workers were on strike, so we rode a bus to a functioning train station that would take us to Florence. I was overwhelmed by the great art and architecture of the city with its pivotal place in the Renaissance. During the trip, Procol Harem's A Whiter Shade of Pale was the top song. I remember hearing it in every country. Despite all the playing time, I could not understand the meaning of the lyrics and still do not. Next, we took a train to Geneva and, from there, went to Amsterdam. In addition to seeing works of the great Dutch masters, we experienced great Dutch beer at the Heineken Brewery. Then, it was a return to Paris on August 5 for the flight back to the United States.

This was an incredible trip during which I experienced much of what I had read about on my own and during college. We saw art, architecture, and history that represented the development and foundation of Western civilization. Recently, much of this has come under attack as being the work of dead white men whose agenda included the suppression and enslavement of other civilizations. Of course, there is truth to that interpretation. However, to understand the human experience, one must understand and appreciate all cultures and their interrelationships. Fortunately, I have been able to travel to all seven continents, learn about the history, art, and perspectives of many cultures, and understand these better because of what I learned about European culture. There is much beauty and valuable insight in what we saw in Europe, which should not be lost. An interesting footnote is that Richie became a cardiothoracic surgeon, eventually leading the adult cardiac surgery program at the University of Michigan.

The Dome, Johns Hopkins University School of Medicine, 1968.

I arrived in Baltimore on the verge of a life-changing experience. The Johns Hopkins School of Medicine was in the middle of an impoverished Black neighborhood filled with dilapidated row houses. The medical students were housed in a relatively new dormitory-style building called Reed Hall. There were two dining clubs. I, along with one of my roommates, chose to join Nu Sigma Nu. It was housed in a dilapidated row house, but the meals were decent. The other club, called Pithotomy, was renowned for its satirical, raucous, obscene, and sexist year-end member-performed shows, which insulted every distinguished faculty member. I thought the club members were less committed academically and thus declined membership. The club has ceased to exist. We were immediately thrown into a challenging curriculum that included gross anatomy with cadaver dissection, biochemistry, neuroanatomy, genetics, and physiology. We also had a wonderful history of medicine course taught by one of the great medical historians, Owsei Temkin, director of the Institute of the

History of Medicine at Johns Hopkins. Today, medical students begin with a white coat ceremony welcoming them to the profession and may have a memorial service for their cadaver, but in 1967, these did not exist. We were just told to get started and learn as much as possible. I had taken the minimum number of science courses at Cornell and did not major in a science, unlike most of my classmates, many of whom had worked in scientific laboratories during their summers. Thus, I was at a disadvantage and needed to spend much time trying to catch up. Also, I believe the faculty had a difficult time with our class and was not sure how to handle it. We grew up during the '60s and had lost our awe and reverence for institutions. One student I remember, Richard Axel, was very disruptive during lectures, making loud, derogatory comments. He did not practice medicine after graduating from medical school but later was awarded a Nobel Prize for discovering the genes of olfactory receptors that regulate our sense of smell, now the second of my former classmates to win a Nobel Prize. He wrote after receiving his prize:

I was a terrible medical student pained by constant exposure to the suffering of the ill and thwarted in my desire to do experiments. My clinical incompetence was immediately recognized by the faculty and deans. I could rarely, if ever, hear a heart murmur. Never saw the retina, my glasses fell into an abdominal incision and finally, I sewed a surgeon's finger to a patient upon suturing an incision... I was allowed to graduate medical school early with an M.D. if I promised never to practice medicine on live patients. I returned to Columbia as an intern in Pathology where I kept this promise by performing autopsies. After a year in Pathology, I was asked... never to practice on dead patients. Finally, I was afforded the opportunity to pursue molecular biology [research] in earnest.[9]

One of the unusual features of the first year was the opportunity to participate in research in a specific clinical area. Our class was highly competitive, so there was intense discussion as to which group would be most advantageous. I was interested in heart surgery and selected the heart physiology group as my first choice. I was fortunate enough to be chosen for it. We measured the cardiac responses of dogs to various stimuli. The group was run by a rather acerbic cardiologist, William Milnor, and a senior fellow who was destined to become chief resident in surgery, Ronald Elkins. They did not get along. Elkins was from Oklahoma, clearly not excited about being in the laboratory, and taciturn with an attitude, not uncommon to surgeons at that time, of infallibility. Milnor took every opportunity to needle him, and Elkins just had to grin and bear it. Milnor, to his credit, invited us all to a pool party at his home at the end of the course.

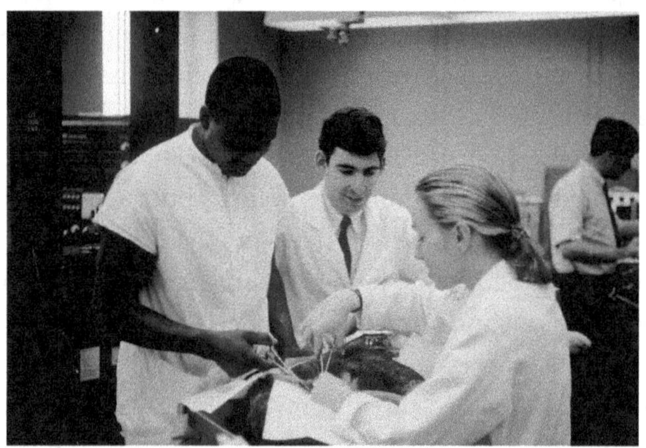

In the cardiac physiology laboratory at the Johns Hopkins School of Medicine with classmate Sharon Pusin (far right), 1968.

The neighborhood around Hopkins was never considered safe. One of my roommates was assaulted. However, none of us was prepared for what happened in the spring. The assassination of Dr. Martin Luther King Jr. triggered civil unrest nationwide, with the riots in Baltimore beginning on April 6, 1968.[11] From our windows in Reed Hall, we could see the chaos below, with angry crowds filling the streets, fires being set, and looting. National Guard troops were called in by Governor Spiro Agnew. We were confined to our dormitory until the rioting ended on April 14.

I made it through the first year. There were no real vacation periods during medical school. Medical students were expected to make some contribution during the summer months. Despite the intensely hot Baltimore summers, I decided to stay and pursue a research project. I had heard about an innovative physician in the new field of nuclear medicine who was looking for medical students for summer projects. He was working with a novel research tool called the microsphere. These extremely small plastic particles (averaging fifty microns in diameter, about the size of a cell in your body) were labeled with various radioisotopes. These particles could be injected in the bloodstream, and the fraction of the heart output going to each region of an organ could be determined by counting the radioactivity in that section of the organ. Methods for measuring cerebral (brain) blood flow experimentally up to that time were inaccurate. The question I was asking was if these particles could be used to measure cerebral blood flow in a dog, which had never been done accurately. Using this technique, our group was successful. The experiments were the first of their kind. I published the research paper as the first author in the prestigious American Journal of Physiology, July 1970.[12] This was my first research publication and the first of many firsts for research discoveries.

The second year of medical school was dominated by the pathology and pharmacology courses. In addition, we began physical diagnosis. This was still an important skill, as computerized tomographic scanning and magnetic resonance imaging had not come into general use. The next summer, I decided to pursue research in the Department of Surgery. I was very interested in cardiac surgery and felt I needed to learn more about surgical procedures and physiology. I met with the chief of surgery, George Zuidema, to see if he would accept me as a research fellow. Zuidema became chief after the retirement of Alfred Blalock. Blalock was the successor to Halsted and was one of the pioneers in cardiac and vascular surgery.[9] He graduated from Hopkins and completed his residency at Vanderbilt after not being selected to continue at Hopkins. He developed the modern treatment for surgical shock based on administering blood transfusions, which saved lives during World War II. However, it was his collaboration with the pediatrician Helen Taussig that brought him international acclaim. Taussig was treating babies with a congenital heart abnormality called tetralogy of Fallot. This complex condition has four defects in the heart: there is a hole between the two lower chambers (ventricles); the pulmonary artery, which brings blood to the lungs so it can be oxygenated, is narrowed; the valve to the aorta sits on top of the hole between the two ventricles; and the muscle in the wall of the right ventricle is thicker than normal. All of this combines to allow blood returning to the heart to bypass the lungs and not become oxygenated. The babies thus have a low oxygen state, and their skin has a blue hue after birth.

Blalock worked in the laboratory with a technician he had brought from Vanderbilt, Vivien Thomas. Thomas was Black, but this did not prevent his hiring at Hopkins, although he never received the credit due to him for helping develop the operation until recently. Blalock and Thomas devised a technique of detaching the subclavian artery (the artery to the arm) and connecting it to the pulmonary artery to increase blood flow to the lungs. When I was performing dog surgery at Hopkins as a student, Vivien Thomas oversaw the Hopkins large animal facility. He was a most kind and gracious mentor to me as I began learning surgical technique. His generous and understanding approach was distinct from the intimidating and abusive behavior of some of the surgeons in the operating room, which, at that time, was thought to be the mark of rigorous and caring surgeons. This convinced me early on that bullying behavior was not only unnecessary but also counterproductive. The first operation was a success, with the patient immediately turning from blue to pink when the clamp came off the subclavian artery. The chief resident assisting Blalock was William Longmire, who later became the chief of surgery and my mentor at UCLA. The intern was Denton Cooley, who later became one of the premier cardiac surgeons in the world and a good friend when I moved to Houston. Vivien Thomas was standing behind Blalock and providing advice during the operation. This operation did not repair the underlying heart defects and was therefore only a palliative procedure. However, it heralded the beginning of a new era that would rapidly develop operations to repair and revascularize the heart.

Playing Trumpet in the Turtle Derby Band Johns Hopkins School of Medicine, 1969.

Although I was not aware of the politics as a medical student, I later heard from a member of the Hopkins faculty that after Blalock retired, the search committee was heavily influenced by the Department of Medicine to choose someone who would be relatively unknown and unlikely to achieve Blalock's fame, which clearly eclipsed that of other Hopkins faculty members. The choice of Zuidema was highly controversial in academic surgical circles.[9] Blalock was vehemently opposed to his appointment, citing his youth, absence of experience, and lack of recognition in the surgical world. Former Blalock trainees who felt they deserved the appointment, as well as disgruntled Hopkins faculty who resigned in protest, prolonged the controversy. But Zuidema survived all this and continued at Hopkins for twenty years. My first meeting with him was to get advice on research mentors in his department. He was dismissive and gave me the names of two other faculty members who "had funding." I decided to work with Robert Rutherford, who was new to the surgical faculty at Hopkins. He was interested in the treatment of patients with traumatic injuries who experienced shock (low blood pressure) and blunt trauma injuries to the lungs. Measuring changes in blood flow to different organ systems during treatment for these conditions was very important, and the radiolabeled microspheres I had helped develop the previous year were the ideal tool to accomplish this. Patients who have lost a large volume of blood and have low blood pressure could benefit if their blood pressure could be raised while they are receiving transfusions. The G suit (essentially a pressurized suit placed around the patient) can do this, but there was concern it would reduce blood flow to vital organs. We measured regional blood flow to all organ systems before and after application and showed that it remained unchanged, with the blood pressure significantly increasing.[13] This was an exciting study as it had direct application to patient care. G suits became routinely used in shock-related emergencies and saved lives. Studies of this type, where there is an opportunity for directly helping patients, are called translational research. It is distinguished from basic research, which addresses scientific questions that may not have direct application. The focus on translational research was to develop into a hallmark of my career.

The third and fourth years of medical school were all clinical rotations. By this time, I was certain I would pursue surgery, although it was still unclear which surgical specialty. The rotations included time on the residents' service, where the residents had major responsibility with attending physician supervision; private services, where the private practice physicians admitted their patients; and outside hospitals, including Baltimore City Hospital. Once again, I decided to spend my summer doing research. G. Melville Williams was a new faculty member in the Department of surgery who was recruited to begin an organ transplant program. He had completed a research fellowship at the Walter and Eliza Hall Institute in Melbourne, Australia, where he studied with Gus Nossal and the 1960 joint Nobel Prize winners Sir Macfarlane Burnet and Sir Peter Medawar, pioneers in the field of immune tolerance. He then worked with the pioneering transplant surgeon David Hume at the University of Virginia and was a Markle Scholar. His research at Hopkins focused on allograft rejection and the role of the endothelial cells, which line blood vessels. We performed aortic allografts in rats by sewing the aorta (the main artery) from one strain of rats into another. Since the two rat strains were unrelated, the aortic graft would be rejected. We then transfused female bone marrow cells into male recipients. The female cells could be identified by sex chromatin bodies in the nuclei of their cells. Some of the endothelial cells in males were female. Thus, in some cases, the damage caused by rejection could be repaired by female bone marrow cells. The concept of bone marrow stem cells was not well developed at that time, but it is likely that was what we were observing.[14] We attempted to culture endothelial cells and received help from George Gey and his wife, Margaret, who developed the HeLa cell line from Henrietta Lacks's cervical tumor. Growing cell lines from cancers was one of the most important technical advances in cancer research. However, the procurement of these cells was a source of controversy many years later.[15] These cell lines would grow indefinitely, providing a constant source of well-characterized cancer cells for experiments. I was awarded the Outstanding Student Research Presentation from the Johns Hopkins Medical Society in 1971. My experiences in the research laboratory were a highlight of my medical education. Research was the key to improving treatment outcomes for patients. In a lifetime of medical practice, you may help hundreds or perhaps thousands of patients. But one discovery resulting in improved treatment would affect many more patients long after your practice has ended.

Johns Hopkins School of Medicine graduation, June 1971. Front row, left to right: David Roth, Julia Saperstein, Bernice Roth, Jack Roth; back row, left to right: Nate Roth, Manny Roth, Richard Roth.

It was time to think about residency. I had decided to pursue surgery and wanted to begin in a general surgery residency that would rotate through various specialty services. Remaining at Hopkins seemed like the best choice. After I talked with several surgical faculty members, it was clear they wanted me to continue at Hopkins. I would be selected if I ranked it first. Out of interest and to gain some insight into other programs, I applied to Brigham and Women's Hospital and was given an interview. When I arrived at Brigham, I was led into a room with around ten of the surgical faculty. They immediately began peppering me with clinical questions, which I managed to answer. Next, I was escorted to the office of the chief of surgery, with the imposing title of Moseley Professor. This was Francis D. Moore, who was a legendary surgeon-scientist and a pioneer in developing quantitative metabolic studies in humans using isotope labeling. He greeted me with an angry frown and then, after a few minutes, said, "How would you like having those microspheres injected into your brain?" He had seen the titles of my research papers but failed to grasp that we had used microspheres as an animal research tool to obtain the most accurate blood flow data. He had also failed to anticipate their potential for regional organ delivery for radiotherapy, which is now being done routinely. It was disappointing to see a prominent department chair have such a lack of scientific insight and be so negative toward a nascent physician-scientist. He was clearly in the twilight of his career and stepped down as chair five years later. I was very happy that I had already made my choice to stay at Hopkins. But this was a useful experience, as it showed how not to conduct interviews for residency candidates, which would be helpful when we initiated our own fellowship program at MD Anderson.

As a surgical intern in 1971, the major role was to gather patient information (computers and the electronic medical record were not available) and hold retractors during surgical cases. Surgical technology was still primitive. The only lights for operating were overhead. The headlight and magnifying loupes now common were not in use. Video camera-guided surgery and robotics were in the distant future. Even though you had never seen a specific operation, you were expected to have mind-reading capabilities to know exactly where to place the retractor, position the lights, and anticipate every move by the operating surgeon. Teaching in surgical residency programs has improved greatly since then. Now, there are simulation centers where residents can practice operative techniques in a virtual environment. Skills can be mastered and evaluated prior to entering the operating room.

The emergency room rotation was chaotic, with frequent severe trauma cases. Patients would come in so inebriated that an accurate physical exam was impossible. Once they sobered up, they would occasionally return with an injury that had gone unrecognized because of their previous unresponsiveness. Despite the long hours and hard work, my internship year passed quickly.

As a second-year resident, I supervised an intern and were able to do a few cases with supervision from a senior resident or attending. I had a week's vacation in the winter. My uncle David had purchased an interest in a ski resort in Waterville Valley, New Hampshire, and invited me to go skiing. I had never skied before, so I signed up for lessons. I was provided with long skis and very uncomfortable rental boots. During the time I was there, the ski conditions were either rain or ice. However, despite the pain and discomfort, I learned to ski, and skiing under those conditions made me very appreciative of the Colorado skiing I would later experience. I really enjoyed skiing, and in future years, I pursued it at many different resorts. Now, I ski exclusively in Telluride, Colorado, at an age when many skiers have dropped out.

During the second year, top residents were selected to be on the chief's service with Dr. Zuidema as the only attending. This was an honor but had the disadvantage that Zuidema did very few cases. Because of his expertise in biliary tract surgery, he did attract complex and difficult cases. I remember one case where the patient had obstruction of the bile duct due to cancer. One way to treat this is to place a stent from the liver into the duodenum to bypass the obstruction. Zuidema tried to position the stent with increasing degrees of frustration. Finally, he called in John Cameron, a young junior faculty member who had trained at Hopkins. Zuidema said, "I can't do this. Why don't you try?" and walked out of the operating room, leaving Cameron to complete the case. Another lesson learned on how not to handle problems in the operating room.

There were faculty members who stood out in their interactions with the residents. Vincent Gott was a cardiac surgeon and the chief of the department. He developed the pacemaker and novel artificial heart valves and led the first heart transplant at Hopkins. He was soft-spoken and kind to the resident staff. I was on rounds with him and the cardiac chief residents and stopped at the bedside of one of his patients, who had received a heart valve and had significant anemia. There were several possible causes for this, including the artificial heart valve, which could be destroying red blood cells, or simply an iron-deficient state, which reduced the number of blood cells that could be made in the bone marrow. I was asked how we might identify the cause and stated that a bone marrow biopsy could definitively eliminate iron deficiency as a cause. Everyone agreed, and I took it as a decision to order the biopsy. However, later that day, a scowling chief resident pulled me aside, asking if I had ordered the bone marrow. I said I did, and the chief resident then said Dr. Gott did not approve it, and it was only part of a discussion. He then took me to speak with Gott. I was really concerned I was in deep trouble, but Dr. Gott understood the situation and could not have been kinder, saying that no harm was done. I nodded to the chief resident and walked away, highly relieved.

One of the highlights of the year was the rotation to the Baltimore Loch Raven Veterans Administration Hospital. It was just me and a senior resident, so I had much more responsibility. The senior resident, whom I met for the first time, was E. Carmack Holmes (Mac Holmes). Mac was the epitome of the Southern gentleman and a calm presence in the operating room. He became a mentor to me and a major influence in my career choices. The chief of surgery was Richard Kieffer. He had been a medical student at Hopkins and completed his surgical training there under Blalock. He was on the surgical faculty at Hopkins. Kieffer specialized in noncardiac thoracic surgery at a time when that was not really a separate recognized specialty. The American Board of Thoracic Surgery, founded in 1948, was a specialty-accrediting board for any surgeon who performed adult or pediatric cardiac surgery or operated on any other organs in the chest, such as the lungs or esophagus. It was not until 1992 that I and others established thoracic surgery training programs specializing in noncardiac surgery that were sanctioned by the American Board of Surgery. Kieffer had never trained in cardiac surgery but had extensive experience in lung surgery for tuberculosis and surgery for cancer of the esophagus. He was an old-school surgeon who would scrub in to help with the most difficult part of the case and then leave all the postoperative management to the residents. Mac and I got along well with him. He did have strong views. We got into a discussion on the economy, and I mentioned John Maynard Keynes's theories. He promptly dismissed Keynes as a "queer communist." The experience on his service was eye-opening in that the surgery, which I had not seen before, was interesting and challenging. The anatomy was fascinating, and operating in the chest was much more pleasant than dealing with the abdomen and all its contents. I decided this would be a specialty I would pursue. There was an unmet need for thoracic cancer surgical oncologists as the incidence and death rate from lung cancer were accelerating. Kieffer left the VA and retired from his Hopkins appointment in 1979. I had heard that he was not happy with the Hopkins Department of Surgery after his son did not advance in the surgical residency program. As I plotted my future career path, it became clear that to be a successful surgeon-scientist in an academic program, I would need additional intensive research experience. Thus, I planned to devote the next two years to research.

6
CALIFORNIA DREAMIN'

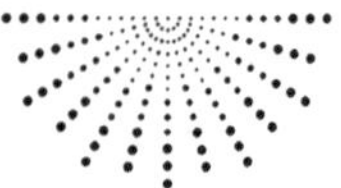

I have no special talent. I am only passionately curious.
—Albert Einstein

It is critical that one's research years be spent with a mentor and group that are leading in one's field of interest and pursuing the highest-quality science. I discussed options with Dr. Zuidema. He strongly recommended Dr. Donald L. Morton, who had recently established a new department of surgical oncology at UCLA. At that time, in 1973, it was a novel idea that a surgeon would specialize in cancer surgery and possibly one type of cancer. The concept of multidisciplinary cancer care was in its infancy, and Morton's group was pioneering this field. New treatments were emerging for cancers, which included drugs, new surgical procedures, and innovative techniques of radiation therapy. In some cases, these treatments were combined. Patients could benefit if their treatment was discussed by a group of physicians, including medical oncologists, surgeons, and radiation oncologists, instead of sending the patient to a surgeon, who, of course, would recommend surgery, or a radiation oncologist, who may be biased toward radiation therapy. I had heard of Morton previously in medical school. During my time on the Osler service, students were required to make a presentation. One of my classmates discussed a paper by Morton that indicated intact cellular immunity, as shown by the ability to develop a positive skin test to dinitrochlorobenzene, predicted a longer disease-free survival, whereas those with impaired immunity had a rapid recurrence of the cancer.[16] This was an intriguing observation. I looked up more of Morton's papers and found that he had identified proteins in mouse tumors that triggered an immune response. This raised the possibility that the human immune system could recognize cancer-related proteins as foreign, and if the immune response was strong enough, the cancer would be rejected or killed for the same reason we cannot transplant unmodified animal organs into humans.

The next step was to travel to UCLA and interview for a fellowship position. Don Morton was tall, youthful in appearance, and had blond hair that he kept in a crew cut—the image of the all-American boy. He was the son of a coal miner and grew up during the Great Depression in a home without running water or electricity. He received his undergraduate and medical education in California.[17] Morton had spent time at the National Cancer Institute (NCI), which is one of the institutes comprising the National Institutes of Health (NIH) in Bethesda, Maryland. He was then recruited to UCLA to establish surgical oncology. I spoke with several members of the group. One of the major attractions was that my mentor from Hopkins, Mac Holmes, who had worked with Morton as an NCI clinical associate, had been recruited to establish thoracic oncologic surgery. Fred Eilber, another surgeon who had been in Morton's research group at NCI, was there as well. Morton had also recruited a cadre of PhD research scientists to study all aspects of the immune response to cancer—cell immunity, antibodies, and viruses. Another member of the group was a medical oncologist, Charles Haskell. It was the first and last time I encountered a medical oncologist as faculty in surgical oncology. All this was extraordinarily impressive. Nothing even close to it existed at that time at Hopkins. Here was a true multidisciplinary group focused on cancer—one of the most challenging diseases in medicine. I was enthusiastic about the fellowship and thrilled to be accepted. I had been at

Hopkins for six years; this seemed like the right time for a change, and Los Angeles would indeed be a major cultural shift from Baltimore. I packed up my few possessions, got in my car, and headed west.

I knew very little about Los Angeles. I needed an apartment close to UCLA to avoid the freeway congestion. A new apartment building had just opened on Veteran Avenue, near a veterans' cemetery, and the price was right. I was amazed at the bright façade and ambiance in contrast to my dismal digs in Baltimore. There was a fitness center and a spa called Cave of the Nymphs. This was all hype, of course, as there were no nymphs on site. I must have looked awestruck and naive to the rental agent as I saw her snicker when I turned on the water faucet in the bathroom to see if it really worked.

The laboratory I would work in was in the Sepulveda Veterans Administration Hospital, located in the San Fernando Valley. The surgical oncology laboratories were divided, with some in the main UCLA hospital building and additional space in the Sepulveda VA Hospital. The surgical fellows were in the VA hospital laboratory. I would be joined by other surgical trainees who were also drawn to the new field of surgical oncology and Don Morton's groundbreaking research. These included Marshal Urist, Arthur Boddie, and Courtney Townsend, all of whom had future stellar academic surgical careers. Don Morton also hired a technician to help manage the laboratory, Elizabeth (Liz) Grimm. Liz had come from Boston, where she worked in laboratories at Harvard Medical School. She and Don Morton shared a common origin in West Virginia, although they grew up in different regions of the state. Liz tells of her interview for the job with Don. He asked if she was a "hillbilly," and of course she said, "Yes, sir", after which he immediately offered her the position, which included helping the clinical fellows, who were spending various lengths of time pursuing translational research projects. I was having an orientation tour, and as we were waiting at an elevator door, I still recall the door opening and Liz walking out. She was strikingly beautiful and soft-spoken. We were introduced, and that is when I realized she would be working with me in the laboratory.

The focus of the research in Morton's group was to determine if cancer elicited an immune response and if the immune system could be directed to reject the cancer. Several case reports existed of patients with cancer who refused treatment, and eventually, their cancer disappeared spontaneously, thus suggesting that the patients' immune systems saw the cancer as foreign and rejected it. The pioneering pathologist Virchow noted as early as 1863 that tumors were often populated with inflammatory cells. The first attempt at cancer immunotherapy occurred in 1891, when William Coley found that mixtures of live and inactivated Streptococcus pyogenes and Serratia marcescens bacteria could cause tumor regression in sarcoma patients.[18] Using bacteria was impractical and potentially hazardous. In 1911, Peyton Rous discovered a virus that caused a type of cancer called sarcoma in chickens. Viruses trigger immune responses and subsequently immunity to the virus, and their proteins could prevent the growth of these cancers.[19]Bacillus Calmette-Guérin (BCG) vaccine is an attenuated strain of Mycobacterium bovisused to prevent tuberculosis. In 1959, Lloyd Old showed that BCG had an antitumor effect by inducing immune stimulation in the tumor.[20] Morton began a clinical trial injecting BCG into melanomas, a highly aggressive form of skin cancer. In some cases, he saw the tumors shrink and the shrinkage of non-injected tumors, suggesting the development of anticancer immunity. Morton's work revived interest in cancer immunotherapy and set the stage for future research breakthroughs. However, it would not be until 1991, when Tasuku Honjo discovered the PD-1 molecule, which prevents immune cells from killing tumors, and developed an antibody that blocked it, that immunotherapy for cancer would become a reality.[21] But when I entered the lab, many questions remained. Did many cancers elicit an immune response? What components of the immune system became activated? Which antigenic foreign proteins was the immune system responding against? In the short space of two years, my research would address as well as provide some clear answers to these questions. To do so, it was critical to isolate molecules from the cancers against which an immune response was directed. Serendipitously, Morton had a collaboration with Ralph Reisfeld, then a professor in the Department of Immunology and Microbiology at Scripps Research.[22]

Ralph was friendly, had a wonderful sense of humor, and was eager to collaborate with cancer clinicians. He was born April 23, 1926, in Stuttgart, Germany. He and his parents escaped persecution by the Nazis in 1938 (two days before their family home was invaded) and went to Switzerland. He immigrated to the United States in 1946. When Ralph was an undergraduate at Rutgers, Albert Einstein convinced him to go into scientific research. He met Morton during his tenure at NIH. Reisfeld trained James P. Allison, PhD, and collaborated with him on the mechanisms of tumor recognition by the immune system. Allison identified checkpoint inhibitors now used to treat some cancers, for which he was a co-recipient of the 2018 Nobel Prize in Physiology or Medicine, along with Honjo. Reisfeld made two important contributions that allowed our group for the first time to convincingly show cancer elicited an immune response in humans. He developed a technique for isolating the molecules recognized by the immune system, called tumor antigens, by extracting them from the cancer cell with a solution of 3 molar potassium chloride (3M KCL). He also perfected a technique for separating the individual molecules in the mixture, named polyacrylamide gel electrophoresis. Individual protein molecules can be antigenic meaning they will elicit an immune response in the host. We were able to isolate antigens from melanoma, show that patients had an immune response to the antigens, and purify and characterize the unique antigen molecules.[23] We developed a rapid test to identify the presence of the antigens in tumors.[24] The antigens and corresponding immune responses were identified in many different tumor types. Importantly, for the first time, we showed that lung cancer patients sometimes mounted an immune response to their lung cancer.[25] Immortalized cancer cell lines were important research tools, and we showed that the antigens were present on cultured cancer cells as well.[26] I published my first paper in the New England Journal of Medicine during my fellowship, showing that skin reactivity to DNCB is a good measure of an intact immune response in cancer patients.[27] Altogether during my two-year research fellowship, I published twenty-two peer-reviewed publications. These established the concept of an immune response to human cancers, paving the way for future immunotherapy research. Of course, the problem was that we did not have a way of stimulating that nascent immune response to a level that would cause tumor rejection. This would finally come with the discovery of PD-1 and the effects of anti-PD-1 antibodies by Honjo twenty years later but would not have been possible without our pioneering work in cancer immunology.

The Society of Surgical Oncology (formerly the James Ewing Society) established a Resident-Fellow Clinical Research Award presented at the annual meeting. This was the most prestigious award in surgical oncology at the time. I received this award twice for papers entitled "Isolation of Soluble Tumor-Associated Antigen from Human Melanoma" (1973) and "Effect of Adriamycin and High-Dose Methotrexate Chemotherapy on in vivo and in vitro Cell-Mediated Immunity in Cancer Patients" (1977). I also received the prestigious Mead Johnson Excellence in Research Award from the National Research Forum in 1980. I was honored to receive this recognition as a resident without yet having completed my clinical training. This award was helpful in bringing me to the attention of senior faculty who were recruiting residents for faculty positions. There was no significant monetary award attached to it. However, the awards caught the attention of Charles Balch, who would later be instrumental in my recruitment to the University of Texas MD Anderson Cancer Center in 1986. I remember attending a meeting and Liz and I playing doubles tennis with Charles and his wife, Carol, probably one of the most important matches of my career, as it resulted in a career-long friendship.

7

DO PRIZES, AWARDS, AND ACADEMIES HELP OR HINDER SCIENTIFIC PROGRESS?

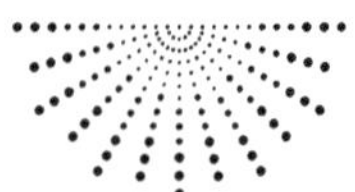

Just remember, it won't be for you. It will be for them.

—Einstein to Oppenheimer on receiving prizes, in the motion picture Oppenheimer

Everyone gets a trophy, and no trophy is worth anything.

—Joseph Epstein

Scientific research in the United States is in critical condition. In a speech on June 26, 2024, National Academy of Sciences president Marcia McNutt stated that the United States was relinquishing leadership in science to other countries. She noted that the United States has a marked decline in the most-cited science papers. Commercialization of new drugs and technologies has plateaued over several decades. China files more patents than the United States and is the site for more than a quarter of the world's clinical trials, as compared with only 3 percent in 2013. One obvious way to address this is through improved K-12 science, technology, engineering, and mathematics (STEM) education. One of my goals in writing this memoir was to document my scientific successes and failures and the factors that both contributed to and obstructed success.

It is my hope that shining a light on these may help pave the way for future successes by others. I have identified certain factors through personal experience, which allows me to comment with some expertise. These include research funding, perverse incentives in a research career, dissemination of scientific findings, scientific misconduct, and criteria for academic promotion. Chapters 7, 11, and 19 are devoted to these important topics.

I was surprised and thrilled to receive multiple prestigious scientific awards so early in my career. These awards increased my visibility and drew the attention of senior faculty who would help in future job searches. However, as the awards, honors, and recognition began to accumulate, I started to question the usefulness of prizes and awards in science. One trend that drew my attention was the startling proliferation of scientific prizes and academies, which has accelerated over the past ten years. When my daughters were young, there was a movement in schools and extracurricular activities to encourage and preserve self-esteem. This was done by always giving positive comments and reinforcement and by giving awards for every imaginable achievement, no matter how minor. If you showed up for every instrumental lesson or practiced a certain number of hours, you received an award, irrespective of the quality of your playing. Now, every professional scientific society has a plethora of awards for some aspect of research. Scientific societies have organized academies to which members elect themselves. No scientist should be without membership in an academy. One society to which I belonged had an active group of officers, senior members, and directors who spent much of their time creating awards and then awarding those awards to one another. Does all this silliness advance science and provide the right incentives for early-career scientists? In my economics class, I learned that increases in the money supply can trigger price inflation, so that the actual value of the currency unit continues to decrease. A similar effect is seen with award proliferation, which reduces the value of the awards to meaningless levels. One of my colleagues was a master at spinning his research and clinical trial results and pulling the most influential political strings. This resulted in numerous awards, to the point that he was called by one faculty member an "award monger." However, much of his science turned out to be unreproducible, leading to expensive clinical trials that showed the treatments to be harmful rather than beneficial. This in no way had any effect on future honors because of his political clout, another example of how the awards process is distorted. One of the oldest scientific awards is the Nobel Prize. Alfred Nobel was born on October 21, 1833, in Stockholm, Sweden.[28]Nobel accumulated great wealth during his lifetime, with most of it coming from his 355 inventions, of which dynamite is the most famous. Nobel died in 1896. His final will specified that his fortune be used to create a series of prizes for those who confer "the greatest benefit on mankind" in physics, chemistry, physiology or medicine, literature, and peace. The prize-awarding organizations are the Karolinska Institute, the Swedish Academy, and the Royal Swedish Academy of Sciences. The Nobel Foundation was founded as a private organization on June 29, 1900, to manage the finances and administration of the Nobel Prizes. A maximum of three laureates can receive the award in each discipline. While this may have been a reasonable restriction based on how science was conducted in the early twentieth century, it seems no longer relevant. Today, many discoveries are the result of team science, with teams comprised of many more than three members. Thus, limiting the prize to three is unfair and detrimental to the scientific community by excluding many, without whose contributions the discovery would not have been made. The prize only recognizes a single discovery when recognition of a lifetime of scientific achievement is also prize-worthy, thus excluding many other scientists. Newer scientific disciplines such as computer science, earth science, and technology are not recognized. Since the first award in 1901, the Nobel Prize, rather than fostering more public recognition of scientific achievement, has evolved to engender criticism, controversy, and division in the scientific community (https://en.wikipedia.org/wiki/Nobel_Prize_controversies). This began with the earliest awards and continues with the most recent awards. The limitations in the number of awardees and political manipulations are primarily responsible for excluding deserving scientists. Nominations are received from all over the world. However, it is ludicrous that a small group concentrated in the Swedish Academy and the Karolinska Institute decides on the most important and noteworthy scientific discoveries. The Nobel Prize is also detrimental to its recipients. A study from the National Bureau of Economic research revealed that post-Nobel, laureates' scientific productivity decreased sharply.[29] Of course, Nobel laureates often receive the award during the twilight of their careers when productivity would naturally decrease, but nevertheless this is still a disturbing trend.

The scientific integrity of the Nobel Assembly was called into question during the Paolo Macchiarini scandal.[30] Macchiarini was the first surgeon to perform a transplant of a biosynthetic trachea. Two of three patients to receive such a transplant died, and the data supporting the clinical trial was falsified. Macchiarini was convicted of involuntary manslaughter. Two high-profile members of the Nobel Assembly were asked to resign because of their participation in a coverup of Macchiarini's scientific misconduct. The complicity of the leadership of the Karolinska Institute and members of the Nobel Committee in the coverup has been well documented in the book The Occasional Human Sacrifice: Medical Experimentation and the Price of Saying No by Carl Elliott (W. W. Norton). Think of how beneficial it would be if the Nobel Foundation used its resources to award scholarships and grants to young scientists both in training and early in their faculty positions. Regrettably, the scientific integrity of several recent Nobel laureates is being questioned. The concerns are not those of scientific controversy but of data integrity[31,32.] These include instances of data duplication in the same manuscript, manipulated images, and retractions that span multiple papers, suggesting that these were not just random errors. Prize committees are not data sleuths and do not have the ability to police scientists. In these cases, a modicum of due diligence would have revealed the problems. If awards and prizes cannot be consistently given to those upholding the highest scientific standards, we should reconsider the process. Joseph Epstein in the Wall Street Journal (May 17, 2024) commented on one prize, “If Bob Dylan deserves a Nobel Prize in Literature, the award doesn't deserve the respect of anyone... I noted that these awards seem to go to two kinds of people: those who don't need it and those who don't deserve it." The science awards face the same degradation in credibility.

Criticizing the Nobel Prize is like jousting at windmills. Nobel's will, the legal founding doctrine of the foundation, and the reluctance of the Swedish Academy and Karolinska Institute to give up their fifteen minutes of fame every October will prevent such changes. However, there has been a tsunami of copycat prizes that continue to divert funds from better uses and amplify the negative effects on science exemplified by the Nobel Prizes. The Fundamental Physics Prize, with a three-million-dollar award; the Kavli Prize, with a one-million-dollar award; and the Breakthrough Prize, with a three-million-dollar award, are recent additions to the prize sweepstakes. The rationale behind these prizes appears misguided, as it is based on the concept that prize money will motivate scientists to make breakthrough discoveries. However, for most scientists, prize money is not a motivation for their scientific work. That motivation arises from within and is accompanied by an insatiable curiosity. What about fame and recognition? This can be bestowed by the academic community with citations, invitations to speak at prestigious meetings, promotions, and non-monetary awards. The money behind these prizes should be used to support young scientists. Current funding mechanisms are either disappearing or, in the case of the NIH granting mechanism, are irreparably broken. I will discuss scientific funding in a subsequent chapter, but the diversion of potential research funds to prizes needs to be reversed, as the priorities and incentives do not align with the current needs in scientific and medical research. Immediate action can be taken to rectify the problem of large monetary prize awards. If these awards are donated to a charitable foundation, there is no income tax consequence for the recipient. Donations to various foundations that distribute the funds to early career scientists based on meritorious applications would significantly increase the available pool of grant funds.

Many honors and awards are bestowed without monetary benefit. They can boost a career, increase a scientist's notoriety, and lead to high-level administrative positions. But do these honors advance the progress of science? It seems in some very prominent instances, they not only interfere with scientific progress but also appear to have incentivized scientific misconduct. Many publications over a long period have been found to have manipulated data for individuals with high-profile research and administrative appointments. Given the number of papers and figures in question, it seems unlikely these were random errors. In any paper with fifty or more individual figures, an occasional duplication could occur. But is it possible these are just random mistakes involving scores of papers over many years? Either there was deliberate falsification and manipulation of the data, or the supervision of the laboratory was incompetent. Either way, this qualifies as scientific misconduct. The individuals involved were promoted to high-level positions, at least in part based on scientific achievements that now appear to be scientific cheating.[33-35] These individuals were members of prestigious societies, including the National Academy of Medicine (NAM). The NAM was known as the Institute of Medicine (IOM) until 2015, when it changed its name to be more in line with other national academies. The IOM selected members with primarily administrative and bureaucratic rather than scientific backgrounds. However, the NAM now emphasizes scientific achievement in medicine. But how did individuals with multiple papers containing highly manipulated data become members? The NAM sends out press releases highly touting new members. But nothing is heard when it becomes apparent that much of a member's scientific output is bogus. Investigations and member expulsions are not publicized. How can an organization nominally representing the highest scientific standards justify this? Granted, it would be very difficult to police the membership process. But when it becomes evident that the scientific record of members is misrepresented, action should be taken.

Membership in prestigious professional organizations is yet another incentive for data manipulation. Although the principal laboratory investigator may not have committed fraud, mismanagement on the scale noted above clearly qualifies as scientific misconduct. By overlooking scientific misconduct and enabling individuals to retain honors, the incentive for scientific misconduct is reinforced. Many scientists want to maintain the status quo, and I expect they will regard my comments as vindictive, self-serving, and sour grapes. But how can organizations presumably dedicated to the highest scientific standards be so lax? However, as seen from the numerous references in this chapter, I am not alone in advocating for change. The facts speak for themselves and cannot be ignored by any scientist with integrity.

Most scientists accept the notion that science is self-correcting. Thus, they maintain that data fabrication is not a problem, as the true data will emerge when other laboratories attempt to reproduce the results. Recent modeling has cast doubt on this assumption. Even if corrective action is taken, time delays may be excessively long, thus allowing cheating scientists to retain positions and honors, further incentivizing scientific misconduct.[36] Detection of manipulated figures and fraudulent data can be challenging. Publishers and reviewers do not police this; however, tools have emerged to detect duplicated and manipulated data. They should be used by journals, and when problems arise, these should be handled rapidly with resources devoted to correcting the scientific literature. Genuine incentives exist for physician-scientists. It is incredibly rewarding to see our work reproduced and cited in the literature. Patient lives saved by novel treatments developed in the laboratory and clinic are an immeasurable reward. Neither honors nor prizes were among the reasons listed by young scientists for pursuing an academic scientific career.[37] It is the accomplishments that are important, not the awards. But enough of this digression. Time to resume my tale.

8
RESIDENCY ENDS, AND I GET A REAL JOB

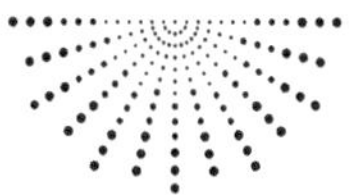

Gravitation is not responsible for people falling in love.
—Albert Einstein

At the completion of my research fellowship in 1975, I needed to decide about my future. Mac Holmes mentioned to me that, based on my productivity during the fellowship, he was asked if I would consider returning to Hopkins to complete my residency training. However, I was impressed with the UCLA surgical residency program. Surgical oncology was a separate division at UCLA, and I would be trained by the best surgical oncologists in the world. I could continue my laboratory research and expand it to include clinical research. Los Angeles and the Westwood neighborhood where I lived were vibrant and exciting. I had also become romantically involved with Liz. She was entering a PhD program in the Microbiology and Immunology Department at the UCLA School of Medicine, and so this was an additional strong incentive to stay.

Dr. William P. Longmire was the chairman of surgery at UCLA and was one of the founders of the UCLA School of Medicine when he moved to Los Angeles in 1948 to become chairman of the Department of Surgery. Longmire had trained at Hopkins and assisted Blalock with the first "blue baby" operation of subclavian to pulmonary artery shunt. When I entered the UCLA residency program, he was about to retire as chair. However, I was still able to operate with him for several remaining years. I was impressed by his quiet demeanor, politeness, and impeccable surgical technique. I have two recollections that stand out because they show his respect and kindness toward the residents and his humility. I was a fourth-year resident at the time and had assisted Dr. Longmire on a descending colon resection for cancer with a primary anastomosis (removing a section of the cancerous colon and then sewing the open ends of healthy tissue together). The patient had a prolonged ileus (bowels stopped working) with some abdominal distension. I obtained an abdominal x-ray that evening and noted a markedly distended cecum, which had increased dramatically from the previous film. It was the weekend, and Dr. Longmire was traveling and could not be reached. As you can imagine, I had considerable trepidation about operating on the professor's patient, but it was clear that if a cecostomy tube was not placed, perforation was imminent. I discussed it with the chief resident, and we went to the OR that evening to place the tube. The patient did well and, by Monday morning, had bowel sounds. I was in the OR on Monday but received a page from Dr. Longmire at the end of the case. I answered it somewhat nervously. However, the professor told me we had done the right thing and expressed his profuse gratitude and thanks for taking care of his patient! There was an audible sigh of relief from me, but I was also impressed with his thoughtfulness in communicating this to a lowly resident.

A second episode that happened shortly after this emphasizes these same traits. We all remember that Dr. Longmire always insisted that the residents (at least the males) wear ties when not in the OR. This rule was never violated. Even on the weekends, proper attire was required. One Sunday morning, I was scheduled to round with him at 8:00 a.m. I was there early with a clean white coat and tie. When Dr. Longmire appeared, something looked amiss. Then I noted his shirt collar was open, and there was no tie. He greeted me and, without a second thought, began apologizing profusely for not wearing a tie that morning. He had either forgotten or left his home in a rush. It was the only time I could remember him not wearing a tie. Of course, I just nodded understandingly, and we began rounds.

As surgical residents, we rotated to several hospitals in the Los Angeles area, including San Bernardino County, Olive View in Sylmar, and Martin Luther King Jr. in Compton. I was one of the first residents to rotate to Olive View, which previously did not have a training program. The residents were required to take overnight calls. The call room was one of the patient rooms in the psychiatric ward. Not only was the bed uncomfortable, but the patients' screams kept me up most of the night. The residents protested as a group and were finally assigned to a more private call room. There was some variation in the facilities and oversight by the attending surgeons in the various hospitals, allowing us to have a considerable degree of independence.

I was interested in pursuing specialty training in cardiothoracic surgery. During my earlier research fellowship, it was evident that very few surgeons specialized in cancer surgery of the thoracic cavity, including cancers of the lung and esophagus. Lung cancer was and still is, the most frequent cause of cancer death in men despite its known association with cigarette smoking. The number of thoracic cancer cases had increased dramatically, and there was an unmet need for cancer surgeons to focus on the care of these patients. This turned out to be a fortuitous choice for me, as thoracic surgeons needed to establish programs were in demand. Then I was rewarded with a lucky break. I was in my second year at UCLA, which was the fourth year of my general surgery residency, counting the two years at Hopkins. One day, I was approached by the chief of cardiothoracic surgery, Don Mulder, about a vacancy in his residency program. The resident who had matched in the program for the next year had withdrawn, and hence, there was a vacancy. He asked whether I would like to become the cardiothoracic resident next year. This was highly unusual, as surgical residents would complete general surgery and then apply for a cardiothoracic position. At the time, it was required to pass the general surgery boards to take the cardiothoracic surgery boards. If I accepted, I realized that I would complete my cardiothoracic residency in two years and then would need one additional year of general surgery residency to be eligible for the boards. However, the excellence of the program, as well as the benefits of not having to apply to multiple programs, travel for interviews, and have no guarantee of acceptance, greatly outweighed any other considerations. I accepted.

At that time in the mid-1970s, cardiothoracic surgery residency programs were designed to provide enough experience that, upon completion, the trainee could perform both cardiac surgery and thoracic (lung, esophagus, ribs, etc.) surgery. Now, a resident can choose a program with an emphasis on one or the other, which makes more sense as the operations and anatomy are very different. When I became chair of thoracic and cardiovascular surgery at MD Anderson, I initiated one of the first approved programs to emphasize training in noncardiac thoracic surgery.

Don Mulder performed pediatric cardiac surgery. He started his residency with Blalock at Hopkins and became one of Longmire's first residents, staying on as a member of the faculty leading cardiac surgery when I became a resident. Another cardiac surgeon, James Maloney, also a Blalock resident, was promoted from head of cardiothoracic surgery to Chair of the Department of Surgery. Gerald Buckberg, yet another Hopkins trainee, was a cardiac surgeon and innovative researcher. He gave me advice when I was finishing my residency and looking for a job. I was most interested in starting up a laboratory to continue my translational cancer research. He told me to make sure I had dedicated space for the laboratory, that I had protected time without patient care responsibilities, and that I work in the lab to establish techniques before hiring research fellows—sound advice that I followed when I set up my lab at the National Cancer Institute. The chief resident in his second year was Henry Fee, who by a remarkable coincidence had been a year ahead of me at La Porte High School.

Jack and Liz were married on November 25, 1978.

The year 1978 was a memorable one. I was completing the first year of my thoracic surgery residency. Liz was completing the requirements for her doctorate and would soon receive her degree in March 1979. And on November 25, Liz and I were married at the Santa Barbara Biltmore Hotel. Liz and I had traveled up and down the California coast following Los Angeles Magazine's recommendations for the most romantic weekend trips. We thought Santa Barbara was the most beautiful location. The ceremony was held in the flower garden at sunset, with music provided by a string quartet. Pachelbel's Canon was played for the processional. My uncle, Dr. David Roth, who was practicing neurosurgery in Boston, was the best man. Both Liz's and my parents attended, along with both my grandmothers. Several people who played an important role in both of our lives were there, including Don Morton and Mac Holmes. When I told Don Mulder, my chief of cardiothoracic surgery, that I was getting married over the weekend, he congratulated me and said, "Of course you will be back to work Monday morning." He was serious, and I was on the job for early Monday morning rounds. I still needed to complete a final year in my general surgery residency to be eligible for both the general and thoracic surgery boards. Now, because of a recent change, one can sit for the thoracic surgery boards without general surgery certification.

Liz's research accomplishments for her dissertation were recognized by her receiving the Intrascience Research Foundation Award, given annually to the UCLA student who has performed the most outstanding research, and she was designated UCLA Graduate Woman of the Year. Liz was then accepted for a postdoctoral research year with Fred Fox, a molecular biologist at UCLA. We both needed to think about our next chapter, which would be a real-world job. After years of education and training, this would be a major change.

In thinking about job possibilities, a major consideration was spending some time at the National Cancer Institute (NCI) in Bethesda, Maryland. Many of the most prominent and successful physician-scientists were associated with the NCI early in their careers. Don Morton, Mac Holmes, and Fred Eilber had all been there. The chief of the Surgery Branch of the NCI was a young physician-scientist, Steve Rosenberg. Steve had been appointed as chief of the surgery branch in 1974 at the ripe old age of thirty-four. This was highly controversial, as he had just completed his surgical residency and had little experience in cancer surgery. Steve was not really interested in performing a high volume of cancer surgery; he was committed to research on the immunology and potential immunotherapy of cancer. The NCI provided him with a substantial budget to pursue this research. The surgical clinical activities of the branch were limited, with relatively low numbers of cases. The major emphasis was on patients with melanoma (a highly aggressive skin cancer) and sarcomas (a heterogeneous group of cancers involving primarily connective tissue and bone). However, many other rare conditions that frequently needed surgical intervention were treated at the NCI. Senior staff at the NCI received financial support for their research without having to go through the laborious process of grant writing and submission. There was also the possibility of collaborating with outstanding cancer researchers. Vince DeVita, who had developed the first effective combination chemotherapy for Hodgkin lymphoma, was the director of the NCI. All this made an appointment to the NCI attractive to both Liz and me.

Liz was offered an appointment as a Cancer Expert with the Rosenberg group, providing her with an opportunity to do cutting-edge immunotherapy research. But there was another offer to consider. Don Morton wanted us to stay at UCLA. This was also attractive because I had ongoing research there, the faculty was excellent, I would learn much from them, and Los Angeles was a great place to live. The one negative was that, having done my research and clinical fellowships there, I would likely continue to be regarded as a fellow and would have difficulty developing an independent program. Rosenberg needed a thoracic surgeon for the NCI Surgery Branch because many patients were seen with unusual lung problems that required surgical evaluation, and there were many sarcoma patients who developed lung metastases that could potentially be removed by surgery. We were both in demand, as I had forty peer-reviewed publications at the end of residency, and Liz had done cutting-edge immunology research as a PhD student. After much discussion, we decided to accept the NCI positions in 1980. I would be a senior investigator and head of the thoracic oncology section. At last, our training had ended, and we both had real jobs.

9
THE NATIONAL CANCER INSTITUTE

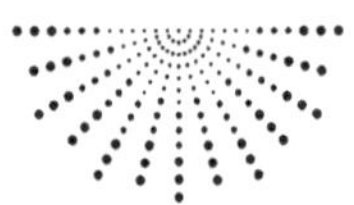

In nature's infinite book of secrecy a little I can read.

—Antony and Cleopatra, William Shakespeare

The NCI is the oldest of the twenty-seven institutes and centers that make up the NIH and has the largest budget and research program.[38] In 1937, President Franklin D. Roosevelt signed the National Cancer Institute Act, which established the NCI as a division of the Public Health Service. The NCI established the Clinical Trials Cooperative Group Program to fund multiple institutions working together to develop clinical trials and began a program of funding cancer centers around the country. Many of the most renowned cancer researchers who had made breakthrough contributions had spent time at the NCI. Combination chemotherapy was developed there, and researchers there were the first to induce long-term remissions in childhood leukemia patients.

I was provided with laboratory space, technicians, and research fellows, all without needing to submit endless grants, as was the case in the real world of academia. I was interested in developing new treatment strategies for the two major cancers that I treated clinically—non-small cell lung cancer, which was the leading cause of cancer deaths, and esophageal cancer. In some cases, because of the policies of the federal government and NIH, I could not always choose the personnel to work in my laboratory. Some technicians had lifelong appointments, and so when I was hired, they were assigned to me. One of the technicians assigned to my lab had spent most of his time in the Navy. He was a good sailor but did not have any experience with the new molecular techniques I was developing. I put him to work taking care of the mice for our animal experiments, but his productivity was less than optimal. I continued some of the work I had begun during my research fellowship several years earlier at UCLA. I showed that human cancers triggered an immune response in patients and that this response was directed against new molecules expressed by the tumors.[39]

A major problem in 1980 in human cancer immunology was finding a way to unleash the human immune system to destroy the cancer while leaving the patient unharmed. We had shown that the patient's immune system recognized some cancers as foreign. Despite this, the immune system seemed powerless to attack the cancer, which continued to grow and spread. Yet there were occasional anecdotal reports of patients with advanced cancers where the cancer spontaneously disappeared without treatment, and one explanation was an immune response elicited against the cancer. Even today, with a drug that blocks a protein that suppresses the immune response to cancer, only a small number of patients respond, and this immune attack is still far from specific, as normal tissues can also be attacked by the stimulated immune system. Our research uncovered one of the reasons the human immune response was ineffective. The cancers produced a protein that directly suppressed the immune response of T cells. Although it would be over ten years until this family of proteins was fully characterized, the protein we identified had the structure of a checkpoint protein. We did not have the analytic methods at that time to fully sequence and characterize it, but this was clearly a member of the family of checkpoint proteins. When these were more fully characterized by Honjo and Allison, antibodies to them could be made that would block the checkpoint and unleash an immune response against the cancer.[40]

The spectrum of clinical diseases that I saw was highly unusual. The National Institute of Allergy and Infectious Diseases had a program in genetic primary immune deficiency diseases. These patients were born with a defect in their immune system that predisposed them to rare infectious diseases that would not occur in an individual with a normal immune system. The infections often involved the lungs. I would be called to do a lung biopsy to determine the cause of the infection because all other tests did not provide an answer. These patients were often very ill and would not recover from anesthesia and surgery. Often, the lung biopsy did not provide any useful information that would alter the patient's treatment. Patients were often treated with antibiotics empirically without a diagnosis and recovered. I decided to organize a randomized clinical trial to determine if the lung biopsy really helped. Randomized clinical trials are the gold standard for determining the efficacy of an intervention. The trial specified the characteristics for which patients were eligible to participate. Eligible patients were then assigned randomly to one intervention group or another. Usually, one group is the standard of care, which in this case was a lung biopsy, while the other group received antibiotics based on the most likely organism to be causing the infection. There was no difference statistically in the survival of the two groups. However, the lung biopsy patients had twice as many severe complications.[41] This was the first clinical trial to address this problem and provided a result that would help patients avoid the severe complications of lung biopsy.

In the early 1980s, a new and much more difficult clinical problem was emerging, and I was on the front lines to deal with it. I was called to see patients in the intensive care unit with a mysterious complex of findings. They looked malnourished and had infections that caused both lungs to be filled with fluid. Several had a very rare skin cancer called Kaposi's sarcoma, characterized by red skin patches. I was called to perform lung biopsies to try to diagnose the infection that might be causing this. The biopsies did not yield an infectious organism. This syndrome was eventually given a name: acquired immunodeficiency syndrome (AIDS). We were among the first to describe its effect on organs in the chest in a paper published with Tony Fauci.[42] Its transmission was linked to sexual activity, with the largest group being homosexual men. It was not until 1983 that Luc Montagnier's team at the Pasteur Institute in Paris discovered that AIDS was caused by a retrovirus, which they named HIV-1, that invaded immune cells and destroyed them.[43] This discovery was rapidly followed by the development of blood tests for HIV, with much of this work taking place at the NIH. Now, at least we could identify patients with HIV and take appropriate precautions. In 1987, the first antiviral therapy was approved, but it was not until 1996 that a highly effective drug combination therapy was developed.

Most of the patients treated in the surgery branch were either melanoma (skin cancer) or sarcoma (bone and connective tissue cancer) patients because they were eligible for clinical trials being carried out at NCI. Melanoma patients were of interest to Steve Rosenberg, as these were patients who could enter his immunotherapy trials. These patients were likely to develop metastases (the spread of the tumor) to the lung, and sometimes this would be the only site of spread. In some cases, there were only five or fewer lung nodules, and they were only one or two centimeters in diameter. This raised the possibility that if these were the only sites of metastases and were removed surgically, the patient's life might be prolonged. Previously, there were anecdotal reports of patients with isolated lung metastases who had them removed with surgery and lived a long time. However, it was important to try to identify which patients would really benefit from the surgery. It turned out that the number of lung nodules was the best predictor, with those having four or fewer nodules attaining a 30–50 percent chance of four-year survival depending on the type of tumor.[44] This was remarkable considering that metastatic cancer was considered incurable and chemotherapy did not greatly prolong survival. Even if the lung metastases recurred, we could perform the surgery again and prolong the patient's life.[45] I reported the first large series of patients undergoing this type of surgery and inspired the concept of removal or treatment with radiation of small numbers of metastases anywhere in the body. I introduced this surgery at MD Anderson. The first randomized trial for the treatment of oligometastases was done at MD Anderson and published in 2016, ultimately providing a high level of evidence that this approach prolonged survival in cancer patients.[46]

Chemotherapy treatment for cancer was still based on drugs that bound to components of the cancer cell that were vital for cell division, such as DNA or microtubules. The drugs were given at the time the patient had spread of the disease. While they could in some cases shrink the tumor, cure was not possible. We knew that for many cancers, even though they had not appeared to spread, that even if the primary cancer was removed, spread would be seen shortly thereafter. Thus, at the time of diagnosis, there must have been small number of cancer cells in organs outside the primary cancer. Perhaps this small number of cancer cells could be killed with chemotherapy. The chemotherapy could shrink the primary tumor, thus making the surgery more successful in controlling the local disease. The first clinical trial of this concept was in breast cancer, but it had never been tried in lung or esophageal cancer, two of the deadliest cancers. I decided to initiate a clinical trial of pre- and postoperative chemotherapy for cancer of the esophagus, a cancer that, at the time, almost no patients survived for five years after treatment. The surgery for esophageal cancer is very difficult. A section of the esophagus is removed with the cancer, and then the stomach is connected to the remaining esophagus. Incisions must be made in the abdomen and the chest. The extent of the surgery combined with the poor condition of the patients who cannot eat a standard diet made the death rate from the surgery alone in the range of 10 to 20 percent. I knew I would need to refine the operative approach to reduce this, and in our clinical trial, the treatment-related deaths were reduced to 5 percent. I designed a clinical trial with patients being randomly assigned to either have surgery only or to receive chemotherapy with three drugs before and after surgery.[47] The results of the clinical trial were dramatic. Five times more patients receiving chemotherapy were alive three years after the surgery than those who received surgery alone. If patients responded —that is, their tumor shrank following chemotherapy—more than 50 percent were alive at three years compared to 5 percent or fewer who either did not respond or did not have chemotherapy. These results eventually led to more trials, with preoperative chemotherapy becoming the standard of care. These results were so exciting that I wanted to apply this strategy to other cancers occurring in the chest. I had the opportunity to do this when I moved to MD Anderson, initiating the first perioperative chemotherapy clinical trial in lung cancer. This would again establish a new standard of care resulting in lung cancer patients living longer, which I will describe in chapters that follow. During this time, other exciting scientific developments were occurring that would revolutionize our understanding of cancer.

Why do the body's normal cells become cancerous? This was a question that had puzzled scientists for over one hundred years. In 1911, Peyton Rous showed that an extract of chicken cancer, which he had passed through a filter too fine for bacteria or cells to pass through, could cause cancer when injected in another chicken.[48] Thus, this was a virus. For many years after these observations, viruses were thought to be a major cause of cancer. It was not until 1964 that the first human cancer-causing virus, the Epstein-Barr DNA virus, was observed, which causes several types of cancer, including lymphoma and stomach cancer. Other virus-related cancers have been identified, including a human T-cell lymphoma-leukemia virus, which is a retrovirus composed of RNA; hepatitis B and C viruses, which can cause liver cancer; and the herpes virus, which can cause cervical cancer. Vaccines against hepatitis B and C and herpes can prevent the cancers from developing. But despite the role of viruses in those cancers, the most common cancers, such as breast, lung, prostate, and colon, do not have a detectable infectious viral origin. However, basic virology research has found that in these viruses, there were certain genes that were responsible for the transformation of normal cells into cancer cells. Furthermore, many of these genes, called oncogenes, without activating mutations, were also found in the genome of normal cells. Such genes could be activated by mutations or by making excessive amounts of the normal protein, called overexpression. These genes function in the cell-signaling pathways, which control cell growth and division. When this control is lost, the cell begins to develop the uncontrolled cell division and metastasis properties of cancer cells. In some cases, it is mutations in these genes that are responsible for the loss of control. They can be characterized as "the enemy within". The mutations can be caused by a variety of cancer-causing agents such as tobacco, ultraviolet light, or alcohol. However, it has also been observed that mutations are constantly occurring in our genes from the time we are born. Why don't we all get cancer at a very young age?

Cells have a mechanism for repairing DNA damage, so many of these mutations are changed back to normal, or the cells are eliminated.[49] Cancer requires the accumulation of cancer-causing mutations in the cell. One or two mutations alone will not change the character of the cell. But there is another type of gene that is important in determining whether a cell becomes cancerous. Certain genes are inactivated in cancer cells either through mutation or deletion. These genes have a tumor suppressor function. They normally regulate the manufacture of proteins and the rates of cell division. When they are disabled, it is like a malfunction of the brakes on a car. The cancerous cells divide uncontrollably and can break loose and spread to other organs. Mutations in tumor suppressor genes are the most common mutations in cancer. Because mutations in oncogenes like the epidermal growth factor receptor cause the gene product, which is a protein, to become hyperactive like flooring the accelerator on a car, small-molecule drugs can be made that block or turn off the hyperactive protein. But a tumor suppressor gene cannot be turned back on if it is inactivated or totally deleted. One strategy would be to insert a normal tumor suppressor gene back into the cancer cell. The development of gene therapy suggested that this was possible. This concept formed the basis for our future gene therapy trials, among the first in the world, which will be described in later chapters.

Steve Rosenberg and his wife, Alice (back left), had a party at their home for NCI Surgery Branch staff in 1983.

Steve Rosenberg was developing a large program focused on the immunotherapy of melanoma. He became interested in a protein that could be used to grow T lymphocytes from bone marrow, called interleukin 2 (IL-2).[50] This observation was made by Gallo's group at the NIH in 1976. A recombinant version of IL-2 was developed, and Rosenberg began giving large amounts of it intravenously to patients to stimulate the immune system against the cancer. I recall Steve catching me in the hall and excitedly taking me to his office to show me some X-rays of a patient with lung metastases. These were very small, but the before-and-after treatment X-rays seemed to show several millimeter shrinkages of the nodules. His new treatment was a success! However, the enthusiasm was soon tempered. Patients receiving IL-2 became very sick with what was called a leaky capillary syndrome. Their lungs filled with fluid, and they could not breathe. This treatment was effective in only a very small number of patients but was too toxic for general use. The FDA declined to approve it, and the company making it went out of business. However, there was another twist to this story. Liz, working with others in the Rosenberg lab, noticed that the cells activated by IL-2 that were able to kill cancer cells did not have the characteristics of T lymphocytes. They appeared to be another class of innate immune cells, which they called lymphokine-activated killer (LAK) cells.[51] These are now an important component of new cancer treatments.

The clinical trials with IL-2 taught me a very important lesson in drug development. Cancer patients have a variety of other illnesses, which are designated as comorbid conditions. They are very susceptible to the toxicities and side effects of the anticancer drugs administered to them. In many cases, these patient's life expectancy is shorter than normal for their age group. Thus, it is critical that they have a high quality of life for their remaining life. New cancer drugs need to be not only highly effective but also do as little damage as possible to normal cells while targeting their toxic effects specifically to the cancer cell. This would become the driving force behind all my future laboratory, translational, and clinical research. Every strategy would be extensively tested to minimize side effects and toxicity to normal cells while maximizing therapeutic efficacy. I would need to develop an entirely novel approach to cancer treatment.

The first human oncogene was identified while I was at NCI, which was incredibly exciting. The proto-oncogene was called HRAS, and the mutant oncogene was derived from a bladder cancer. There was only a single missense mutation, which caused the oncogene to be in a permanently turned-on state.[52] This raised the possibility that if this single abnormal protein could be targeted and turned off, it could cause the cancer to stop growing or to die.

I developed a collaboration with the Gallo laboratory to look for new molecules expressed by cells that had been turned cancerous by the introduction of an oncogene. In this case, we used the acute lymphocytic leukemia oncogene. In the past, these cells were injected into mice or rabbits to see if they formed antibodies to a new molecule. However, there was a new technique recently developed called monoclonal antibodies, which revolutionized antibody production. A mouse is injected with the cells or protein of interest. The spleen or other white cells are then separated and fused with a type of cancerous cell that produces antibodies. They are diluted until single clones are obtained. The resulting antibodies can then be screened to find an antibody that specifically binds to a single molecule. We found that the cells with the oncogene expressed a new protein that could be detected with monoclonal antibodies.[53] Thus, this antibody could be used to deliver an anticancer drug directly to cancer cells and not to normal cells that do not have the protein. We were able to produce such a drug and show that it was highly specific for the oncogene-transformed cells.[54] This research set the stage for the future development of antibody drug conjugates that are now highly successful in clinical trials and approved by the FDA.[55]

As a thoracic surgeon, my primary clinical interest was in lung and esophageal cancers. There was no one in the surgery branch with similar interests. When I was conceptualizing the esophageal cancer clinical trial, I tried to get medical oncologists interested in collaborating, but none of them wanted to participate. So, I elected to administer the chemotherapy myself. As a surgery resident at UCLA, I had given chemotherapy in some of the clinics, but I had no formal training in medical oncology. Nevertheless, our team administered the complex three-agent chemotherapy and had minimal complications. It was not so difficult. There was another institution across the street from the NIH that had a major program in lung cancer research: the Bethesda Naval Hospital. John Minna, a translational lung cancer researcher, and Adi Gazdar, a pathologist, had moved there from the Veterans Administration Hospital to establish a lung cancer laboratory and clinical research program. Their group was one of the first to establish immortalized lung cancer cell lines. I read about this and realized that I needed this model to establish my own lung cancer research program. John and Adi were very generous in supplying the cell lines. Their lung cancer cell lines, which eventually numbered in the hundreds, became some of the most important research reagents and were fundamental to the discovery of new treatments.[56] Shortly after I moved to Houston, John and Adi moved to the University of Texas Southwestern in Dallas. We continued our collaboration, which included a joint highly prestigious NCI Specialized Program of Research Excellence that completed twenty-eight years and is continuing, the longest continuous funding for this type of grant in NCI history.

My laboratory in the Surgery Branch of the National Cancer Institute. Front row, left to right: Emil Trahan, Jack Roth, Stanley Leong; back row, left to right: Phil Scuderi, Bill Putnam, Bob Ames, Bill Funkhouser.

It had been an incredibly interesting, rewarding, and productive six years in the surgery branch of NCI. During that short period of time, we confirmed the immune response to human cancer, identified a major protein that blocked the anticancer human immune response, performed the first randomized clinical trial for lung biopsies, performed the first randomized clinical trial for perioperative chemotherapy for esophageal cancer (establishing it as a new therapeutic approach), clarified which patients benefited from surgery for their lung metastases, identified new targets related to oncogenes, and developed the concept of antibody drug conjugate to target oncogene-related proteins. But this was only the beginning. How could Liz and I expand our translational research and clinical trials programs? Most of the resources in the surgery branch were directed toward Rosenberg's immunotherapy program. It was impossible to expand the clinical trials program because few patients would travel to NCI, and there was only a small community directly served by the program. But it would be difficult to leave NCI and Bethesda. By 1984 Liz had a tenured position at the NCI neuro-oncology branch, and for both of us our research could continue without any need to write grants. We loved our home in Potomac, Maryland, a beautiful, idyllic suburb of Washington, DC. And we had two wonderful additions to our family—our daughters, J and K, born in 1983 and 1986, respectively.

Liz and I were being recruited by many excellent academic centers. Many medical schools were now focusing on oncology. It was apparent that the number of cancer patients was increasing and that unique training and abilities were needed in a specialized multidisciplinary group to provide the highest level of cancer care. This was the model established by Don Morton, and now many other centers were adopting it. We were invited to consider faculty positions at Johns Hopkins School of Medicine, Indiana University, Memorial Sloan Kettering Cancer Center, and Ohio State University, where Arthur James, a cancer surgeon, was creating a new cancer center. We also visited the University of Texas MD Anderson Cancer Center in Houston, Texas. I was not impressed by my initial visit to MD Anderson and turned down their offer to become department chair of thoracic surgery. MD Anderson seemed to be primarily a state cancer hospital with little national reputation. The emphasis appeared to be on clinical patient care, whereas I was looking for a program that emphasized translational and clinical cancer research. Several months later, I heard that Charles Balch, a surgical oncologist with a strong translational research interest, was recruited to head the Division of Surgery at MD Anderson. I remember the tennis Liz and I played with Charles and his wife at a Society of Surgical Oncology meeting. We had remained friends. Thus, I was not too surprised when he contacted Liz and me about reconsidering jobs at MD Anderson. He told me the institution was changing rapidly under its new president, Charles (Mickey) LeMaistre. LeMaistre was to turn MD Anderson into the best clinical and research cancer center in the world. He was committed to recruiting top translational and clinical researchers and providing them with the resources they would need to develop world-class programs. LeMaistre was a very persuasive fundraiser, and there were multiple corporations and individuals in Houston with extensive financial resources who thought donating to a cancer center was a worthy cause. He had established many endowed chairs, meaning that the endowment would yield thousands of dollars each year that could be used for research. I believed that MD Anderson was an institution on an accelerating upward trajectory. I would receive space and financial support for research with a generous startup package, and there were large numbers of patients for clinical trials. I would be the chair of a new department of thoracic surgery and hold an endowed position, which meant additional funds to support research. Liz was offered a tenured appointment as an associate professor. This was too good an opportunity to pass up. Liz and I accepted and began planning our move to Houston.

10
DEEP IN THE HEART OF TEXAS

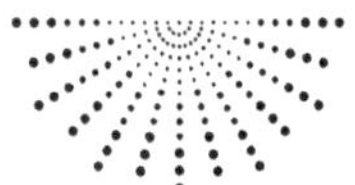

Glendower: I can call spirits from the vasty deep.

Hotspur: Why, so can I, or so can any man; but will they come when you do call for them?

—Henry IV,Part 1, William Shakespeare

The MD Anderson Cancer Center is named for Monroe Dunaway Anderson, born June 29, 1873, in Jackson, Tennessee.[57] He began working in his father's bank but then decided to go into business with his older brother, Frank, and Frank's brother-in-law, Will Clayton, buying and selling cotton. Anderson moved his company to Houston in 1907 for access to larger banks and the ship channel and port that opened in 1914. His company became the largest cotton merchant in the world. Anderson was a lifelong bachelor. His death would result in taxes and the dissolution of the company. His lawyers advised him to put his $21 million estate (worth over $300 million today) into a foundation, which Anderson stipulated should support "the promotion of health, science, education, and the advancement and diffusion of knowledge and understanding among people." Anderson died from a stroke in 1939. The trustees of the MD Anderson Foundation favored using funds for health care. In 1941, the Texas legislature authorized the University of Texas to build a cancer hospital for both research and treatment and set aside $500,000. The Anderson Foundation agreed to match those funds if the hospital was built in Houston and named after Anderson. There was public land by the recently constructed Hermann Hospital, and the Anderson Foundation acquired it. This was an exceptional concept, as oncology did not exist as a specialty at that time.

The construction would take time, so a temporary hospital was set up on the James A. Baker estate. James Addison Baker Sr. was the grandfather of James A. Baker III, who served as chief of staff for two presidents. A surgeon, Randolph Lee Clark, became the director and surgeon-in-chief of the new cancer hospital. He had previously had a vision of a pink hospital, and so the exterior of the first building was covered in pink marble, and the hospital acquired the nickname Pink Palace when it opened for patient care on March 19, 1954. In 1961, Clifton Mountain, a general surgeon, became head of thoracic surgery. He and David Carr, a medical oncologist at the Mayo Clinic who subsequently came to MD Anderson, established a staging system for lung cancer, which had not previously existed. This system classifies the extent of lung cancer by tumor size, lymph node spread, and spread to other organs, which is helpful in predicting survival and determining the appropriate treatment strategy. I was appointed to establish a separate department of thoracic surgery and take over the leadership role from Dr. Mountain.

Moving to a new state for new jobs with two children, a three-year-old and a six-month-old, was unexpectedly difficult for us in the summer of 1986. We had purchased a home earlier that was still under construction, and it was not yet ready to move in, so we ended up staying in an apartment building that MD Anderson made available for patients who needed prolonged housing for treatment. We immediately encountered the administrative roadblocks that were pervasive throughout the institution at that time and have only increased. With a toddler and an infant, we obviously needed childcare, but MD Anderson had none to offer, and we were told our Jamaican nanny, who had come with us, could not stay in our building. We would need to get her a separate hotel room a few blocks away. This was not the way to welcome new faculty and help with their move. Several weeks later we could finally move into our new home, but the nanny did not feel welcome, and returned to the DC area.

Prior to my arrival, there was no department of thoracic surgery. In fact, there were no board-certified thoracic surgeons in the institution. Thoracic surgery was performed by general surgeons, as thoracic surgery was considered a part of general surgery. It soon became evident that these surgeons were concerned about their positions and working under the new sheriff in town. None of them was adequately trained in current thoracic surgery practice, and they were not supportive of the academic clinical and laboratory research direction I wanted to steer the department in. One of my highest priorities would be the recruitment of thoracic surgeons certified by the American Board of Thoracic Surgery who would contribute to the research mission of the department and institution.

The chair of a department at MD Anderson has many diverse responsibilities. My department had both patient-centered clinical responsibilities and an academic mission to perform high-quality research that generates publications and grant funding. There were numerous administrative responsibilities, including developing the annual budget for the department, hiring and evaluating staff, and ensuring that the fellowship training programs provided mentorship and adequate cases to fulfill training requirements. The chair must decide how to accomplish these goals and what type of leadership style to adopt. My primary goal was to develop a department that provided exceptional clinical care and conducted cutting-edge research to improve patient outcomes and care. I had been in multiple departments in various institutions and had experienced a variety of leadership styles. I wanted to build a department where everyone worked together, where it would be enjoyable to come to work, and where each member of the faculty could pursue their passion. Building the department began with careful recruiting of surgeons from the best training programs who had a collaborative mindset. My goal was to provide advice and resources to help them build a program around their major interests. Thus, my leadership style was that of a servant leader who facilitated faculty goals at every step. I also worked to inspire and motivate by example, establishing excellence in clinical care and research in my own practice. Thus, faculty would not be competing but developing unique programs that would benefit from cross-collaboration. Although I stepped away as chair sixteen years ago from the date of publication of this book, the department continues to flourish as a center of clinical and research excellence with the subsequent department chairs being my trainees demonstrating the durability and value of this concept.

There were many administrative issues that needed attention. At that time, desktop computers were in their infancy, Windows operating systems did not exist (remember the C-prompt command line?), and data was stored on 1.2-megabyte floppy disks. I needed to set up offices, hire an administrative staff, recruit thoracic surgeons, and supervise the renovation of laboratory space in addition to establishing a cutting-edge laboratory and clinical research program. Charles Balch, who was now the overall head of surgery, and I were the first faculty members in surgery to have a strong academic focus with plans to develop both laboratory research and clinical trials programs. Perhaps the heads of the other clinical departments felt threatened, but they were not very welcoming or willing to develop their own departments in that direction. In fact, some were downright hostile.

The administrative structure of MD Anderson was also odd. LeMaistre was the president, but his background was neither cancer treatment nor laboratory research. He appointed a cadre of vice presidents to supervise the various programs. In a strange twist, the head of the clinical program was a basic scientist, and the head of the research program was a pathologist. Although LeMaistre and Balch were enthusiastic about my recruitment, it was not clear that the other administrators shared their enthusiasm. The vice president for research was an acerbic individual who did not really support clinicians who were also doing laboratory research. I would have multiple run-ins with him over various administrative issues until he left the institution. In contrast, fairly soon after my arrival, Waun Ki Hong, the chair of thoracic and head and neck medical oncology (which had been combined in one department as they could not find a qualified individual for lung cancer alone) came personally to welcome me. Waun Ki Hong was Korean and had trained at the VA in Boston and Memorial Sloan Kettering. His major interest was head and neck cancer, but the head of medical oncology asked him to take over lung cancer when the prior chair, David Carr, retired. Hong was also research-oriented, although he had no laboratory research background. He seemed collaborative, and we would lead several projects together over our years at MD Anderson.

However, we had our disagreements. In academic settings, one of the most important resources is space, and space allocation is a source of endless administrative disputes. Shortly after I arrived, a radiation oncologist, James Cox, was appointed as physician-in-chief. Hong and the head of medical oncology, Irv Krakoff, thought that Hong's department needed additional space. As I was the new kid on the block, the space allocated to my department looked like easy pickings. Besides, why do surgeons need space if they are always in the operating room? So all three teamed up, thinking their combined authority would carry the day. But they had not considered my obstinacy. The space allocated to our department was part of my contractual recruitment package, and I needed it for future recruitment. Fortunately, the administration saw it my way, and I won the first of many academic battles. Someone once said that academic disputes are so vicious because the stakes are so low.

Renovation of my laboratory space was finally completed. I needed to hire research staff for the laboratory and was able to recruit Bob Ames, who had worked with me at the NCI. One of my first research fellows was Steve Yang, a surgery resident from the University of Texas Health Science Center, across the street from MD Anderson. Steve did some pioneering work showing that combining IL-2 and tumor necrosis factor, another cytokine that activates the immune response, greatly increased immune cell killing of cancer cells.[58] This led to a clinical trial that showed that metastatic lung cancers respond to this immune therapy and paved the way for other combination immunotherapy clinical trials. This was an excellent example of how research from the laboratory could be directly translated to treating patients in the clinic.[59] Steve ultimately became the head of thoracic surgery at Johns Hopkins, the first of many of my fellows to attain leadership positions.

A dinner at our new home in Houston with colleagues from MD Anderson, including Mien-Chi Hung, currently president of China Medical University and chancellor of the China Medical University - Asia University System in Taichung, Taiwan.

Paul Schneider was a surgeon from Germany who was interested in learning about cancer research. In our laboratory, he was one of the first to detect abnormalities in the epidermal growth factor receptor tyrosine kinase domain, an important on-off switch for this oncogene, which later explained the activity of drugs targeting the epidermal growth factor that only worked well in cancer cells with a mutation in that domain.[60] We did not have the technology to do extensive DNA sequencing, but fourteen years later, these mutations would be rediscovered. Paul also found that the p53 tumor suppressor gene was mutated in Barrett's esophagus, which is a premalignant condition that can lead to cancer of the esophagus.[61] He returned to Germany to practice surgery and participated in one of the biggest surprises of my life. Unbeknownst to me, Liz was plotting something very unusual and special for my upcoming fiftieth birthday. She contacted Paul to see if he could obtain tickets to the Bayreuth Festival. Attending this is the dream of every fan of Richard Wagner's music, but the waitlist for tickets can extend for years. However, in an amazing coincidence, Paul was treating a singer scheduled to perform at Bayreuth, and she was able to obtain two tickets for the Ring cycle. When Liz presented me with them, I could not believe my eyes. We had an incredible time in Bayreuth, which I will describe in the following chapter.

Over the years, I trained many research fellows who made important discoveries. I always tried to remain in touch with them after they left the laboratory and follow their careers. MD Anderson had an arrangement with the Texas Heart Institute (THI) for residency training. THI trained three cardiothoracic residents each year. To qualify for board certification, each resident needed a certain number of noncardiac thoracic cases, and they rotated to MD Anderson to obtain that experience. The head of THI was Denton Cooley, a very prominent cardiac surgeon and a major presence in the Texas Medical Center. He trained at Hopkins with Blalock and assisted on the first "blue baby" operation (Chapter 5). Blalock liked athletes, and Cooley had played basketball at the University of Texas and was a good tennis player. Blalock enjoyed arranging matches with Cooley when he was a resident at Hopkins. Cooley was initially at Baylor with another prominent heart surgeon, Michael DeBakey.[62] However, in 1969, Cooley implanted the first artificial heart without DeBakey's knowledge or permission. This created a lifelong enmity between the two. Cooley left Baylor to establish THI across the street from DeBakey. They finally made amends in 2007. A lawyer supposedly asked Cooley during a trial if he considered himself to be the best heart surgeon in the world. Cooley replied that he did. "Don't you think that's being rather immodest?" the lawyer replied. "Perhaps," Cooley responded. "But remember, I'm under oath." I found Cooley to be a congenial and collaborative person. He invited me to all his resident end-of-the-year dinners. Toward the end of his career, he gave me a tour of a museum documenting his career, newly established in the THI building.

Resident training programs are an important component of an

academic program. Providing excellence in education is challenging but necessary to produce the next generation of cardiothoracic surgeons. The residents from THI were competent but were not interested in surgery outside the heart. They acquired the number of cases they needed, but their future careers would be focused on building a practice in cardiac surgery. It was becoming evident to me and others who focused on cancer care and other noncardiac surgical patients that cardiac and noncardiac thoracic surgery had little in common. It was important to have experience with heart surgery and the great vessels, but cancer surgery was becoming more complex, and clearly, a higher level of specialty training was needed. In Canada, the residencies for cardiac and noncardiac surgery were separate. We were one of the first institutions to offer a noncardiac thoracic track residency, which we began in 1992. This provided residents with extensive experience in cancer surgery, along with the experience in cardiac surgery at THI needed for board certification. I soon realized that one of the benefits of the program was the ability to recruit and train future faculty for our program. Many of our trainees have gone on to become department chairs at MD Anderson and other institutions, as well as faculty at MD Anderson. The separate fellowship program continued to provide an opportunity for thoracic surgeons who had completed their residency to obtain a year of advanced training in thoracic surgery.

But in 1986, my priority was to build a department, and I was going to do it by recruiting the best surgeons, all certified by the American Board of Thoracic Surgery. Bill Putnam had been a clinical associate under me at the NCI. His goal was to become a noncardiac thoracic surgeon, and Bill was accepted in an outstanding thoracic surgery program at the University of Michigan, where noncardiac surgery was under Mark Orringer. I knew Mark from Hopkins during the time he was a chief resident. Mark was very detail-oriented and driven, and I knew anyone in his program would be well trained. Bill saw the potential for developing thoracic surgery at MD Anderson and accepted my offer to join our thoracic surgery faculty. In 2005, he left to become the chair of thoracic surgery at Vanderbilt and eventually moved to the Baptist MD Anderson Cancer Center in Jacksonville, Florida, where he became the medical director.

John Nesbitt was recruited in 1992 after a career in the Navy with service in Desert Storm. John played a major role in developing our educational programs. He eventually returned to his hometown of Nashville and became head of the Division of Cardiothoracic Surgery at St. Thomas Hospital.

Our training programs offered an exceptional opportunity to train and then retain top thoracic surgery talent. Garrett Walsh was one of our first fellows who had completed his surgical residency at McGill in Montreal. After completing his fellowship in our program, we kept Garrett on as a faculty member. Steve Swisher was recruited to our faculty after completing his thoracic track fellowship in our program. Steve completed his general surgery residency at UCLA and had done research with Don Morton's group. Steve eventually became the chair of thoracic and cardiovascular surgery at MD Anderson when I stepped away in 2008. Subsequently, he became head of all surgery at MD Anderson. Ara Vaporciyan, another of our thoracic track fellows, became chair of the department after Steve moved up. Thus, our department and MD Anderson surgery have been led by a legacy of our trainees.

One of the primary attractions of moving to MD Anderson was the large population of patients with cancers of special interest to me. Lung cancer, at that time and today, is the leading cause of cancer deaths in men and women. It is over twice as high as the second leading cause, cancers of the colon and rectum. Lung cancer was relatively rare in the early years of the twentieth century. As cigarettes became more popular, the cases of lung cancer skyrocketed. It was not until the 1950s that studies definitively associated smoking with the development of lung cancer.[63] Fortunately, because of successful anti-smoking campaigns, the incidence of lung cancer has decreased dramatically during the twenty-first century. This has been the driving force behind the decrease in cancer deaths during the same time. However, lung cancer is still a major problem. In 2024, it is estimated there will be 234,580 new cases of lung cancer (116,310 in men and

118,270 in women) and about 125,070 deaths from lung cancer (65,790 in men and 59,280 in women).[64] If someone stops smoking, there is still a lifetime increased risk of lung cancer, although the risk decreases over time. Of greater concern is that 10–20 percent of lung cancers in the United States occur in people who have never smoked.[65] The causes of this are not clear. There may be some genetic predisposition. Also, exposure to secondhand tobacco smoke or other cancer-causing agents, such as radon, may play a role. A small number of lung cancers were diagnosed at an early, potentially curable stage. Most patients presented with symptoms, such as chronic cough or pneumonia, which were associated with advanced cancer. The five-year survival rate was less than 20 percent. Better treatments were urgently needed.

At NCI, I completed a randomized clinical trial where chemotherapy was given before surgery, the first of its kind for esophageal cancer. If there had been any spread of the tumor that could not be detected by preoperative testing, those cells could be killed by chemotherapy at a time when only a few were present. The chemotherapy could be more effective then, as opposed to when the metastases were finally visible on imaging. Also, patients would tolerate chemotherapy better before surgery than afterward, when they are recovering with part of their lung removed. The clinical trial with esophageal cancer was successful in improving survival.

Then I wanted to apply the same concept for the first time to lung cancer treatment. I decided to focus on a stage of lung cancer that was locally advanced and rarely cured with surgery alone, designated stage 3A. The tumor had spread to mediastinal lymph nodes (located in the middle of the chest), but these could be removed surgically along with the primary tumor. Once again, I designed another first—a randomized clinical trial to test this. Patients would either be offered standard surgery or receive chemotherapy before and after surgery. This would all be determined randomly. If the patient's tumor progressed and the patient had not received chemotherapy initially, chemotherapy could be given at that time. The trial began in 1987. I was young and optimistic when the trial began, but it became one of the most difficult research projects to complete in my career. There were many obstacles. Stage 3A patients were not all that common. The surgeons in the department at that time, who were there before I arrived, were not interested in clinical trials, as it meant considerably more work in explaining the trial and obtaining informed consent. However, I pushed ahead. Would the trial succeed in accruing enough patients, and would the addition of chemotherapy prolong the survival of lung cancer patients? Only time would tell.

11
PAYING THE BILLS—THE FUNDING CRISIS FACED BY CANCER RESEARCHERS

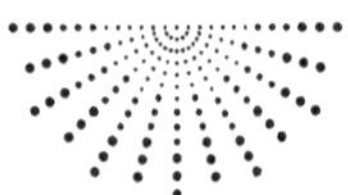

Everything is theoretically impossible, until it is done.
—Robert A. Heinlein

Earlier at the NCI, my research budget was part of the overall surgery branch budget, and I did not worry about raising money to pay for fellows, technicians, or reagents. It was great while it lasted, but the NCI was not the real academic medicine and research world. The process of funding research at an academic research institution is complex and time-consuming. Institutions expect researchers to pay their own way, including all or a substantial part of their salary. The three mechanisms for grant funding most used are grants from the National Institutes of Health or foundations, direct philanthropic gifts, and sponsored research agreements from industry. Grants from the NIH are the most difficult to obtain. NIH funding is limited and has not increased with inflation, so there has been a real decrease in the value of the funding over time. There are several types of grants. The research project (R01) grant is the oldest funding mechanism, generally awarded to an individual investigator or small group of investigators. It is considered the most prestigious grant. In general, tenure-track and tenured faculty members are expected to have one or more of these grants. With current reductions in federal research funding, fewer than 10 percent of applications for R01 grants are funded. If you are considering a career in academic research, the odds are not in your favor. Would you make a career choice with a 90 percent probability of failure? This, in part, explains the influx of PhD researchers into industry, which has reached record levels.[66] There are other grants for early-career investigators and for larger groups of researchers focused on a specific research topic, but these are also funded at extremely low levels.

When I arrived at MD Anderson, one of my first projects was to submit an R01 grant to the NCI. I had never written one before, but I had an extensive research and publication record. I wanted to continue my research that linked the immunology of cancer with the newly emerging field of cancer molecular biology. I assembled a grant that would investigate new proteins (tumor antigens) expressed by cells made cancerous by oncogenes, titled "Tumor Antigens Expressed by Oncogene Transformed Cells." The new proteins, which would be limited to the cancer cells, could be targets for drugs. They could also be useful for early cancer detection if they were shed into the blood. In 1987, when I submitted the grant, it could be up to twenty-five pages long. This limit was eventually reduced to twelve pages to alleviate some of the reviewers' burden. Preparing one of these grants is a long and arduous process that may take months. The quality of the science proposed will ultimately determine whether the grant is funded. However, the budget must go through an approval process by one's institution. There are then multiple forms and compliance approvals that must be obtained relating to animal care and use and to patient-derived specimens. I had never done this before. Could I possibly succeed?

The current administrative burden in the preparation of NIH grants is costly and difficult to justify, given the 10 percent probability of success with each submission. The submitted grants are reviewed by a study section, which consists of researchers from around the country outside the NIH who perform research similar to the applicant's and are considered experts in the field. Each study section member may be assigned multiple grants to review. This takes many hours, and each study section may require two days of reviews several times a year. In earlier years, when grant funding was more plentiful, this system worked, but now, with most grants not being funded, it is very difficult for reviewers to differentiate among many excellent grants. There is also a tendency to be very conservative. The grant must have extensive preliminary data showing that there is a high chance of the research succeeding. This puts novel or out-of-the-box concepts at a disadvantage. The highly competitive environment for grants distorts the peer-review process. Those experts in your field who are reviewing your grant in the study section are also your competitors. How objective and impartial can they be when you are both competing for the same small number of grants?

The increasing difficulty in obtaining grant funding has another insidious consequence. The number of physician-scientists, physicians who both practice medicine and conduct scientific research, has dropped precipitously.[67] Today 1.5 percent of physicians in the United States are physician-scientists, compared with 4.7 percent thirty years ago. This decrease has enormous implications for progress in medicine. Physician-scientists are uniquely capable of making discoveries in the laboratory and rapidly translating them to medical practice in the clinic through clinical trials. Many recent advances in cancer treatment, such as immunotherapy and targeted drugs, were developed by physician-scientists.

There are multiple reasons for the demise of physician-scientists, but the lack of research funding is a central cause. Promotions in academic centers usually require having grant funding. The 10 percent award rates for grants mean the odds of funding your research and obtaining promotion are stacked against you from the beginning. No wonder physicians never enter or rapidly exit the physician-scientist track, to the great detriment of medical progress.

I was fortunate; the first NIH R01 grant I submitted was funded. But I was in for a pleasant surprise. It received one of the best scores of all the grants reviewed during the funding cycle. This resulted in my grant receiving an NCI Merit Award, which means an extended period of funding beyond what was requested. Unfortunately, the funding situation would only get worse, and I would need to be very creative to maintain my unbroken over-40-year funding record with NIH grants.

The lack of funding may be contributing to a general decrease in research productivity. More effort is required to produce smaller incremental gains in knowledge.[68] Furthermore, the disruptiveness of scientific findings has decreased.[69] With the continuing reduction in research funding, it will be impossible to address these problems. How can this critical issue with funding be alleviated? Funds from research prizes could be repurposed into grants for young investigators (Chapter 7). Prize foundations would award the grants based on merit review. This would potentially increase the funding pool available. Wealthy individuals banding together can bankroll research organizations with a specific focus.[70] An example is Arena BioWorks, privately funded for $500 million. Profits from resulting patents and drugs would remain private. The scientists would be working outside academia, using infrastructure created by the organization. Thus, they would not need to be concerned about grant funding, publications, or the tenure process and would furthermore have a much higher salary.

Another approach would be to fund people rather than projects. This would, in theory, incentivize higher-risk projects with potentially bigger payoffs. It also relieves the investigator from constant grant submission pressure. This is not a new idea. The Howard Hughes Medical Institute, founded in 1953, funds researchers for seven or more years. Howard Hughes fellows have been awarded thirty Nobel Prizes.

As a society, we need to recognize and prioritize the value of scientific research in improving our health and quality of life. Funding cannot be the sole responsibility of governmental organizations, as political and fiscal pressures will continue to reduce their ability to adequately fund research. Structured sources from the private sector are a potential solution that needs further development.

12
DESIGNER GENES—CORRECTING THE CAUSE OF CANCER

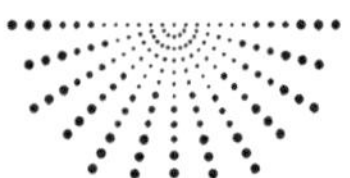

> There are genes inside cells that tell cells to grow, and the same genes tell cells to stop growing. When you deregulate these genes, you unleash cancer.
>
> —Siddhartha Mukherjee

In Chapter 1, I wrote about oncogenes and tumor suppressor genes, which contribute to the development of most cancers. DNA (deoxyribonucleic acid) consists of chemical molecules that make up our genetic code. DNA molecules appear in specific sequences in the chromosomes of our cells. Using ribonucleic acids (RNA) that are made to mirror the DNA, proteins are produced in the cell that regulate the myriad of cellular functions, including cell differentiation (specialization) and cell division. There are families of genes that signal cells and control cell life and death. While many normal cells are constantly being renewed in the body as a normal process, such as cells lining the gastrointestinal tract or bone marrow blood-producing cells, this growth and cell division are tightly regulated so the cells do not grow uncontrollably. In cancers, mutations (which are mistakes in one or more bases in the DNA code) in this family of growth-controlling genes are detected. These mutations are likely caused by the effects of molecules from cancer-causing agents (carcinogens), which can naturally or unnaturally exist in the environment or can be the result of lifestyle choices such as tobacco consumption. The effects of the mutations depend on the function of the gene. If the mutation occurs in a gene that turns on cell growth, the mutation may cause that gene to be permanently in the on position, like an accelerator that is stuck to the floor. Opposing this family of genes is another family called tumor suppressor genes. These genes balance the cell growth process by applying the brakes at the right time. Mutations can inactivate these genes, which is akin to the brakes failing.

Cancer treatments in the 1980s were based on drugs that bound to DNA or otherwise inhibited DNA from mediating cell division. The problems with these drugs included severe side effects because they were not selective just for cancer cells but could inhibit rapidly dividing normal cells, such as those in the bone marrow, from dividing, thus causing anemia and loss of white blood cells, resulting in a predisposition to infections. The drugs had low response rates of around 20 percent, so most patients, while experiencing the side effects, did not receive any benefit in terms of tumor regression. Could a drug be designed that would have few and mild side effects but was still effective against the cancer, even in patients whose tumors progressed on current cancer treatments? The recent insights into the genetics of cancer suggested novel treatment strategies to me that had never been attempted.

The concept of gene therapy had been proposed as a way of treating inherited monogenic disorders, which are genetic defects that occur in one crucial gene with disastrous consequences. An example is adenosine deaminase deficiency, which is caused by a mutation in the adenosine deaminase gene and results in severe combined immunodeficiency (SCID). Patients are susceptible to viral, bacterial, and fungal infections that a person with a normal immune system could easily fight off. If a normal adenosine deaminase gene could be placed in the patient, it would completely cure the disease. In 1991, this was only a concept. However, progress in this field over the past thirty years has now made this a reality with dramatic successes.[71] But when I began work in this field, there had been no gene therapy successes in cancer treatment.

First, we needed to prove the concept. What would happen if we could turn off an activated oncogene in a human cancer cell? Would the cancer cell die, simply stop dividing rapidly, or would nothing happen? KRAS oncogene mutations occur in about one-third of patients with a type of lung cancer called adenocarcinoma. Because of the high incidence of lung cancer, this translates to about thirty thousand patients per year. To test this concept, we used a new technique called antisense. We made RNA that was expressed and was complementary to the mutant KRAS RNA. That is, each base was the binding partner for the sense RNA nucleotides. When the sense and antisense strands of RNA bound together, it prevented the production of the mutant KRAS protein.[72] When we did this, the cells stopped growing. It worked in the test tube, but would it work in a living organism? Our next test would be in mice.[73]

In designing animal experiments, the investigator tries to closely resemble what is occurring in the patient. There is a strain of mice called nude mice because they have no fur. This strain has been bred with a defective immune system, which allows them to accept transplants of human cancer. The mouse is quite closely related to humans and shares 97.5 percent of its working DNA with humans. The next time you look in a mirror, think about that—the only difference between you and a mouse is 2.5 percent of your DNA. We took an aggressive human cancer cell line and injected the cells directly into the lungs of nude mice, which formed lung tumors. The antisense KRAS gene was inserted into a retrovirus. Antisense means that the sequence of bases is made up of the complementary bases so that the antisense binds to the sense strand of RNA preventing it from making its protein. A retrovirus is a type of RNA virus that has an enzyme (reverse transcriptase) that can make a complementary DNA copy of the viral RNA, which then is integrated into a host cell's DNA which is the opposite of the usual process where DNA makes RNA. This type of retrovirus is in the same general family as HIV, but it is engineered so it cannot cause disease. However, it is still able to enter the cancer cell and deliver the antisense payload. The retrovirus with the antisense and a control without the antisense were injected into the windpipes (tracheas) of the mice so the retroviruses would travel directly to the cancer cells. The results were dramatic. Ninety percent of the mice treated with the control retrovirus developed tumors, while 87 percent of the mice treated with the antisense KRAS had no tumors. For the first time, we had shown that targeting the KRAS oncogene and stopping it from continually stimulating the cancer cell prevented cancers from developing. This was also the first use of retroviruses and antisense for the treatment of cancer. This would lay the foundation for our first cancer gene therapy clinical trials. These studies provided the rationale for the development of drugs targeting KRAS mutations and antisense drugs, but this would not occur until twenty years later.

Another diverse family of genes, called tumor suppressor genes because they are the brakes on cell growth and division, commonly develops mutations, resulting in cancers. The p53 tumor suppressor gene is mutated in over half of lung cancers. There is a rare genetic syndrome, Li-Fraumeni, where p53 has a germline mutation, resulting in the development of multiple cancers at a young age.[74] We studied p53 in esophageal cancers and found, for the first time, that the mutations occurred in premalignant cells called Barrett's esophagus, which led to the development of adenocarcinomas.[75] We also detected p53 mutations in head and neck cancers. It turned out that patients who developed a second primary head and neck cancer usually had different mutations in their second cancer, showing that it was a new cancer and not a recurrence or spread from the original cancer, which would be treated very differently.[76] It of course, was impossible to reactivate a missing or deactivated gene with drugs at that time. Gene therapy provided a solution. The missing gene could be replaced in the cancer cell with its normal version. We could use the same strategy used for the delivery of antisense, a retrovirus inactivated so it would not cause disease. First, we would need to show this worked in experimental systems and that re-expression of the normal p53 gene in cancer cells with a defective p53 caused the cancer cells to die. In two landmark papers, we were able to show that the p53 retrovirus infected the cancer cells and resulted in a normal p53 protein being expressed. Furthermore, when p53 was expressed, it caused the cancer cells to die.[77,78] Now we had a treatment we could take into the clinic.

I was optimistic but did not realize the enormous effort and time needed to develop this gene therapy drug and initiate a clinical trial. At the same time, we continued the exploration of the clinical potential of immunotherapy and had some success! In 1991, in collaboration with Liz and others, we had just finished an immunotherapy clinical trial with promising results.[59] Four of the twelve patients had tumor shrinkage, and seven had their tumors stop growing for up to four months. All patients showed activation of their immune responses. Immunotherapy worked in lung cancer patients, although it would also take twenty years until it became a standard of care.

13
FAMILY MATTERS

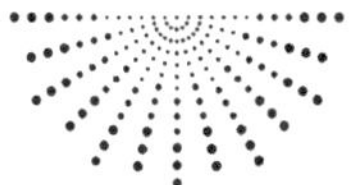

I have found the best way to give advice to your children is to find out what they want and then advise them to do it.

—Harry S. Truman

This chapter may seem choppy and disconnected, but that was our life at that time. I was thinking about science every day—seeing and operating on patients with complex cancers, running a large department, teaching residents and fellows, and always looking for new ways to continue to fund our research. However, there was a very important part of my life that revolved around my family. This and the following chapters will provide a look into my days during this incredibly hectic period. As I write this, looking back, I cannot believe we did all of this, but it was documented in a diary format written while it was happening. Liz was incredibly busy with her laboratory research. Keeping all of this going involved a very complex balancing act.

It was now 1991. Cancer Research published our article on the inhibition of activated KRAS expression by antisense RNA. Experiments were well underway to put this construct in retrovirus and adenovirus vectors for delivery to tumors. The story was picked up by several newspapers, including the Los Angeles Times. My parents called on Sunday morning to tell me their friends had called about the article.

A major component of academic life was attending research conferences to learn what others were doing, network with other scientists, establish collaborations, and present your own work. There was a time before Zoom when meetings were held in person. At that time, personal appearances at national and international meetings were an important component of academic life. Travel included annual society meetings, guest lectureships at other academic centers, and invitations to speak at national and international meetings. All this travel provided opportunities to see how other institutions were working, network with colleagues and collaborators, and educate audiences on state-of-the-art research. While many of these meetings were held in interesting and fun environments, the travel and time away from family was ultimately burdensome. All this was possible because of childcare from grandparents and a live-in nanny. I was attending a conference on Biology and Novel Therapeutic Approaches for Epithelial Cancers of the Aerodigestive Tract at Steamboat Springs, Colorado, which I helped organize. Liz was attending a cytokine conference at Keystone at the same time. Presentations identified new oncogenes that may be involved in lung cancer genesis, new growth factor mechanisms, and new opportunities for chemoprevention. The weather was beautiful during the conference, and I was able to get in some spring skiing. I prepared a meeting summary for the journal Cancer Cells, which was published by Cold Spring Harbor Press. Papers were also published as supplements for the Journal of the National Cancer Institute.

Then the unexpected occurred. My parents called and revealed that Dad had prostate cancer. In a routine checkup, his PSA was 70. He wanted to be treated in Houston. The first step was a CT scan, which detected an enlarged pelvic lymph node. This was biopsied and was positive for prostate cancer. At his age, seventy-three, neither surgery nor radiation treatment was advised for this advanced stage. Instead, he began treatment with Lupron, which suppresses testosterone production. Testosterone is a hormone that drives the growth of prostate cancer. He had a remarkable response to this drug. His PSA went to near zero. He lived to eighty-eight and never had a recurrence of prostate cancer. Our family history of prostate cancer is extensive. Two of my dad's three brothers developed it, with one brother dying from it. Thus, the possibility of developing prostate cancer from that point on shadowed my life. Screening for prostate cancer with annual PSAs was still recommended, and I had annual PSAs from then on until I had a very unpleasant experience with a urologist. But that was twenty-four years in the future.

Meanwhile, the week consisted of preparation for my keynote address at the Annapolis NCI conference on Detection and Treatment of Early Cancer. Tuesday, I had a single case: the removal of lung metastases (spread) in both lungs from a sarcoma, which is a tumor of the connective tissue. Wednesday was a busy clinic. By Friday, the keynote address was completed. On Saturday, we traveled to Trinity, Texas, to see Camp Olympia, where J would spend three weeks that summer. On Saturday night, we all had dinner at Casablanca, a Moroccan restaurant.

Liz was busy working on a grant concerning the use of gene-modified tumor-infiltrating lymphocytes. On Monday, I prepared my keynote address for the meeting sponsored by the NCI in Annapolis called Strategies for Detection and Intervention in Early Lung Cancer. This summarized the Steamboat Springs meeting and presented new technology for early detection and therapy, including our proposal for viral therapy. Then I had a very packed day in the operating room. All the cases were challenging. I performed three difficult cases Tuesday, including lung lobectomy for metastatic renal cell cancer, chest wall resection for a tumor involving the ribs, and removal of metastases to the lung. Fortunately, the patients did well.

When I submit a paper for publication, hope springs eternal. Scientific journals are ranked by their impact factors. Science rejected the p53 Barrett's manuscript. Editors were unable to recognize the seminal contribution that p53 is mutated in premalignant lesions. However, p53 mutations may be an important marker for patients who will develop cancers. Rejections are frequent. Journals are evaluated by a metric called the impact factor, which is a measure of how often journal articles are cited in other papers. It is an imperfect metric. Review articles that summarize all the recent work in a specific scientific area of interest are the most cited, but these are not original research articles. The journal with the highest impact factor is CA, which publishes primarily cancer statistics and thus is quoted in every paper that cites current cancer incidences. One or two highly cited articles may have an outsized effect on the impact factor. But journals such as Science and Nature have developed mystiques around their impact factor, which often influences promotion and tenure decisions. High-impact journals reject over 90 percent of their submissions, further adding to their glamour. These factors create a biased, time-consuming, and ultimately resource-wasteful environment for scientific publication. I will discuss this and propose solutions in Chapter 19. We submitted our paper to Cancer Research, another excellent journal, and it was accepted.

Music was a major part of early childhood for both Liz and me, and we both felt it was important to provide musical experiences for our children. Our older daughter, J, began piano lessons, and our younger daughter, K, began both piano and violin. J was playing well and won a superior rating in a Gold Cup piano competition. Music was becoming a major part of our daughters' lives. Two years later, K was studying violin using the Suzuki method. Her instructor was incredibly patient with the children and really made them feel accomplished. She also provided a course on music theory, but the lessons were very immersive and required that the parent (in our case, mostly Liz) be there. Of course, everything was done to maintain the student's positive attitude. If there was a problem, the parent took the blame. There were also many outside events, including competitions and workshops, which were time-consuming. For the latest Suzuki workshop, which was fortunately in Houston, the instructor was staying with us. Houston has first-class music and theater companies. The Houston Grand Opera has consistently excellent productions, and we took our daughters to see Mozart's The Magic Flute. We had a videotape of a production filmed by the great Swedish director Ingmar Bergman. Our daughters would watch it repeatedly and then walk around the house singing the Queen of the Night's aria.

The Annapolis meeting in April 1991 was highly successful, and my keynote address was well received. The meeting recognized the importance of the lung cancer problem, the necessity to focus on the diagnosis and treatment of early lung cancer, and the identification of high-risk premalignant lesions. Intermediate endpoints for clinical trials must be validated. Over thirty years later, these problems have still not been solved. Screening of smokers with computerized tomographic (CT) scanning can identify early lung cancers in a small percentage. However, people are reluctant to undergo these scans, and a significant number of lung nodules requiring follow-up or biopsy are identified that turn out to be benign. Better tests and tools are needed. Of course, the ultimate solution is the elimination of tobacco.

Two important papers were accepted for publication. The first was the paper describing the synergistic interaction of OKT3, IL-2, and TNF in the abrogation of established pulmonary metastases in a mouse model. This was accepted without revision in the Journal of Immunotherapy. The second paper described the results of the IL-2/TNF trial in lung cancer patients.[59] The paper indicated that major responses could occur with this regimen. An astonishing finding was that IL-2 levels remained elevated even after the therapy stopped. At the Thursday lab meeting, it was shown that both the antisense KRAS and p53 genes had been successfully integrated into retroviral vectors. This set the stage for the virus therapy experiments. If this worked, it would establish the feasibility of an entirely new concept for treating diseases. Instead of simply trying to kill cancer cells, we would be able to modify their genetic makeup.

Liz struggled, too, with grant writing and was not happy with the time it was consuming. I gave her a break by taking the children shopping for Mother's Day presents. J was playing Indiana Jones in her drama class, and I helped her buy a costume over the weekend. Liz and I had a date night with dinner at a good Houston restaurant, Charley's 517, and heard the Houston Symphony under the direction of Christoph Eschenbach perform Mahler's Das Lied von der Erde. It was a magnificent performance.

There are two major scientific meetings each year devoted to cancer research and treatment: the American Association for Cancer Research (AACR) and the American Society of Clinical Oncology (ASCO). ASCO is usually pronounced ass coe. A business executive who was not familiar with the society and thought it was a business once told me that this company really needed to change its name! For many years, both organizations held their meetings during consecutive weeks. This meant a long time away from work and family if you were attending both. ASCO, with twenty thousand attendees, dwarfed AACR, and because of difficulties securing venues, the organizations went their separate ways. Meetings were held in Houston that week. Our lab had ten presentations at the AACR and four at ASCO. Our grant with Margaret Spitz, chair of the Department of epidemiology at MD Anderson, for the study of lung cancer in minorities was funded. It was ranked third of sixty-eight.

One of the major challenges thoracic surgeons faced was training the next generation. At the time, trainees for a career in noncardiac thoracic surgery needed to complete extensive training in cardiac surgery, which they would never practice. I wanted to develop a thoracic tract program at MD Anderson. However, residents would need some experience in cardiac surgery, and the Texas Heart Institute was the logical place, as we already trained residents from that program. I met with Denton Cooley to discuss a separate slot for a thoracic resident in the residency program. He was very accommodating and genial. I assured him it would not reduce the training his residents needed, as we had more than enough cases. He approved.

Friday was the annual Department of Thoracic Surgery dinner honoring the residents and fellows. It was held at the Colombe d'Or (originally the mansion of William Fondren, founder of what is now Exxon). Over sixty people attended, and everyone seemed to have an enjoyable evening. Violin continued to consume more time. On Saturday, Liz and K departed for Ottawa, Kansas, for the Suzuki violin camp. I was experiencing a quiet week with both Liz, J, and K away, but surgery was keeping me busy. Patients with cancer of the esophagus (tube connecting the mouth to the stomach) were among the most challenging in my practice.

The operation requires an incision in the abdomen to mobilize the stomach. Another incision must be made between the ribs for access to the chest cavity. The stomach is then pulled into the chest and connected to the esophagus remaining after the cancer has been removed. Patients undergoing this operation are often debilitated because the cancer prevents them from eating a full diet. Sometimes, because the tissues are weak or have a poor blood supply, the connection between the esophagus and stomach breaks down. Fortunately, this does not occur often, but it delays the patient from eating normally and prolongs hospitalization. The surgeon faces these problems with every case, and I performed an esophagectomy that Monday along with a lung resection for pulmonary metastases on Tuesday. Fortunately, both patients did well.

My office was busy with the completion of the grant and the application for the additional residency position. On Thursday, I attended the executive committee of the medical staff meeting. The plans for the new clinical research building were devised without any consultation with the scientists using the facility. This can be a persistent problem at large academic institutions where the management is top-down. On Friday, I took half the day off to take J and her friend to Water World. Liz and K returned on Friday, and both had had a very good time at the Suzuki workshop.

J had been at camp for two weeks, and we missed her. Her letters discussed only how good the food was. She was involved in riflery, horseback riding, waterskiing, and baseball. I was reminded of the swift passage of time when I received a book of personal sketches from my Hopkins class for the twentieth reunion. It made for fascinating reading. I was the only member of my class to be chairman of an academic department at a major university. Several class members had administrative appointments at their hospitals. Most sounded content.

Planning for our program project grant for Studies in Early Lung

Cancer began. This would take a massive amount of effort. I took a much-needed break by touring the Houston Zoo with K on the Fourth of July. The following week, I traveled to Toronto for a major lecture at the International Congress of Radiation Research and spoke on our research on the molecular biology of lung cancer.

Scientific progress is neither linear nor rapid, which has always frustrated me. In preparing for a clinical trial to test our gene therapy, a cell line had to be made that could produce the retrovirus in large quantities for injection in the patient. But progress was quite slow in the lab. Transfecting (infecting) cells with retroviruses and getting them to grow was not easy.

Just before I became board certified in thoracic surgery, the board decided that a periodic recertification process would be necessary instead of simply granting certification for life. It is not unreasonable to make sure surgeons remain competent. However, the process that was developed was cumbersome and irrelevant. Cardiothoracic surgery is made up of many subspecialties, including adult cardiac surgery, pediatric surgery, and noncardiac thoracic surgery, the last of which was all that I practiced. Regardless of the surgeon's practice, it was required to take exams in all these areas, which I had not practiced for the past ten years. This was a painful process, but I completed it. At the same time, I had to begin planning for our next large grant, which would be funded under a new initiative from the NCI called Specialized Programs of Research Excellence.

My position as department chair was highly visible, and I often received referrals from high-profile patients. For example, the director of the development office at MD Anderson called me the previous week. His wife, who had smoked for thirty years, had a new left upper lobe nodule on a routine chest X-ray. I removed it on Thursday, and fortunately, the prognosis was favorable. In addition, the first Specialized Program of Research Excellence organizational meeting was held. From the very beginning, the chair of thoracic/head and neck oncology, whom I had hoped would be an active collaborator, was very negative toward the projects. I believe the underlying issue was that SPORE was originating in our department and not his.

Liz met with her Chair about her promotion, as she had more than fulfilled all the requirements for promotion to full professor and was told that her major problem was teaching, although her immunology lectures and multiple grad students did not count. Eventually, she became the director of the Cancer Biology Program and was awarded their first training grant, providing stipends for graduate students. He was an unsupportive chair for her, and it was unfortunate that she had to continually deal with these problems. Politics was an integral part of academic life, even at MD Anderson. But sometimes there were events that were so strange that one could not believe they were happening. If these events were included in the plot of a novel about academic life, I would dismiss them as preposterous. Nevertheless, the following sequence of events occurred. The chair of Liz's department had been trying to get an appointment for his wife at MD Anderson. He even came to me to see if I would give her a research position. I did not think she was qualified in areas that were relevant to our research program. I checked with several colleagues and was told to avoid hiring her, so I declined. Liz was told by a colleague that her chair wanted her out of the department. This was likely retaliation for the executive committee of the science faculty turning down his wife's appointment. The position for his wife was then proposed in the Department of Pediatrics, so Liz's chair provided space and salary, but the appointment was nominally in Pediatrics. The letters of recommendation were from a close friend of the chair and his deputy chairman. Liz would continue to have problems with her chair in this department.

Then more curious events occurred. A letter surfaced, written by the chair's wife explaining her life story. The letter was a rambling dialogue filled with bizarre happenings. For example, whenever she became ill, a messenger named Mary would bring her holy water from the pope. In short, she believed she was the heir to the Vatican empire. Her family had many enemies, including the Rothschilds and Bronfmans, who eventually apologized to her. At the end of the letter was a description of what were called "ill-advised germ warfare experiments," which had led to the Desert Storm syndrome, the subject of what she described as a massive cover-up. These beliefs reverberated throughout MD Anderson, and their denouement would be swift and unanticipated. This was followed by a rambling seven-page article in a publication entitled Criminal Politics, which considered itself "the magazine of conspiracy politics." The first five pages described her harassment, persecution, and poisoning of the chair's wife.

We then learned that Liz's chair's stepdaughter returned from service in the Gulf War with a chronic fatigue syndrome that she thought was the same as that suffered by other veterans. Because Liz's department chair and his wife had postulated that the syndrome was caused by mycoplasma, a genus of bacteria that can cause pneumonia, they advised the stepdaughter to take the antibiotic tetracycline, which, according to the article, cured her. She references a JAMA article as being authored by her and her husband, but they were not listed in the journal. This was followed by their story being published by the Houston Press. The department chair was quoted: "Just focus on the issue and what we're doing, because this other stuff sounds kind of crazy." They had concluded that biological weapons were being produced by a company in Houston and tested on inmates in the Huntsville penitentiary, all of which was refuted as nonsense. The appointment of the chair's wife at MD Anderson was terminated. But despite her dismissal, she continued to work in the department, with one secretary feeling so harassed that she resigned. Faculty in the department complained to the faculty senate and administration concerning the chair's research presented to the public without peer review, prescribing drugs and offering medical tests without a license, and not obtaining the required approvals for working with pathogenic agents. Both the chair and his wife carried guns because of their fear of assassination. All this ended with dramatic flair when Houston police escorted the chair in handcuffs out of his office and out of MD Anderson forever.

But that is not the end of the story. The former chair and his wife surfaced in Irvine, California, where he began work at a nonprofit called the Institute of Molecular Medicine. His wife was the CEO.

Investigations by government laboratories and other investigators failed to confirm the mycoplasma hypothesis.

During the summer of 1991, J appeared in a production of Starlight Express. It was a splendid production. The next day, we left for Keystone, Colorado, for a much-needed vacation. Keystone is near the continental divide and, during winter, is a ski resort. The summers there were a welcome change from Houston, with cool temperatures and low humidity. We heard several performances by the National Repertory Orchestra, including three new works in a composer competition. The playing was outstanding that year. We also went horse riding several times. Liz was an experienced rider, but she was thrown off her horse during a trail ride, much to my horror. Fortunately, she was not hurt. However, I could not escape work and was forced to spend an hour and a half on a conference call during a department chairs' meeting regarding anesthesia. The anesthesia department continued to have problems recruiting.

K gave a nice recital on Saturday at a venue in Houston called Ovations. School began on Monday. Both K and J were enrolled at River Oaks Elementary in the HISD public school system. Both were off to a good start. The educational programs looked excellent. The pace in the lab was still slow. Difficulties were still occurring with sequencing. Labor Day weekend was fun; we gardened, barbecued, and relaxed.

I was dealing with a major problem at MD Anderson that fall. Only thirteen or fourteen operating rooms could open because of anesthesia shortages and nurse featherbedding. Yet demand for operating room time was increasing. New ideas were emerging for the SPORE program. I was using modular grant writing to prepare the proposal and thus could use segments from a variety of previously unfunded grants. It was reassuring that lung cancer was no longer a forbidden topic in the research community.

Liz and I attended a fall open house at River Oaks Elementary and met J and K's teachers. The family attended the opening night concert of the Houston Symphony and heard Midori perform the Paganini violin concerto in a passionate and technically superb way. A Bulgarian soprano, Stefka Evstatieva, substituted for Renato Scotto and sang Verdi and Puccini arias beautifully.

On September 20, I went to Snowbird, Utah, for the American Association for Thoracic Surgery (AATS) retreat. Fifty of the leaders in American thoracic surgery met to plan future directions for the specialty. Clearly, research needed to be addressed. Funding and directions for this area were lacking. Of interest was a 2-to-1 vote to abolish the American Board of Surgery in general surgery for thoracic surgery board certification. This eventually happened.

From Snowbird, I flew to Los Angeles to be a visiting professor at UCLA, where I was scheduled to present a lecture at Tuesday afternoon rounds. The room scheduling was so mixed up that half the staff missed the lecture. However, my lecture at Grand Rounds on molecular approaches to cancer therapy was well received. The SPORE grant then became all-consuming. My parents arrived and looked well. Liz was off to Asilomar, California, for a neuro-oncology meeting. Her talk was well received. Work continued on the SPORE grant. There were some further complications with getting the Radiation Therapy Oncology Group as the data management center because the other clinical trial cooperative groups did not recognize it as an approved center. This political nonsense and territoriality made my life miserable.

On Tuesday, Liz and I traveled to Charlottesville, Virginia, for a conference on biomolecular recognition and targeting. The meeting, held at the Boar's Head Inn, was attended by about thirty people. The fall foliage was spectacular, and our talks went well.

Back in Houston, we saw a splendid performance of Rusalka at the Houston Grand Opera. This is a little-known opera by Dvorak. It is a variation of the Little Mermaid story, and we took K and J. The performance was exquisite, with a superb portrayal of Rusalka by Renee Fleming.

I went to San Francisco to give three talks at the American College of Chest Physicians. In general, these were well attended. Liz was busy with talks at the Texas Immunology Conference and the MD Anderson Melanoma Conference. She received excellent priority scores in two study sections simultaneously (ninth percentile in one). It also looked like my grant would be renewed, but the SPORE application was still extraordinarily time-consuming.

Steve Rosenberg was given the Gottlieb Award at the MD Anderson conference. We attended a dinner in the wine cellar of the Doctors Club. The dinner and wines were superb. Steve was in a good mood. His older daughter was taking a year off from Princeton, and the middle one was starting Dartmouth. He had been on a Sierra Club hike, developed a kidney stone, and had to be evacuated by helicopter.

Over Thanksgiving, we went to Magic Island to celebrate Liz's birthday and had a great time. One of the acts was a juggler with chainsaws. While in San Francisco at the American College of Surgeons, I saw a Chagall lithograph from the Meyerovitch Gallery in San Francisco. It was titled The Magic Flute and was the lithographer's first strike of a plate created by Chagall for the Metropolitan Opera in 1967. The Magic Flute was beloved by our family, and I purchased the lithograph, which still hangs in our living room. After returning home, K discussed her science class at dinner. She told us about her "taste bugs" that crawled in and out of her tongue.

Still, the SPORE application was not complete, and I was concerned. All the projects had weaknesses. Funding would probably hinge on which applications had the fewest weaknesses. We celebrated with Thanksgiving dinner at home for a change. Liz and the girls went horse riding on Saturday at Hermann Park Stables. We attended a madrigal dinner at the Shepherd School on December 5. The singing was beautiful, with magic acts and other entertainment. Work on the SPORE grant continued. The staff was working late and on weekends. The proposal was shaping up. The submission date was January 17. Several sections came in at the last minute, and one still had not been received. Only ten institutions applied for the lung cancer SPORE (twenty-one for breast and twenty-three for prostate). However, it would still be very competitive to be selected for funding.

We departed for Keystone early Sunday morning for skiing. The snow was adequate. November was the wettest month on record, but it only snowed once while we were there. The skiing was excellent.

We had a traditional fondue dinner in the new lodge on North Peak. The lodge was spectacular, with high-beamed ceilings and a stone fireplace. We then all went on a sleigh ride to the historical Smith Cabin for dinner. J and K steadily improved in their skiing. By the end of the trip, K was doing parallel turns and skiing down blue runs. The weather was warm and sunny almost every day. Both Liz and I raced NASTAR. Liz won two bronzes and a silver. I won my first bronze after taking a racing clinic. My handicap was 47 (47 percent slower than the U.S. ski team). The day after we returned, I spent twelve hours at the office finishing the SPORE grant. Only polishing details and figuring the budget remained.

The SPORE grant was finally submitted after some last-minute changes. From January 15–20, 1992 the whole family went to Captiva Island, Florida, for the General Thoracic Surgery Club meeting. At first, the weather was quite cold. The meeting included some interesting talks. The most interesting presentation was on thoracoscopic surgery, which involves the use of a video camera and special instruments to remove parts of the lung through very small incisions. The children enjoyed the ocean. I then took a two-day trip to Frankfurt to present a paper on new directions in esophageal cancer. The quick turnaround was necessary because of all the work remaining at home. On February 29, Liz and I attended a gala for the Jewish Community Center at the Westin Galleria. As I write this, I look back on these years mystified and incredulous. How could we possibly have accomplished the trips, time with our children, and all our responsibilities at MD Anderson?

14
SPORE-ULATION

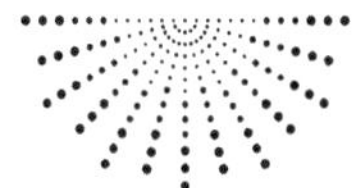

Art is I; science is we.
—Claude Bernard

In 1991, the news that the new funding initiative developed by NCI director Sam Broder for translational research would include lung cancer electrified the lung cancer research community. For many years, it was very difficult for researchers applying new laboratory research findings to the clinic to receive NCI funding. The prevalent funding mechanism, R01 grants, was designed to fund basic laboratory cancer research without any regard to whether it might result in advances in the care of cancer patients. Now a new funding mechanism was developed exclusively for translational research so that we could take our research discoveries and bring them directly to the patient.

I began an effort at MD Anderson to develop a SPORE program. But there was other good news. John Minna and Adi Gazdar, my former collaborators at NCI, were coming to Texas. Wouldn't it be great if we could submit a combined grant? I had spoken with John, and initially, he seemed enthusiastic about a joint grant. However, in the beginning, getting MD Anderson and UT Southwestern to work together was a challenge. My colleagues at MD Anderson warned me that no collaboration between MD Anderson and UT Southwestern had ever been successful in the history of the two institutions because of cultural and political differences. UT Southwestern had a stable of Nobel laureates who felt their institution's basic science was superior, and, of course, MD Anderson faculty felt they had the upper hand in cancer. I sent a summary of our SPORE program to John and Adi and was disappointed when it was returned unopened with a note that they were submitting a single-institution SPORE.

Things did not go well. My SPORE was not funded, and UTSW received a P20 planning grant rather than a full SPORE. When I received the reviews from the SPORE grant, I recognized that two of the reviewers had direct conflicts of interest, including one who had a financial interest in a laser bronchoscopy company that could compete with one of our projects. Finally, there were numerous factual errors throughout the review. This made a mockery of the concept of peer review, and I was disappointed. I appealed this to NCI, but as usual, this was to no avail. It became clear to John and me that our programs were complementary in translational science and clinical research and that, together, we would have a much stronger SPORE program. In 1996, we were awarded the first University of Texas Lung Cancer SPORE. Now we really had to work together as a team to harness the potential of both institutions. John and I agreed we needed SPORE investigators from both institutions to meet at least once a month to monitor progress and plan new research. At first, we began flying between Dallas and Houston. Those of you who have flown Southwest know that its schedules are suggested as opposed to actual arrival and departure times, so we were spending as much time in airports as we were discussing research. Video conferencing was in its infancy, but we had this available at both sites. I suggested we try it, and our SPORE video conference became a monthly tradition. This morphed into Zoom with the pandemic. When our SPORE program was funded, it was unique as the first multi-institutional SPORE. This set a precedent, as now 70 percent of SPOREs involve more than one institution.

Swag from the SPORE investigator meeting in Chantilly. Note the mug is made in China.

The SPORE program was rapidly expanding. Jorge Gomez became the director of the SPORE program and was primarily responsible for the increase to over fifty SPOREs. Under Jorge's leadership, we experienced a golden age of SPOREs. There was an annual SPORE meeting for all SPOREs. This was frequently held at very elegant venues such as Westfields in Chantilly, Virginia. Attendees received tote bags and coffee mugs. I looked at the base of my SPORE-emblazoned mug and saw that it was made in China. NCI had contributed to the trade deficit! In 2016, Jorge joined the University of Arizona, where he remains as Assistant Vice President for Translational Research in Special Populations.

SPOREs became a family affair in our home. Liz was the principal investigator on the first MD Anderson skin SPORE awarded in 2005. Liz and I attended an AACR meeting together in San Francisco and met Jorge as we were walking to the meeting. He had a puzzled look seeing us together, and Liz explained that we were married. He had no idea. Jorge told us we were the first SPORE couple. In this case, the SPORE promoted both research and romance.

NCI directors have had varying levels of enthusiasm for the SPORE program. Harold Varmus convened multiple review panels to curtail SPOREs, but each panel gave the SPORE program glowing reviews. Andy von Eschenbach, who came from MD Anderson, again tried to curtail SPOREs. He proposed reducing SPORE funding from five to three years. When this was announced, David Carbone, a SPORE investigator from Vanderbilt, showed a slide at the SPORE annual meeting that referred to the SPO grant. Our SPORE was invaluable in moving translational science forward. I will provide one example from a single SPORE project.

In 1982, when John was at the NCI-Navy Medical Oncology Branch, their group had a series of publications on 3p chromosomal deletions in lung cancer. I was in the NCI Surgery Branch at the time and was collaborating with John and Adi. The work continued when we all moved to Texas. Mike Lerman and John identified genes in a frequently deleted region of 3p. One of my first SPORE projects was to functionally characterize the genes in this region. Working with the superb molecular biologist Lin Ji, we found that multiple genes in this region had tumor-suppressor properties.[79] Genes delivered systemically by an adenoviral vector dramatically reduced lung metastases in a human non-small cell lung cancer xenograft metastases model. One of the genes, originally called FUS1 (now known by its Human Genome Organization [HUGO] name, TUSC2), was of great interest. Its expression was reduced in most lung cancers. It also mediates multiple critical cell and immunologic functions, including kinase activity, apoptosis, and cytokine production, which regulate the maturation and activation of natural killer cells. We developed a nanovesicle to encapsulate a plasmid expressing TUSC2 so it could be injected intravenously for systemic delivery.[80] Recent phase-1 and -2 trials as a single agent and combined with a tyrosine kinase inhibitor have shown safe gene delivery to the tumor, as well as tumor regressions—the first successful systemic gene therapy for cancer (chapter 33).

One of the critical questions was whether the TUSC2 protein produced by the gene would be expressed in cancer cells in metastases throughout the body. Patients consented to have biopsies of their tumors pre- and post-treatment with the gene therapy. Using an antibody to the TUSC2 protein, we were able to show expression of the protein throughout the tumors, including centrally after treatment.[81] But could this gene therapy enhance or overcome resistance to immunotherapy with checkpoint blockade? To answer this question, I felt we needed a preclinical model more representative of the cancer patient. Existing mouse models had mouse tumors in a mouse microenvironment and did not adequately represent the heterogeneity of human lung cancer. The first step was to grow human lung cancers in immunosuppressed mice, called patient-derived xenografts (PDXs).[82] Bingliang Fang, a researcher in our department whom I recruited from Baylor, led this effort. We now had more than two hundred PDXs with sequencing in over half. But these tumors were grown in immunosuppressed mice, so immunotherapy could not be tested. We needed to give the mice a human immune system. Ismail Meraz developed a humanized mouse using fresh CD34+ stem cells from umbilical cord blood. Mice were reconstituted rapidly and at a cost of one-tenth that of a similar model from commercial sources.[83] Now we could test the combination of nanovesicle TUSC2 + anti-PD-1 in a human lung cancer lung metastases model that was resistant to checkpoint blockade. The tumor had both KRAS and LKB1 mutations, which promoted drug resistance. The combination therapy significantly prolonged survival.[84] In other studies, we showed this was primarily due to the activation of natural killer cells by TUSC2.

Next, we combined TUSC2 with carboplatin and pembrolizumab.

Here again, we saw that TUSC2 increased efficacy in the same model. For the first time, we observed complete responses. In a highly aggressive metastasis model refractory to checkpoint blockade with human cancer and a human immune system, an immunotherapy combination can induce complete responses. This single project and its spinoffs resulted in clinical trials, which include novel targeted drug combinations identified by our PDX studies.

Original lung cancer SPORE investigators Paul Bunn, John Minna, and Jack Roth.

The SPORE program has been a resounding success and has benefited the cancer research community in many ways. Our SPORE grant was continuously renewed, and John and I received an award from the NCI for having the record for the longest-funded SPORE grant.

15
THE RAC

> Conventional people are roused to fury by departure from convention, largely because they regard such departure as a criticism of themselves.
>
> —Bertrand Russell

Spring 1992 was a season of personal reawakening filled with milestones, scientific breakthroughs, and one of the most frustrating experiences in my life up to that time. J was finishing a school science project. Together, we plunged into the enigmatic world of bean sprouts and the factors that make them grow. This was juxtaposed against my own endeavor to combat lung cancer with groundbreaking genetic therapy. I began preparing a protocol for the injection of a retrovirus expressing cancer-fighting genes into patients' lung cancers in the airways (endobronchial) that could not be removed with surgery and were obstructing airflow. This was the first attempt to reverse genetic mutations in cancer cells in humans. The bustling weeks led me to the Big Apple, where an accolade awaited: the Lucy Wortham James Award, a token of recognition for my relentless pursuit of new cancer treatments and accomplishments in cancer research. On Sunday, March 15, I left for New York to receive the

Award for Basic Research from the Society of Surgical Oncology. The meeting was held in the ballroom of the Waldorf Astoria. Liz flew up on Monday to be there with me for the presidential dinner and my talk. Charles Balch gave a presidential address using interactive video with a laser disk, which was novel at that time. That evening, the black-tie presidential dinner was held at the Whitney Museum. A Wegman exhibition with fantastic dog photos was being held. I delivered a talk entitled Molecular Surgery for Cancer, which was well received. Liz and I had lunch with Paul Rumely, my high school classmate, whom I had not seen in over twenty-five years. He looked well and was a vice president for recruitment at Moody's. The award was presented at a dinner that evening. I sat next to Murray Brennan, chief of surgery at Memorial. An astronaut named Story Musgrave gave the after-dinner speech, recounting his flights on the space shuttle with spectacular photos. He would go on to be the specialist who fixed the Hubble Telescope.

Liz and I were at the awards banquet where I received the Lucy Wortham James Award from the Society of Surgical Oncology on March 16, 1992.

On March 23, I had my first executive physical. During the cardiac stress test, I observed premature ventricular contractions and runs of ventricular tachycardia. These are serious arrhythmias that can precede cardiac arrest. I was concerned. In discussing it with my cardiologist, I was informed that these abnormal heart rhythms can occur as a benign condition in young, healthy, asymptomatic adults. I was still very worried. On my cardiologist's recommendation, I had a stress thallium scan to rule out organic heart disease. This was normal. I began increasing my exercise routine to involve more heart conditioning. To date, I have had no further episodes of abnormal heartbeats.

Liz left for England on March 29 to participate in an immunology meeting, so I was the designated caregiver for the kids. I took K to her violin lesson, the first time without Liz, and she did very well. On Sunday, I left for the American Surgical Association meeting in Palm Desert, California. I was inducted into the organization, which is the oldest and most prestigious surgical organization. The average age of members appeared to be older than sixty-five.

The grant writing and search for research funding were endless. I was preparing grants for two large new program projects, including one in lung cancer with Ki Hong and one with Al Diesseroth in gene therapy. More data was needed to show some uptake of retroviruses by human tumor cells before starting the direct injection protocol. Would these experiments work, and when would the data be available?

On April 26, I went to Los Angeles for the American Association for Thoracic Surgery meeting. I was the inaugural speaker for the Thoracic Surgery Biology Club, an organization aimed at stimulating research in thoracic surgery. I returned on April 28, just in time to miss the Los Angeles riots. The main thrust of our laboratory research during this time was to get the retroviral constructs into clinical trials. The preliminary data from the subcutaneous injection of supernatants in three-day established tumors looked very promising. I talked with the technology development staff about forming a company to attract venture capital. I estimated we would need about $2.5 million to complete the clinical trials. The final touches were in place on our manuscripts for p53 in second primary tumors and retroviral vectors for the delivery of antisense constructs, and now we could submit them for publication.

K attended a Suzuki workshop and had been making good

progress. J won second prize at the district science fair for "Changes in Growth of Sprouts." We had dinner at the brownstone for two departing faculty members, Drs. Bernadette Ryan and Rolando Colon. Liz left to chair a session at the AACR in San Diego. I spent the weekend with the children. J was riding her bicycle all over the neighborhood with her friends. Summer approached with scholastic triumphs for J and musical accomplishments for K, intertwined with scientific progress and societal engagements. Amid festive family gatherings and institutional politics, the race for funding and protocol approvals for our medical endeavors reached a crescendo. This was the last week of our daughters' school. At the awards ceremony, J received a certificate for scholarship and citizenship. She had straight As. K received a citizenship certificate and had an excellent report card. The music recitals were on May 31. I had to take K and then drive to Dudley Hall to hear J. The resident dinners were also held that week. Liz and I went to the University of Texas Medical School dinner, having received an invitation from Steve Yang. The MD Anderson thoracic dinner was held at the Warwick. J had her taekwondo orange belt test on June 7 and passed. The children began summer school for the first time. We hosted my parents' fiftieth wedding anniversary celebration from June 12 to 14 in Houston. It included dinner and a show at Magic Island, dinner at the Wine Cellar of the Doctors' Club, and brunch at the Warwick. Dad's brothers and sister all arrived on time. I provided some remarks for the occasion, which I recently found buried with some old papers; the speech below was accompanied by slides long since lost:

Elizabeth and I are delighted that y'all (as they say in Texas) could join us to help celebrate this auspicious occasion. A fiftieth wedding anniversary is a rare and joyous occasion. Marriage is an institution to which many of us have been committed, but these two individuals provide an example of how it should be done. One pundit recently said, "A man is incomplete until he's married—then he's finished." Not all marriages are made in heaven. This was exemplified by Winston Churchill when he was addressed by a female member of Parliament: "Mr. Churchill, if you were my husband, I'd give you poison." Churchill replied, "Madam, if you were my wife, I'd drink it." Nevertheless, Richard and Bernice Roth have had a marriage that has survived and thrived for fifty years. We might ask how they accomplished this. I think they followed the philosophy of Mae West, who said, "Too much of a good thing is wonderful." My mother has instructed me not to give an emotional or sentimental talk. And no matter how old you are—and, children, remember this—you must always obey your mother's wishes. I will also dispense with any levity. This talk will be kept on a very high scientific plane. Fortunately, recent archaeological discoveries have shed new light on the Roth and Saperstein clans. Recent excavations in the La Porte and New Castle regions have uncovered some rare and unusual artifacts, which I will share with you tonight. Richard Roth was born on December 26, 1917. He was born into one of the most turbulent periods in American history. Just eight months earlier, the United States had declared war on Germany. The first slide shows Richard at the age of two. Note the resolute expression. Bernice Roth was born on January 17. The year is classified information. This slide shows her at an early age. It is difficult to imagine now what it was like to live during crises that dwarf our present events: the Great Depression, the rise of the Nazis, and the Second World War. On the other hand, today, we must deal with Bush, Clinton, and Quayle. Many of you do not realize the enormous sacrifices these two individuals made. A little-known fact is that my mother was a child prodigy ballerina. She was so good that there is a rumor that the legendary Sergei Diaghilev tried to recruit her for his corps de ballet. But she turned him down and instead attended Indiana University. K and J should also note that there are cheerleading and tap dancing genes on the Roth side of the family. Life at the Roths during these years was unpredictable and exciting. From recently obtained tapes, I understand there were undercurrents of jealousy, murder, and election fraud. Dad began a military career. This ended after the war, but had he pursued it, it is clear who would have been the commander of Desert Storm. My parents met at Indiana University and were married on June 14, 1942. I was able to obtain a newspaper published on this day. It is a copy of the Hartford Daily

Courant, which I will present to the guests of honor. The wedding was not covered by the national news services. The paper provides some interesting insights into the times. At that time, a four-piece bedroom set was on sale for $49.50. Humphrey Bogart and Irene Manning were starring in The Big Shot, and Glenn Miller and His Orchestra were in town. Three years after they were married, another event occurred. Our family settled down in La Porte, Indiana, in the idyllic comfort of small-town life during the '50s. Although life did not approach the situation comedies that were popular at the time, such as the Donna Reed Show and Leave It to Beaver, La Porte was a pleasant and stimulating environment. Dad was certainly not Ward Cleaver. On the other hand, I was hardly the Beaver. I learned many lessons from my parents that have remained with me all my life. For example, from my mother, I learned that no salad should be eaten until the tomatoes are removed. From my dad, I learned that there is a time for work, and there is a time for more work. My dad had a quiet strength and authority that were unchallenged. My friends would come up to me and say, "My dad can beat up your dad." And I would reply, "How much would it cost?" One of the highlights of that time was a trip to California and the newly opened Disneyland. At that time, travel was still accomplished by train. As time passed, Mom's dancing abilities were still evident. My parents supported me through college. With the helpful counsel of uncles David and Nate, I decided to attend medical school, and they again supported me. This is not a picture of a mafia family but was taken during my graduation from medical school in 1971. Notice all the hair and dark glasses. When I decided to relocate to California, once again my parents were very supportive. They grew to love Southern California so much that they made it their home. In California, I met a flower child, shown here in San Diego. We married, and my parents welcomed her into our family like their own daughter. From California, we relocated to Bethesda, Maryland. Mom and Dad were always there to help us. We then moved to Houston. Here, with vigor and vitality, they assumed the role of grandparents. Mom even lost her fear of dogs. They have provided help with the children in their usual, unselfish, and spirited way. When I could not go, they accompanied Liz to receive her Distinguished Alumni Award at Randolph-Macon College. So let us help them celebrate this great event and offer a toast to those party animals, Richard and Bernice Roth.

The season matured into a blend of solitude and strategy as Liz honed her executive acumen, and I navigated the tides of venture capital to fund our gene therapy clinical trials, all while a novel bystander effect in our experiments hinted at unforeseen avenues in cancer treatment. Our protocol for the modification of oncogene and tumor suppressor gene expression went to the Surveillance Committee at MD Anderson that week. This was the first step in the approval process. We were required to receive local approval before the protocol was approved by the Food and Drug Administration. I spoke with Nelson Wivel, chair of the NIH Recombinant DNA Advisory Committee (RAC), about our submission to the RAC in September. I was still trying to line up venture capital funding. Writing the protocol for submission was an arduous process, with detailed points to consider. The intratracheal instillation of retroviral supernatant in the experiment completely suppressed orthotopic tumor formation. The proliferation experiments indicated there was a bystander effect; that is, the cells taking up the retrovirus released some protein or stimulated the immune response, causing a much more robust anticancer effect. This was an unexpected and fortuitous finding that suggested gene therapy might be more effective than we had anticipated.

I was invited again to participate in the executive development course given at Rice University. Liz had previously taken the course. It was a six-month time commitment. However, I had been invited three out of the last four times and did not believe I could turn it down again, despite my feelings that it was a waste of time reiterating platitudes and the obvious, supported by anecdotal case studies. My opinion did not change after I completed the course. Institutional politics was a constant accompaniment to life at MD Anderson. Without warning, the political atmosphere there became murkier.

Jim Cox was a radiation oncologist. He and his wife, Ritsuko

Komaki, also a radiation oncologist, came to MD Anderson when Jim was recruited to become physician-in-chief and vice president for patient care. Ritsuko was an infant when her family's ancestral home in Hiroshima was obliterated by the atomic bomb.[85] When one of her classmates died of radiation-related leukemia, she was inspired to become a physician and use radiation to cure cancer. The institution was growing, and there were continuing problems with clinic operations and staffing. Jim and two of his deputies decided they could solve all these problems with a top-down approach. He began by firing the chief of hospital and clinic operations. He unilaterally decided that he and his two deputies could run the institution. The structure that the president had established consisted of large divisions, including medicine and surgery, each of which administered multiple departments. This structure was set up so that the president would only need to deal with a few division heads instead of the heads of multiple and continuously proliferating departments. Cox sent a memo around that stated the positions of the division heads were abolished. Imagine occupying the prestigious and well-paid position of division head and then, out of nowhere, receiving a memo (this was before email) that your job position was eliminated. The president began receiving multiple urgent phone calls.

Several weeks later, I received another memo indicating that Jim Cox was stepping down as physician-in-chief and VP for patient care. Rumors had been circulating for weeks. Apparently, the combination of the bizarre attempt to dissolve the Divisions, along with the firing of the Chief of Hospital and Clinic Operations, had taken its toll. It was ironic that he was demoted to division head of radiation oncology, one of the positions he had tried to eliminate.

Funding my clinical trials in gene therapy was a massive challenge. The NIH did not provide grants to fund clinical trials. Pharmaceutical companies were reluctant to fund trials outside their priorities. Thus, the only solution to bring this technology to patients was to set up a new biotechnology company and attract venture capital. This was risky business, but I reached a point where there was no alternative. I began the process of raising venture capital for a company to produce our retroviral supernatants for clinical trials. This involved presentations to potential investors. I took J to the bus for summer camp. Liz and K were in Fort Worth for yet another in a long series of Suzuki workshops, so I was all alone that week.

The major project that week was completing our submission to the RAC. When gene therapy appeared to be possible, resulting in clinical trials, it was felt that a special review panel was necessary because of the potential risks of this new treatment both to the patient and to the population at large. The NIH RAC was comprised of both scientists and laypeople. In practice, the term RAC was most appropriate as it was reminiscent of the medieval torture device (the rack). Their review process was interminable and was carried out by individuals who had competing interests. This review process would introduce long delays before our gene therapy clinical trial could begin. For clarity, the timeline for our research, from its beginning until the first gene therapy for human use was approved, is shown in Table 1.

Year	Publication	Scientific Discovery
1991	Cancer Research[72]	Reversal of single genetic lesion (mutant KRAS) causes regression of human cancer in vivo
1992	Cancer Research[73]	Retroviral vector antisense-KRAS and wtp53 prevent the growth of orthotopic human lung cancer xenografts.
1992		RAC approval for the first retroviral vector p53 clinical trial.
1993	Cancer Research[77]	Retroviral p53 penetrates spheroids.
1993		Adenovirus vector expressing wtp53 is developed.
1994	Cancer Research[86]	Cancer chemosensitivity is induced by adenovirus-p53.
1994		RAC approval for the first adenovirus-p53 clinical trials in lung and head and neck cancers.
1996	Nature Medicine[87]	Publication of retroviral vector-p53 clinical trial.
1997		Completion of Phase I Adenovirus-p53 clinical trials in 86 patients.
1997-2008		Begin phase II/III clinical trials for adenovirus-p53.
2003		Adenovirus p53 gene therapy becomes the first gene therapy approved for human use.

Table 1: Timeline for Cancer Gene Therapy from Laboratory to Clinic, detailed in subsequent chapters.

I picked up J at camp, and the next day we left for Keystone, which was beautiful that year with warmer weather. The girls were more independent that year and spent time alone in the village. Liz and I went mountain biking up to the Outback and almost made it to the top. We played lots of tennis and heard several NRO concerts. Then school began.

I received our reviews from the RAC. This was a difficult week because all the experiments to answer the reviewers' comments on our lung cancer therapy protocol needed to be completed. We finished the reply on time. One of the reviewers was Dusty Miller, a virologist. He called me and sounded somewhat apologetic for his unreasonable review. I answered all the reviewers' points and submitted our reply.

Our group had developed a technique for changing the expression of cancer genes that could be used in patients. This was a completely new approach to cancer treatment. The treatment was directed at the genes that caused cells to become cancerous. New genes were inserted in cancer cells. The new genes switched off the cancer-causing genes. This treatment had the exquisite specificity for which I had been searching and lacked acute toxicity. This would be the first treatment to directly target cancer genes. It was the first application of oncogene research in the treatment of patients. In a second clinical trial, we used a retrovirus to insert the p53 tumor suppressor gene into cancer cells that had lost the tumor suppressor function of p53 because of a mutation. It was also the first application of p53 research in the treatment of patients, and it was the first application of gene therapy to a common cancer. This clinical trial was made possible because of the development of a novel virus system for delivering the anticancer genes to the cancer cells in large amounts and because of the discovery that tumor cells that take up the virus stop the growth of cancer cells that have not taken up the virus. This was a surprising and revolutionary discovery. The mechanism for this includes the release of proteins by the infected cancer cell, called cytokines, which can both kill uninfected cancer cells and trigger an immune response against the cancer.

I was scheduled to depart at 4:00 p.m. on September 13, 1992, for Bethesda, Maryland, to present this to the NIH Recombinant DNA

Advisory Committee. The committee had twenty-four members, but only four of them were physicians, and of these four, only two dealt with cancer patients. Nevertheless, I answered the critiques from the reviewers, and I was confident that the protocol would be approved. It seemed impossible to get funding to develop this further from the NIH, as the study sections were composed of individuals with very limited scientific horizons who did not approve high-risk projects until shown definitively that they would work. Thus, I continued to make efforts to form a company to produce these reagents and carry on with the research.

I met with Columbine Ventures representative Carl Stutts and Ventures Medical's Archie Kuo to discuss our proposal. During all these efforts, there were problems to address with the clinical faculty. It was becoming more difficult to retain faculty. Bill Putnam was looking at a job in Birmingham to replace Richard McElvein, who was retiring. Bill was fed up with the treatment he received at Hermann Hospital, where he had a joint appointment, being shut out of the case referrals. He was also dissatisfied with the operations in the clinic and the operating room, which remained inefficient with long delays between cases.

I was picked up by the taxi at two-thirty for the trip to Intercontinental Airport for the flight to National Airport. Sunlight was pervasive, and the flight was turbulence-free. This was obviously a favorable omen. With me was Tapas Mukopadhyay, a molecular biologist in our research group who had developed the retroviral constructs that we would use in the clinical trial. After arriving, Tapas and I took the Metro to the medical center stop in Bethesda and were picked up by the Marriott shuttle. The next day, Dr. Chiang picked us up and drove us for a visit to Genetic Therapy, Inc. (GTI), located on I-270. We were considering having GTI produce the clinical-grade retroviral vectors. The company employed about seventy people and consisted of several labs and offices. I had presented a seminar that was well received. Tapas and I discussed the project with several of their scientists; however, they were still concerned about the transcripts being produced by the retrovirus. Therefore, we designed our next experiments to determine if the KRAS transcript was genomic or cDNA. Sets of primers for reverse PCR would be synthesized, with one binding to the intron region and others binding to the exons. Following the meeting, Tapas and I returned to the afternoon session of the NIH Recombinant DNA Committee meeting at the Bethesda Marriott.

Next, the RAC considered a protocol from the Fred Hutchinson Cancer Center presented by Dr. Schuening. This was a protocol to mark peripheral blood stem cells with a genetic marker to determine their fate after autologous bone marrow transplantation. Gene marker protocols were proliferating rapidly. They did not benefit patients but provided some potentially useful scientific information on the lifespan of genetically engineered cells. The discussion was so long that the last protocol for the day had to be postponed. Although my protocol was scheduled to be first, it was now postponed until second. This was fortuitous. Strategically, I planned to have the protocol presented on the second day when the RAC was less apt to scrutinize in detail because of reviewer fatigue. This extra delay worked in my favor.

I talked privately again with Dusty Miller, who raised some additional objections about the bystander effect. I could see this would be a major point of contention. Even though he agreed with our response to his review, he clearly had an agenda to sink our protocol. Dr. Barbara Murray, an infectious disease specialist from the University of Texas Medical School at Houston, had no concerns. The membership of the RAC was unusual, considering that they were concerned with medically related gene therapy protocols. Only four of the members were physicians. Two were in infectious diseases, one was a hematologist, and one was a pediatric oncologist. None had expertise in adult solid cancers. There were also basic scientists, lawyers, and ethicists. The dynamics of the RAC were critical to negotiating the review process. Expert opinion by one member of the RAC could sway the entire committee. It was clear that I either had to persuade or neutralize the primary reviewers.

That evening, I had difficulty sleeping. Thoughts about the next day's presentation kept going through my mind. I put the slides together for the talk. I realized I had to emphasize the efficacy in the animal models and present the bystander effect as convincingly as possible. Someone in the room next to mine was playing the television so loudly that I could not sleep. Finally, I called security. They had to call the room several times and knock on the door before the occupant could be roused, and the music stopped.

Dr. Albert Diesseroth, a hematologic oncologist from MD Anderson, presented his protocol first. This was yet another marking protocol, which marked autologous marrow cells in patients with chronic lymphocytic leukemia who were undergoing marrow transplantation. The RAC spent a surprisingly long time deliberating. Apparently, some aspects of the presentation differed from the written protocol. In addition, they were concerned about a protocol that conferred no benefit to the patient. At 9:30 a.m., the discussion ended, and it was time to present my study.

Dusty Miller presented his comments first. It was clear that he continued to be critical of the protocol. Why did he persist? He was involved with a new company in Seattle that was pursuing similar gene therapy, and I was surprised there were no questions about his potential conflict of interest. His first concern was that the gene inserts could mutate. Secondly, he thought many different gene products might result from the different promoters. Lastly, he stated he was not convinced by the bystander effect. He did not see why normal cells that contain p53 would not continually produce substances that would prevent the formation of cancer. Dr. Susan Hirano questioned whether high enough titers could be achieved with the new packaging cell line and queried who would produce the final product. Fortunately, all the top management from GTI were there and were able to respond. She was also concerned about toxic effects with multiple administrations and transduction efficiency in patients. Mr. Capron, an attorney, was concerned about risks to other hospital personnel. He also wanted to be sure that the consent stated that patients would not be compensated only for non-negligent injuries. Dr. Robert Parkman asked about foreign proteins from the fetal calf serum that was used to help the virus-producing cells grow. Dr. Post wanted control data from transduction in tumor cells without a mutation. Someone from the FDA queried whether there might be an incentive not to resect all the tumor. I stated that just the opposite would be the case because we wanted to reduce tumor burden to a minimum and could not remove all the tumors.

I then gave my presentation. The first thing I did was thank the RAC for their reviews. I noticed that during the entire day, no one had bothered to acknowledge the hard work of the RAC. I started off with a chest X-ray in a patient with a whiteout of one lung, meaning that the obstructed airway caused the lung to collapse. I thought this would be especially dramatic and would emphasize the human aspect of the study. Next, I presented the preclinical data and the animal studies. I then reiterated the evidence for the bystander effect. After that, I answered the questions. I focused on the stability of the cell lines and the preliminary focus-forming assay data. I also emphasized all the lines of evidence for the bystander effect. My high school debate training was clearly helpful here. With help from GTI, the questions on the packaging cell line were answered. One of the RAC members said that if the bystander effects were real, then the proportion of cells at day 9 should be equal to the starting proportion. Fortunately, this experiment had just been completed before I left. In fact, that was exactly what happened. It was clear that the dynamics were right. Dr. Parkman made a statement that I had done exactly what the RAC wanted—that is, bring in relevant animal models with convincing preclinical data. Finally, Dr. Miller made a motion for approval of the protocol. The only stipulation was that tests for the transforming virus should be repeated with better controls. The vote was 18 in favor and 0 against.

I received calls from the Houston Chronicle and the New York Times. I spoke with Natalie Angier at the New York Times, who had written a book on cancer research in Bob Weinberg's lab. I realized I needed to be very careful with any interactions with the press. Steve Rosenberg's experience with the press was an excellent lesson in what not to do. A recent Time Magazine article commented, "Rosenberg has also been criticized for inflating patients' hopes by publicizing his experiment before there are any results to report. "It's a very high-profile research activity that Steve Rosenberg is running," Dr. Philip Leder of Harvard University School of Medicine told the New York Times. 'He didn't come to you after the experiment was successful. He came at the beginning, because it might be quite uninteresting when it's all finished.' Given all the attention and elevated hopes, Rosenberg should reveal his results even if they are uninteresting with the same alacrity he shows in announcing the start of an experiment." I took extreme measures to avoid this trap by qualifying all commentary and holding any conclusions until the data was published.

Bruce Johnson, whom I had known from the NIH, came over in the afternoon to discuss the future IASLC Lung Cancer Research Meeting to be held in Airlie, Virginia, April 13–16, 1993. I would be a co-organizer. After exercising at the hotel health club, I returned to the room to find a tray of fruit and cookies with a note, "Congratulations, Love, Liz," yet another example of her thoughtfulness and support that have continued to this day. The next day, I must face the FDA.

16
THE END OF THE BEGINNING

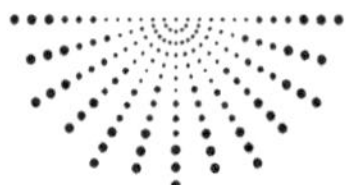

Excellence is never an accident. It is always the result of high intention, sincere effort, and intelligent execution.
—Aristotle

Finally, I presented our protocol to the FDA, and they were very receptive. There were suggestions for additional experiments, such as determining the sensitivity of the detection assays. However, there were otherwise no major problems. This was a marked contrast to the RAC review. After returning to Houston, I was besieged with calls, including some from London and Germany about the upcoming clinical trials. I would then need to push for the FDA approval and manufacture and quality control testing of the gene therapy product so it can begin human tests.

After I returned to Houston, Judah Folkman, a pediatric surgeon and translational scientist, presented the annual Mike Hogg Lecture at MD Anderson. The lecture was superb. He was an expert on angiogenesis, the formation of new blood vessels, and established the concept as an important cancer research topic. For years, no one believed that angiogenesis factors existed. However, he persisted and is now highly regarded. I had dinner with him at Charley's 517 following his lecture. His achievements were eclectic. He produced one of the first heart defibrillators and invented controlled release technology for the Navy. However, when I tried to discuss my research, all he could do was quote Vogelstein's work and was apparently unaware of our studies. It was disappointing that a fellow surgical scientist was so unsupportive and only focused on the narrow perspective of his own work.

I later met with Sherman Muller and Carl Stutts from Columbine Ventures. This was now the third meeting. Sherman Muller had a father who died of lung cancer and was therefore very interested in our work from a personal perspective. They wanted to finance a company, but the initial amount offered was relatively small. The company would be financed in stages. This group funded early companies primarily at medical centers and had recently funded a company with another MD Anderson faculty member. They must go through a process called due diligence, so I recommended Bill Benedict from Baylor (one of the co-cloners of the retinoblastoma gene (Rb) which is another tumor suppressor gene) and Al Diesseroth. I met with Al on Monday. He struck a deal with Ngenex to give two million dollars to MDA to create a retroviral production facility. This company was primarily interested in multiple drug resistance. This was an opportunity for synergy with our company. Liz and I had lunch at the Faculty Club and discussed names for the company. We came up with Intron.

I had an extremely difficult and interesting case on Tuesday, October 13. A three-hundred-pound man had three primary tumors. He presented with a right lung cancer and a kidney cancer and an undiagnosed left lung nodule. I removed the left lung nodule through the thoracoscope, and it turned out to be a primary bronchoalveolar cancer. The man was so fat that anesthesia could not insert a double-lumen endotracheal tube, and I had to perform a difficult right upper lobectomy without the lung deflated. The patient did well post-op. This was one of the most extreme examples of multiple primary cancers that I had seen.

Financing for my company appeared to be moving rapidly. I had another meeting with Archie Kuo and Bill Maleny of Ventures Medical. They seemed to be very interested and wanted to work with Columbine. They were talking about arranging additional financing through Chemical Ventures in New York, which was the largest venture capital company in the world, with $1.5 billion in assets.

I continued with the executive development course. This was a circus. We were split into groups to complete a task. Each group was given incomplete materials. Our group had the least. This was meant to demonstrate the importance of collaboration but degenerated into a fiasco. How would this improve the performance of our administrators?

This week, I was absorbed in preparing for three lectures. The first was given at an antisense workshop and was highly attended, even though it occurred on a Saturday afternoon. On Wednesday, I traveled to Gaithersburg, Maryland, to present at an NIH workshop on biomarkers and early cancer detection. I met David Sidransky, who worked with Bert Vogelstein, one of the first to identify p53 as a tumor suppressor in human cancer and who now has his own lab. He was an arrogant individual who had a rigid way of looking at data and had difficulty seeing two sides of a question. At the meeting, I believed our data was convincing to him about mutant p53 as an early event in upper aerodigestive tract cancers. Several additional papers had come out showing our results were correct. I presented our data on Barrett's esophagus. It appeared we had discovered a new pathway for the development of malignancy. Mutations in the p53 gene were seen primarily in metaplasia and increased when the metaplasia was associated with cancer. This appeared to be an alternate pathway for the development of malignancy, bypassing the step of severe dysplasia.

There were now three major problems I must solve if the gene therapy clinical trials were to begin. I must obtain the final RAC approval, the clinical-grade supernatant production must be initiated, and all this must be funded. I continued to meet with the GTI people during the conference and was told there would be a two-month delay in starting the clinical trial because of production issues. After this, I flew to New Orleans for the fall ASCO meeting, where I presented our data on esophageal cancer. I made it home in time for Halloween.

The next two weeks were filled with presentations to venture capital groups. These included Ventures Medical, Domain, and Texas Biomedical Ventures Partners. Domain was the most prominent of the group and had financed such companies as Amgen and Immunex. They were interested, and negotiations were to have begun that week. On November 14, Liz and I attended an MD Anderson dinner to support science in the schools. It was called "Back to the Future." A group called the Rock 'n Roll Retreads played, and we danced the night away.

On Friday, November 20, another member of the Domain group visited. They were very interested but wanted to fold our company in with Viagene. Furthermore, they wanted to have input on all aspects of the company. Their micromanagement style, plus their obvious desire to eliminate the independence of our company, was undesirable. Texas Biomedical Development Partners was a new group that could come up with the twenty million dollars necessary to bring the company to an IPO. They had a hands-off management style. Most critically, they were willing to put up the money immediately without further hassle, which would allow us to proceed with the clinical trials.

The next week, our family went to Charleston, West Virginia, to visit Liz's parents, brother, and sister. We had Thanksgiving dinner at the Marriott Hotel and then went to Fairmont, where Liz's sister and her husband live, to enjoy the fresh country air and their avocation of raising purebred spaniels and Friesian horses. The following Thursday, I flew to Los Angeles to speak at a UCLA course on lung cancer. The frequent-flyer miles were accumulating. Also, this was an active and exciting week in research. My sponsored research agreement with Texas Biomedical Development Partners was signed on December 16, and they advanced $815,000 for research and support of the clinical protocol. This would be a celebratory holiday season.

Retroviruses are problematic for delivering genes to cancer cells. They are difficult to produce in the large quantities needed for clinical trials. They can be unstable. Retroviruses are inactivated by normal serum complement and thus cannot be injected intravenously. Finally, retroviruses have a limited capacity for DNA. A new approach was needed if gene therapy was going to advance. Adenoviruses are common cold-causing viruses but can be engineered so that they do not cause disease in humans. Adenoviruses also have a large capacity for gene DNA, exist in the cell as extrachromosomal DNA, so they cannot cause genes in the chromosomes to be damaged or turned on, and can be made in large amounts. Adenoviral vectors for cancer gene therapy will be the subject of the next chapter.

On December 18, 1992, my family and I left for Keystone, which can be extremely frigid in the winter, but the sun was bright, and the snow was excellent. We entered the ski racing competition called the National Standard Race, or NASTAR. A professional ski racer sets the pace, which is then handicapped based on your age. Liz won a silver NASTAR medal on her second run. On December 23, after taking a racing clinic, I finally won a bronze. Although I was getting older, I was not getting old fast enough to achieve the handicap I needed for a gold medal! J was taking skating lessons. K, only age 5, had advanced rapidly in ski school and was now level 5 (green and blue runs). Her instructor described her skiing as "awesome." On December 29, J and K entered NASTAR for the first time. They both won silver medals on their first runs. They were each one second off the gold.

The new year of 1993 was off to a good start as I received the sponsored research agreement, which totaled $865,000, the largest agreement yet executed by MD Anderson. The pace of new findings in the laboratory continued to increase. Toshi Fujiwara was a Japanese surgeon who originally came to Liz's laboratory as a research fellow, and after he successfully completed projects in immunotherapy, he joined my lab. He had been working in my lab for the past year, studying the effects of normal p53 on the growth of 3D cancer cells that have a mutant p53 gene. Normal p53 dramatically slowed the growth of these spheroids. This showed that the gene can affect microdeposits of a tumor with a 3D configuration, like what would occur in a patient. In collaboration with Laurie Owen-Schaub, the mechanism appeared to be apoptosis, or programmed cell death. Apoptosis is a Greek word meaning "falling off." The dead cancer cells fragment and look like dead leaves that have fallen from a tree.

On January 15, I flew to New Orleans to give the first Plenary Lecture to the Radiation Therapy Oncology Group. Over three hundred attended, and the lecture was well received. J was in my lab doing her school science project. She was conducting a test called the polymerase chain reaction, or PCR, to see how few mutant p53 cells could be detected in a mixture of cells with deleted p53. For her 10th birthday, we hosted eight friends who first went horse riding at Hermann stables, followed by a dinner and slumber party, in our home which turned into a madhouse.

Production problems for the gene therapy protocol appeared to be endless. GTI began to exert pressure to control all our technology. They said they would not proceed with the clinical trials unless they had an exclusive license for our technology. After checking with the Texas General Counsel in Austin, it appeared that if we collaborated with them, it might give them potential claims on our technology. They sent us two supernatants, one for KRAS and one for p53, but both were inactive in our assay system, which completely undermined my confidence in the company. I contacted the FDA and determined that our lab could produce the reagents under conditions that were adequate for approval. I then obtained permission from Dr. Arthur Bank to use his packaging cell line. Finally, I discovered that Microbiological Associates in Rockville, Maryland, could perform the safety tests for the reagents and possibly produce the material for the clinical trial. This removed all obstacles to using our own reagents and running the trials ourselves without GTI's assistance. A letter was sent saying we would no longer consider using GTI reagents, but then I received a call from them asking for a conference in Houston. I scheduled the conference, although I was doubtful it would accomplish anything.

The Rice University executive development course ended, and I gave a presentation to the class summarizing my experiences. I felt that the changes that would most positively impact MD Anderson's clinical operations would be an incentive system for clinical activity and more decentralization of the administration. Years after my comments, these changes have gradually been put in place at MD Anderson.

I was traveling again, but this time the destination was very attractive. Liz and I left for Hawaii. I was to make a plenary presentation on our gene therapy studies at the Japanese American Summit. We stayed for two days in Honolulu and then rested for three days at the Hyatt resort on the Big Island. This island was much more volcanic than the other islands we had experienced, with vast expanses of black volcanic rock. But there were also lovely gardens. We had the experience of swimming with dolphins.

It seemed those days I was always airborne. After a brief respite at home, on February 22, I left for New York to present at Cancer Progress '93. This was a gathering of biotech executives and companies. The day I presented, Synergen, a biotech startup stock, collapsed from 58 to 15 because its sepsis drug trial was inconclusive. The mood was somber.

We had a double-header in the prestigious journal Cancer Research. Chung's paper on p53 mutations in second primary tumors was accepted without revision and given a high-priority status. It was published on April 1. Renee's paper on in vivo gene therapy in mice was accepted for Advances in Brief.

We returned to Keystone for spring break skiing. The base was over seventy inches, and it snowed almost every day; yet, the weather was warm. We had an owner's closet in our condominium that was stuffed to the breaking point with skis, clothes, and food, and it presented a major hazard every time we opened it on arrival. For the first time, the girls did not go to ski school once during the trip, skiing well mostly on blue runs.

Jerry Cobbs sent GTI a letter stating I did not want to use their vectors. Yuan Chiang from GTI called me to set up another meeting. They wanted to come to Houston to try to work out the problems with the viral vectors. David Nance then insisted that we make them sign a confidentiality agreement. They did this, and now the president of the company, Barrett, wanted to visit as well! The contract with Microbiological Associates was nearing completion. I had also identified producer cells that we could send.

The problems seemed endless in preparing the vectors for the clinical trial. We needed to find a new gene delivery system. It was discovered the packaging cell lines were grown in media incorrectly prepared by the core facility, and the cells became sick. We lost all the cells with the old KRAS antisense construct that were mycoplasma-free. Fortunately, the new constructs seemed to be almost ready. That coming week, they would be tested for biologic activity.

The paper Discordant p53 Mutations in Primary and Second Primary Cancers of the Aerodigestive Tract was published in Cancer Research.[76] An article describing the findings appeared in the Houston Chronicle. The paper was accepted without revision and was published within one month of receipt. For forty years, it had been thought that multiple primary cancers arise because of a field effect. The entire mucosa of the aerodigestive tract is exposed to a carcinogen. However, the molecular basis of this had never been identified. In our study, p53 mutations were identified in head and neck primary cancers and second primaries. The mutations were all discordant. This indicated that a common carcinogen was affecting the aerodigestive tract. However, the distinct mutations showed that the cancers arose independently. This was the first molecular demonstration of theory of field cancerization which postulates that there is a field of cell and molecular changes which predisposes to cancer in that field.

On April 12, I left for the IASLC Workshop in Lung Cancer in Airlie, Virginia. I was an organizer along with Bruce Johnson and Adi Gazdar. The workshop lasted for four days, featuring enthusiastic discussions. I stayed in a manor house overlooking the beautiful countryside emerging in the spring. After we were both disappointed with the outcomes of our SPORE submission, John Minna and I decided to submit a joint SPORE. It would be a challenge for our two rival institutions to work together, but team science was the future.

On April 15, our article on retroviral therapy of human lung cancer in mice appeared in the Advances in Brief section of Cancer

Research.[73] I received calls to present seminars at Boston University and Memorial Sloan Kettering, but I turned them down. My travel schedule was too tight, and I needed to devote more time to family and to get the clinical trial going. The new p53 construct was finally tested and proved to be better than the old construct, but we next faced more frustrations. The new p53 construct was shipped to Microbiological Associates to go through the fifteen safety tests required by the FDA. Meanwhile, I received another fax from Arthur Banks revoking his previously granted permission to use his packaging cell line. As it turned out, he had formed a company, and we had to deal directly with them. Their first materials-transfer agreement specified that they had exclusive rights to anything packaged in their cell line. This was not acceptable. On April 20, the top brass from GTI finally showed up. They expressed their surprise at the partnership we had formed but also expressed their willingness to strike a deal. K's violin studies were intensive, and during the weekend, she spent both days in the Suzuki workshop.

I received a letter inviting me to apply for consideration for the departmental chairmanship in surgery at the University of Miami. I went ahead and threw my hat in the ring. It was always helpful for the administration at MD Anderson to know that you were wanted elsewhere. The frustrations of the budgeting process at MD Anderson were mounting. Without a clinical incentive plan and with an inadequate departmental budget, I needed to keep looking for a better administrative structure.

My parents had arrived on May 16 to care for our daughters while we were traveling and stayed for J's piano recital, which was on May 23. She played Fur Elise beautifully and won a special award as the most improved student, as well as numerous trophies. On May 19, 1993, I left for the AACR. Liz was already there to chair a session. The morning of May 20, I gave a symposium presentation on our work in a session on antisense chaired by Jack Cohen. The room was packed, and the talk received much attention. We stayed for the AACR presidential reception and dinner. Margaret Kripke was the incoming president. On May 22, I had the first clinical research retreat for our department. Several potential research topics were discussed.

On May 29, I left for Genoa, Italy, for an International Lung Cancer Conference sponsored by Dr. Motta. On arrival at the airport, I was not met and had no lira. I had to negotiate with a cab driver who spoke only Italian, and I ended up paying one hundred dollars for the cab ride. The meeting site was lovely. The meeting itself had a few interesting presentations. John Minna and I discussed more strategy for obtaining our joint SPORE grant. I returned on June 3. Immediately after my British Airways flight from Genoa to London took off, British Airways went on strike. Liz had her lab party on June 5 at our home, and K's violin recital was on June 6.

Our new company, Intron, was going through the incorporation process as a Delaware corporation. We finally negotiated with Art Banks's company, Genetix, for the use of their packaging cell line. Preliminary contact was made with Canji, another small biotech company in San Diego that was working with tumor suppressor genes. They were very interested in our work. An extensive network of alliances was forming. They also had a patent position on p53.

I received a fax from Dusty Miller rejecting our reply to meet the RAC stipulation. The experiment required adding retroviral supernatant (liquid from the virus-producing cells) to NIH3T3 cells to ensure there was no transformation to cancer. This was a ridiculous experiment because neither antisense KRAS nor p53 is transforming. He wrote that we needed to test 100 mL instead of what we tested. Also, there were questions about the consent form and a mixing experiment that were never mentioned previously. I had not received a single written communication from the RAC since our protocol was approved. Miller was duplicitous, changing the rules in the middle of the game. In addition, he had an intellectual bias against our research. There were conflict-of-interest issues because he had his own company, Targeted Genetics, which was associated with Immunex. I called Wivel to resolve this. On June 11, we had our departmental dinner honoring the residents at the Wyndham Warwick. It was fun, with Garrett Walsh presenting some humorous slides of the faculty.

It turned out the RAC stipulations were in the transcript of the minutes. However, they were never sent to me. The RAC did not require that our Surveillance Committee make all the changes suggested by the RAC. However, I needed to show that the changes were submitted and rejected. On top of this, the lab that had a virus producer cell line that gave us the positive control for the focus-forming assay had lost the cell line because of a freezer breakdown. It took us almost a year to locate this cell line. Now I had to write Robert Weinberg to retrieve the cell line.

I met with Mike Shepherd from Canji on Tuesday. His company's primary project was tumor-suppressor protein therapy with the Rb protein. I was looking for potential alliances with this company. Liz and K left on Saturday for another Ottawa, Kansas Suzuki workshop. These workshops were unending, but it was a great chance for Liz and K to spend time together. K played in the orchestra ("William Tell Overture," "Can Can," "British Grenidiers"). She also played a solo. J was leaving for Camp Olympia on Monday. On her return, Liz immediately left for Atlanta for an American Cancer Society study section to review grant applications.

Surprises continued at MD Anderson. The chief of hospital and clinic operations, who had been fired by Jim Cox during the division head purge, was leaving and had taken a job as CEO of Georgetown. Charles Balch, currently the head of the Division of surgery, assumed the CEO's job. Helmut Goepfert, the chair of head and neck surgery, would assume Balch's job, at least temporarily, to complete the musical chairs. Ironically, Goepfert was one of the most vocal opponents of the division of surgery being formed, which he now headed.

Plans were proceeding to begin the formal organization of a gene therapy company now called Intron. A prospectus was being prepared. There was continued frustration with sending the antisense KRAS retroviral supernatant. Wei-Wei Zhang from Intron traveled to Canji in San Diego to scout out their scientific expertise to determine if Intron wanted to work with them. The trip to Canji showed that they were six months to a year behind us in the development of their adenovirus vector. They did not have any other science that would benefit us. They wanted to buy us, but their plan was to buy us for Canji stock. As they would run out of cash in April, this did not seem promising. I also met with Lou Buccollo, the CEO of Ngenex. The company was focusing on the multiple drug resistance gene and was collaborating with Bill Benedict in the development of a modification of the retinoblastoma gene, which is another tumor suppressor gene. They were very interested in the system we had for delivering our genes; however, a collaboration never developed.

17
LUNG CANCER BREAKTHROUGH

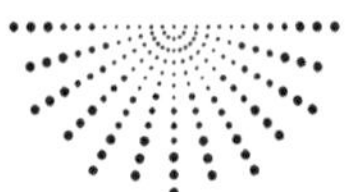

Medicine, the only profession that labors incessantly to destroy the reason for its existence.

—James Bryce

Earlier, when I was at the NCI, my clinical trial in esophageal cancer suggested that giving chemotherapy before surgery increased the number of patients surviving long-term without increasing adverse events associated with the complex surgery. In 1987, I began a clinical trial investigating this concept in non-small cell lung cancer, the most common form of lung cancer and the leading cause of cancer deaths in the world. The clinical trial would only include patients with locally advanced lung cancer that had not spread to other organs, except to the lymph nodes around the lung. This was a very difficult clinical trial to complete. Patients at this stage were not common and frequently not candidates for surgery. The faculty I inherited when I arrived at MD Anderson were not academically oriented and were not willing to consider entering patients. It is interesting to remember and share the origins of our study. I invited one of the faculty members to write the protocol, but he was unable to do it. When we finally completed the study, he had entered only one patient on the protocol. He moved to private practice at St. Luke's Hospital, where he ran the thorax clinic, and eventually ended up in Switzerland.

Despite multiple obstacles, sixty patients were eventually entered in the trial. Would this number be sufficient? In designing a clinical trial, the principal investigator works with a biostatistician to make an informed guess as to what the difference in outcome will be between the two treatment arms. However, if one treatment is better than the other, the principal investigator would like to try to stop the trial as soon as that is statistically confirmed so all patients can receive the better treatment. The mechanism for this is the interim analysis, which is a statistical comparison of the treatment groups midway through the trial. The statistician on the trial informed me that it was time for an interim analysis. The interim analysis showed a survival difference in the two arms that was statistically significant at a very high level. The degree of significance is indicated by a p-value, which is the likelihood that you would obtain a difference if there were no difference. The smaller this value, the more confidence you have that the study findings are accurate. A value of 0.05 or less is usually considered significant. For the analysis of our clinical trial, the p-value was more than ten times lower at the 0.004 level of significance. This was so significant that entry into the study was stopped. This was the first randomized study showing the benefits of perioperative chemotherapy in stage 3 lung cancer patients. The patients receiving the chemotherapy had a six-fold increase in the length of their median survival, an astonishingly positive result in a group of patients with a generally poor outcome. I planned to present this at an upcoming lung cancer workshop in Bruges, Belgium, but I was in for a shock.

Liz and the girls were off to West Virginia to attend a family reunion, see her parents, and attend her niece's wedding. Finally, Intron Therapeutics, Inc. was now a reality. The company had been incorporated in Delaware. The antisense KRAS retroviral producer cell line was sent to Microbiological Associates for safety testing. There were continuing problems with this, and I decided I needed to focus on the retrovirus p53 for the clinical trial. Our new construct, which had modifications, was not as effective as the old construct, so we would need to revert to the previous design. Fortunately, the family could leave Houston to escape the oppressive heat and humidity to spend two weeks in Keystone, Colorado. K won third place in the Colorado State Fiddle Championships in her age group, which was held in Keystone that summer, and improvised a fiddle version of Twinkle, Twinkle, Little Star she picked up at her Ottawa Suzuki summer workshop.

On my return, I left for Bruges, Belgium, for the IASLC workshop in the treatment of advanced non-small cell lung cancer. Bruges is a perfectly preserved walled city from the Middle Ages, well known for its highly detailed lace. At the conference, I presented our randomized study on perioperative chemotherapy compared to surgery alone. I had heard that a group in Spain had copied the design of our trial and initiated the clinical trial three years after ours began. The principal investigator of the Spanish trial, Rafael Rossel, presented his study. I had heard a rumor that it had been submitted to the New England Journal of Medicine, and he confirmed this. This was shocking news, as they had copied our idea and now could be the first to publish their results. I would urgently write up our results so they could at least be published together. I stopped by Paris on the way home and was president of one of the sessions of the Organization for Specialized Studies on Diseases of the Esophagus. I saw Paul Schneider, one of my first MD Anderson fellows, and discussed our multi-institutional study on p53 in Barrett's esophagus. He presented a paper confirming our previous publication on p53 in Barrett's esophagus.

Writing up the results for our lung cancer clinical trial was a huge undertaking, made more difficult because of the time pressure forced on me by the potential publication of the competing paper. Fortunately, most of the data had already been gathered. In one day, our new research nurses, Julie Han and Faye Martin, contacted all the living patients. However, it was still a formidable task to get a New

England Journal of Medicine paper submitted in one week to try to beat the other group to publication. And to make things worse, our data manager resigned. I began working day and night. On September 10, I went to Vancouver to receive the Cosbie Honorary Lectureship bestowed by the Royal College of Physicians and Surgeons. In Seattle, I waited three hours because a Canada International flight had to replace a tire, and the tire did not clear customs. I was writing feverishly in the airport on my laptop. After my lecture, Wally Temple, president of the Canadian Society of Surgical Oncology, and Henry Shibata took me to a great sushi restaurant. All during the trip back, I was writing furiously to complete the manuscript. When I returned, it was completed in draft form, and I faxed a copy to Ki Hong, who was in San Francisco as he was a coauthor and his department had been a major collaborator. Then I made a frantic effort to get Neely Atkinson, the statistician, to perform the final statistical analysis. There was an incredible difference between the two groups, with a sixty-five-month median survival in the perioperative chemotherapy group and an eleven-month median survival in the surgery-alone group. This was the first randomized trial of induction chemotherapy in lung cancer. Along with the confirmatory trial from Barcelona, it began a new era in the treatment of lung cancer. It was reassuring that the Barcelona trial confirmed our results. This treatment alone would save five thousand lives per year in the United States and seventy thousand lives per year worldwide. I traveled to Dallas to present a talk at a lung cancer course given by John Minna and presented our randomized trial results there.

The time was racing by, and many family concerns were pressing. It was time to investigate middle schools for J. This involved an incredible amount of time in filling out applications and touring schools, but it was important to find the right fit.

On October 12, I flew to San Francisco for one day to present at the American College of Surgeons on the resection of pulmonary metastases. The following Monday, John Minna and his group from Dallas came to meet with us to plan SPORE grant submission strategy. The Public Affairs office called and wanted me to work with a reporter from the Chronicle, who was doing a story on patients at the MD Anderson Cancer Center. The reporter was very nice, but it was disconcerting having a newspaper reporter follow me around in the clinic and the operating room. On October 22, I flew to Newark, New Jersey, to be a distinguished professor at the University of Medicine and Dentistry of New Jersey, where I presented a talk on molecular surgery for cancer. The dinner at an Italian restaurant was excellent.

Now yet another problem had arisen with respect to the lung cancer gene therapy protocol. The minor stipulation to show that our virus had no transforming activity had been met with a series of ten experiments. In May, after the RAC failed to send me copies of the minutes where I discussed the design of the experiments with Dusty Miller, he rejected our experiments again with requests for additional experimentation. Here it was over a year after my initial RAC approval, and the protocol was still pending final approval in an ongoing bureaucratic nightmare. It appeared this was a passive-aggressive tactic to prevent our protocol from beginning. The tests from the Microbiological Associates master cell bank looked good, although there were some heart-stopping false alarms concerning viral titers and replication competent retrovirus.

I called the New England Journal of Medicine, and both reviews were in, but as of that time, I did not know the status of the lung cancer paper. Also, to add to the complicated MD Anderson political atmosphere, I heard that Balch was looking at the chairman's job at Duke when David Sabiston retired. Other candidates included two other friends, Mike Zinner and Glen Steele. None of them got the job.

I flew to San Diego to attend the International Gene Therapy of Cancer Meeting and present our work. When I returned, I found a fax of Miller's comment saying that he wanted more experiments done and wanted the issues brought before the RAC at its December meeting. I called Leroy Walters, who was chairman of the RAC, and told him this was unacceptable. Miller had ties with Targeted Genetics, which represented a possible conflict, as he knew I had a company developing gene therapy.

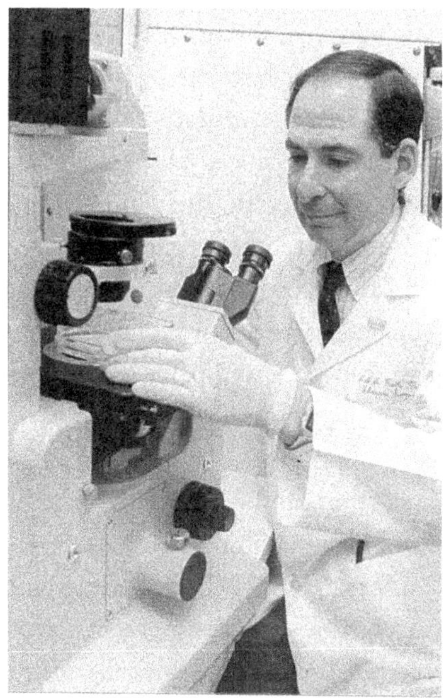

The author at the research microscope from the 1993 Houston Chronicle article

My parents arrived on Thanksgiving, and Liz prepared a feast. On Saturday, we took the girls to the NASA Space Center Houston. On Sunday, the Houston Chronicle supplement appeared with a picture of me in the operating room on the cover. In general, it was well-written. However, there was not enough about our research effort. My assistant, Carol, had made some comments to the reporter. She really thought I should take more of a personal interest in the secretaries and compliment them on their clothes! I would be accused of sexual harassment for sure. The article was published in the Houston Chronicle Magazine with a picture of me and my fellow, Paul Morris, operating. It included the story of my patient, Bill Logue, a state district judge from Waco. He was the juvenile court judge responsible for finding new homes for the children living in the Branch Davidian cult compound, which earlier in the year had become a burning funeral pyre. Bill had presented to my clinic over five years ago with a diagnosis of adenocarcinoma of the esophagus. He had noticed that some foods seemed to stick in his throat. He had an endoscopy, which showed cancer in the lower part of the esophagus, and then came to see me. At the time, we had not initiated any new clinical trials with chemotherapy or radiation for cancer of the esophagus, so I proposed using the standard surgical operation to remove the cancer. Bill recovered rapidly and, instead of retiring, continued as a judge. Now five years had passed, and there was no sign of cancer. It was very likely that he was cured. Bill was a very emotional and demonstrative man. When I told him his cancer was operable, he gave me a hug and repeated that gesture at every clinic visit. If only all our patients had such great outcomes.

The New England Journal of Medicine had a reputation as a leading journal for the publication of research articles. The journal returned our article after three months in review with a rejection. One of the reviewers was obviously incompetent. Each of the criticisms was not just arguable but incorrect. A journal with this influence has an ethical obligation to choose competent reviewers and employ editors who can recognize incompetent reviews when they are received. If this is not managed well, important medical findings are delayed in their presentation, and patients ultimately suffer. The Rosell paper, however, was accepted. I was astonished, as the design of the clinical trial was identical to ours, which preceded theirs by three years, and the results were identical. It is unusual for two trials in the same patient population to be completed at the same time with similar results. Such an occurrence would further validate the findings of both trials. Yet New England Journal of Medicine ignored this despite obvious errors in the review of our paper. I later identified one of the reviewers as a medical oncologist with a reputation for being unreasonably critical and arrogant. This is conjecture, but he may not have been able to accept the possibility that a surgeon could conceive and complete a successful clinical trial that incorporated chemotherapy. I have heard this at meetings and study sections. On the contrary, surgeons are highly knowledgeable about the biology, clinical course, and needs of patients with potentially surgically resectable cancer, and our trial design was copied by a medical oncologist. Res ipsa loquitur. I was desperate to get our paper out immediately. I decided to submit it to another high-impact journal, the Journal of the National Cancer Institute. The hypocrisy of New England Journal of Medicine and its failure to live up to the highest standards of medical journalism was evident in its most recent mandate to limit access to journal articles for news organizations,[88] with a statement that "News outlets that report for physician readers will no longer meet criteria for embargoed access." This was a simple ploy to restrict access to increase market share. This order was rescinded later because of protests from medical correspondents. The crisis in scientific publishing will be discussed in more detail in chapter 19.

It was the December holiday season, and the RAC made yet another ridiculous request. They wanted to give our protocol to three new primary reviewers to resolve the impasse created by the Miller request. This would create an enormous amount of work for everyone. I needed a break, and the family would benefit from time together unimpeded by work. On December 18, our family flew to Grand Cayman Island. One of the highlights was a trip to Stingray City, where we could snorkel with the stingrays.

After returning, I frantically worked in the lab to do the transformation experiments required by the RAC. Fortunately, the Abelson retrovirus that we received from Naomi Rosenberg in Boston (suggested to us in a fortuitous call to Jeff Ostrove at Microbiological Associates) worked. We had to set up thirty plates showing that if we added a small amount of virus to our supernatant, we could still get transformation. Southern blots of the infected cell line showed there was no rearrangement. Miller had claimed for six months that the presence of a SV40 polyadenylation site caused rearrangements, but this was incorrect.

It is 1994, and what better way to begin the New Year than with a Suzuki workshop in Lafayette, Louisiana, which K and Liz attended? On January 27, I went to Washington, D.C., for a BioEast meeting to give a presentation on gene therapy. I was interviewed afterward by

Susan Jenks, a reporter for JNCI. She was interested in the scientific aspects of our gene therapy trial. I needed to rush back to Houston to meet with representatives from Rhône-Poulenc Rorer, a French pharmaceutical company with four billion dollars in yearly sales. In 1999, it would merge with Hoechst to form Aventis, which would become part of Sanofi in 2004. They had written to me about developing a relationship with Intron. They wanted to move very quickly. Interestingly, we would need to change the name of the company because Schering-Plough said it infringed on their drug, Intron A. The name of the company was changed to Introgen. Washington was in the middle of a severe ice storm, with freezing weather gripping the East Coast. My plane was delayed coming in from Newark and, after one hour of de-icing, was on the runway when the airport closed. I spent the night in Washington and flew back at 6:30 a.m. the next day. At this point, we were frantically doing experiments to meet the RAC deadline. Unfortunately, they were not working. The focus-forming experiments were always difficult. These needed to be done with mouse cells called NIH3T3 cells, which were derived from a mouse embryo. These cells could spontaneously transform to become cancer-like, and they did this on a regular basis. Nancy Yen, my technician, had set up over 150 plates. Only a single band was detected with a restriction enzyme, which cuts DNA at specific sites, KpnI, in a mixture of lung cancer cells infected with the p53 retrovirus. However, the control did not migrate at the appropriate size. The research scientist who did the experiment told me that because the gels were 1 percent, the difference in migration would not be seen. Unfortunately, he made a big error in estimating the size of the KpnI fragment, which I did not pick up until it was pointed out to me by Miller in a letter. After the scientist conducted the experiments, he left for India and was unreachable.

Thoracic oncology was now a recognized subspecialty, and multidisciplinary management of patients, with the participation of surgeons, medical oncologists, radiation oncologists, pathologists, and radiologists, was essential in the management of every patient. It was time for a textbook on this emerging field. I had suggested this to Steve Rosenberg, but he had just completed his own oncology textbook and was not receptive to potential competition. However, I persisted and found a publisher, and the first edition came out in 1988.

On February 17, I went to Tampa to meet with Jack Ruchdeschel and Tom Weisenberger, my coeditors, to complete the editorial tasks for the second edition of our textbook, Thoracic Oncology, which eventually went into three editions. Jack took us to a hockey game between the Tampa Bay Lightning and the Montreal Canadiens, which Tampa won in a very electrifying match. The next day, we spent twelve hours editing chapters. I toured the Moffitt Cancer Center. Jack had done a great job building up the cancer center, and I thought then it had a bright future, which it has realized under the current leadership of its new president and CEO, Dr. Patrick Hwu, also a friend and colleague who had been recruited from MD Anderson.

On March 4, I went to face the RAC again. They focused on the rearrangement issue, and the data I showed were very weak. With the scientist gone and no explanation for the aberrant migration of the control band, I was in a bad position and took some flak. Nevertheless, the RAC approved the protocol with the stipulation that the unsequenced 1 kb intron must be sequenced and we must have restriction maps of the vectors.

I ran to the airport and caught a plane for Orlando to deliver a lecture at the American Cancer Society regional meeting in Florida. Back at home, J got a superior plus rating at the Gold Cup Competition playing Chopin Waltz in A minor. Liz and I celebrated an evening together and went out to dinner at an elegant restaurant.

It was spring break and time for spring skiing. On March 10, we all left for Keystone. The weather was incredibly warm, but the snow was still decent. I got my NASTAR handicap down to 41. We returned from Keystone, and on Saturday, I presented a Meet the Professor session at the Society of Surgical Oncology with Mike Burt on esophageal and lung cancers. On March 22, I left for Montreal to present the E. J. Tabah lecture on surgical oncology. Dr. Tabah was one of the founders of surgical oncology in North America. I presented three lectures: one at McGill University on gene therapy, one at Montreal General on lung cancer, and one at McGill surgery rounds on esophageal cancer. I was feted with dinner at several excellent restaurants, including the University Club. I returned on Friday, and my parents arrived on Saturday. This was fortuitous, as more travel was imminent.

RPR had expressed continued interest in funding our research. They requested that representatives from Introgen (including me) fly to Paris to meet with scientists and executives of RPR. I left on April 4. We toured the RPR facility with Joe Bossart, the director of business development. That evening, we all went to the Lido, which had a spectacular show with ice skating, helicopters, and live animals. The following day, we went to their biotechnology research facility. Bruno Tocque and his colleagues gave an impressive presentation. RPR was focused on the potential for gene therapy. Their annual report had a double helix on the cover.

I returned on April 7 so I could be present for an award Liz was receiving. She received the Texas Federation of Business and Professional Women's Clubs Past State Presidents Award for her research. I went to the breakfast, presentation, and lunch, with my parents also in attendance. This was a very prestigious award and well-deserved by Liz. Incredibly, I then left for the AACR on April 12 to fly to San Francisco. Here, I gave a symposium presentation on the gene therapy of lung cancer. John Minna chaired the session. I finally returned home for some rest. I played tennis with Ki Hong on Sunday and managed to stay on the court.

Now that Charles Balch had an executive position, the search continued for someone to head the division. I was approached to see if I would take the position, but I declined. Taking such a position would eliminate the time I needed for research and clinical trials. Administration was my least favorite activity. Helmuth Goepfert, the ad interim head, was the leading candidate for the new division head. He had been endorsed unanimously by all the department chairs. This was odd because Helmuth was one of the most vocal critics against establishing the division structure. However, he had presided over it well as the ad interim head. He did not get it, though. The division head position went to a surgical oncologist and physician-scientist, Dr. Raphael Pollock.

Our proposal for using an adenovirus p53 expression vector with cisplatin was submitted to the RAC for presentation at the June 10, 1994, meeting. I could hardly contain my enthusiasm at having to face the RAC again. However, the adenovirus delivery system had many advantages and was the future of gene therapy clinical trials. The girls were in the last stretch, with lots of work for the end of the school year and recitals.

Our thoracic track residency program was finally approved by the Residency Review Committee. Although I had delegated one of our faculty to complete the application, I ended up doing it myself. This was one of the first such programs in the United States and set a new standard for training surgeons in thoracic surgery. I had the faculty and Paul Morris, our first thoracic resident, over to the house for dinner. Paul became the thoracic surgeon at the University of Hawaii in Honolulu, a great position and location.

K and J's recitals were on the same day. The playing at the violin recital was superb. A lot of the senior students were leaving. J did beautifully playing the "Chopin Waltz" in A minor, although I only got to see the tape.

The head of technology transfer called me on Friday and presented me with a stockholder agreement, which he wanted me to sign by Monday so it could be sent to the Board of Regents for approval. He essentially tried to bully me into signing what were very unfavorable terms that completely changed the original agreement. Apparently, everyone met and decided to eliminate my 10 percent non-dilute provision and divide with UT, which suddenly wanted a piece of the action. The agreement was very complex, had some noncompetition provisions in it that would prevent me from essentially breathing if I left Introgen, and made my stock illiquid. I called Doty and told him I could not sign it. They would need to adhere to the original terms.

Our paper on the prolongation of survival with perioperative chemotherapy for lung cancer appeared in JNCI to general acclaim. Articles on the study appeared in several newspapers, and there was a story on the evening news both locally and nationally. I also presented the paper at ASCO, which was held in Dallas that year. A press conference was held the following day. Our findings have since been reproduced in multiple subsequent clinical trials. The next chapter describes how preoperative drug treatment has evolved to the present day and continues to be a lifesaving strategy.

18
EVOLVING ROLE FOR SURGERY AND NEOADJUVANT THERAPY IN STAGE 3 LUNG CANCER

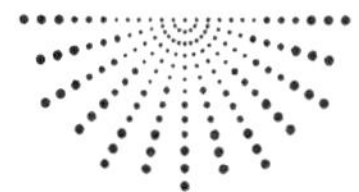

Every disease is a musical problem; every cure is a musical solution.
—Novalis

When a patient's cancer is discovered, a procedure called staging is performed to determine if it is localized to the organ of origin or if it has spread to lymph nodes or other organs. This is accomplished with imaging studies such as a PET scan or by a procedure to biopsy lymph nodes. If these studies are all negative for cancer, it is still possible the cancer has spread, but the number of cancer cells may be so low that they elude detection. With lung cancer designated as stage 1, about a third of patients will eventually show spread to other organs. The concept of adjuvant therapy, which is giving systemic treatment such as chemotherapy or immunotherapy to patients with no sign of spread, was developed to attempt to kill these small deposits of cancer cells before they were detectable, grew, and continued to spread. Adjuvant therapy is given after local treatment and may last a year or more. Neoadjuvant treatment, such as the one I developed, as described in Chapter 17, can be given for a much shorter period and at a time when the patient is in the best medical condition before surgery or radiation, both of which can be debilitating. Thus, the patient is more likely to receive a full course of treatment. There is also the possibility that shrinking the tumor will make the surgery more successful in controlling the local tumor. How has this concept advanced? Here I summarize progress in the treatment of stage 3 lung cancer.

When I began my oncology research fellowship, treatment for stage 3A operable non-small cell lung cancer (NSCLC) was primarily single modality, either surgery or radiation therapy; the staging system was less refined, with each stage being very heterogeneous; and preoperative staging was inaccurate. In highly selected patients, surgery at best, could obtain a 20 percent five-year survival. In 2024 there are 2.21 million new cases of lung cancer yearly worldwide.[89] Among those with newly diagnosed NSCLC, it is estimated that about 20 percent of patients present with stage 3A disease.[90] Although five-year survival has improved to 40 percent with multimodality treatment based on the results of the clinical trial I published and other studies, outcomes remain unsatisfactory for most patients.

The recognition of poor outcomes from stage 2A NSCLC and the heterogeneity of this group was dependent on the development of an accurate clinical and pathologic staging system. In 1964, Dr. Clifton Mountain, a surgeon at the University of Texas MD Anderson Cancer Center, and Dr. David Carr, a medical oncologist at the Mayo Clinic, realized the importance of a staging system for lung cancer. No such system existed at that time for lung cancer, although the tumor size, lymph node metastases, and distant metastases (TNM) system was already being used in Europe for other organs. Together, Dr. Mountain and Dr. Carr developed the first TNM staging system for lung cancer, supported by a large database of clinical material. This work was undertaken under the auspices of the Task Force on Lung Cancer of the American Joint Committee on Cancer Staging and End Results Reporting (AJCC) and was subsequently adopted by the AJCC. Dr. Mountain continued to refine this system throughout the rest of his career, and his staging system became the standard worldwide in the management of lung cancer. Recognizing the need to coordinate international efforts in lung cancer research, Dr. Mountain was one of the founders of the International Association for the Study of Lung Cancer (IASLC) in 1973. He carried the message of the multidisciplinary care for lung cancer developed at MD Anderson to physicians and researchers worldwide, seeding the framework for national guidelines to come and establishing the foundation for the IASLC Staging Committee.

Despite the refinement of the staging system for NSCLC, now entering its ninth edition, stage 3A is one of the most heterogeneous stages with T descriptors ranging from T1 to T4 (referencing the size and invasiveness of the tumor) and nodal descriptors ranging from N0 to N2 with single or multiple stations. Most clinical trials have focused on classic 3A, which would be primarily T1–T2 N2. However, this is a small group, making completion of such trials difficult, and many of the subsequently discussed clinical trials failed to meet accrual goals.

Converging clinical advances in the 1980s set the stage for the development of the multimodality treatment of stage 3A NSCLC. Preoperative staging improved with the wider use of more accurate CT scans and mediastinoscopy. Clinical trials with cisplatin in NSCLC lung cancer began in the 1970s with a 21 percent single-agent response rate.[91] This was the highest response rate achieved for a single agent in NSCLC up to that time, and additional trials showed that responses to combination drug treatment (e.g., etoposide) were higher. This stimulated the hypothesis that the addition of systemic drug treatment either pre- (neoadjuvant) or post- (adjuvant) surgical resection could improve long-term survival. It was possible that more drugs could be delivered prior to surgery than afterward, with deterioration of the patient's performance status. A second benefit of neoadjuvant therapy would be a more accurate assessment of the tumor response to chemotherapy, which could influence postoperative treatment. Based on this rationale, the first neoadjuvant chemotherapy clinical trial in NSCLC was initiated.[92] Patients with stage 3A NSCLC were randomized to receive either immediate surgery or up to three cycles of cisplatin combination chemotherapy followed by surgery followed by up to three cycles of chemotherapy if the tumor was initially stable or responded. The trial showed a highly significant difference in overall survival in favor of the neoadjuvant chemotherapy group. The results were first presented at an IASLC Symposium in 1993. A second clinical trial begun three years later confirmed these findings.[93] The publication of a large, randomized adjuvant (postoperative) chemotherapy trial for stages 1–3 showing a modest survival benefit with adjuvant chemotherapy shifted interest away from neoadjuvant trials.[94]

Adjuvant chemotherapy has its greatest survival benefit in stage 3 patients. The overall magnitude of the benefit is similar to that of neoadjuvant chemotherapy when compared to adjuvant chemotherapy. However, it is more likely that full-dose chemotherapy will be given preoperatively compared to postoperatively. Brandt and colleagues showed that patients who received neoadjuvant chemotherapy, compared to adjuvant chemotherapy were more likely to receive the full-dose (78 percent versus 63 percent) and full-cycle regimen (91 percent versus 78 percent)[95]. Patients receiving adjuvant chemotherapy were more than twice as likely to have an adverse event compared to patients who had neoadjuvant therapy (38 percent versus 15 percent). These findings are like the NATCH trial, where 97 percent of neoadjuvant chemotherapy patients began their planned course of treatment compared to only 66.2 percent of adjuvant therapy patients.[96]

During this period, developments in the treatment of lung cancer with radiation therapy combined with chemotherapy showed that concurrent chemoradiation was more effective than sequential administration.[97] This observation stimulated many randomized clinical trials attempting to define the benefits of surgery compared to nonsurgical chemoradiation in stage 3 patients. In the Intergroup (INT) 0139 trial, patients were treated with neoadjuvant chemoradiation and subsequently randomized between surgery or further radiotherapy.[98] Overall, survival did not differ between both arms, although progression-free survival was better in the surgical resection group. Mortality following pneumonectomy was very high, emphasizing the high morbidity of neoadjuvant chemoradiation in this group and likely neutralizing any survival advantage for surgery. An unplanned subset analysis was done by matching patients who had lobectomy after neoadjuvant chemoradiation to a matched group treated with chemoradiation alone. There was a highly significant difference in survival favoring the surgical group.

In the ESPATUE trial, patients with 3A and selected patients with 3B NSCLC received neoadjuvant chemotherapy, as well as concurrent chemoradiotherapy. Patients were then randomly assigned to receive a chemoradiotherapy boost or to undergo surgery.[99] No difference in overall survival was observed between the two arms. In the European Organization for Research and Treatment of Cancer (EORTC) 08941 trial, only neoadjuvant chemotherapy was given, followed by surgery or radiotherapy in the case of a response to chemotherapy, also randomizing those patients with a minor response.[100] Once again, overall and progression-free survival did not differ between the two randomized groups. These trials were completed at a time when mediastinal staging by positron emission tomography (PET) and endobronchial ultrasound-guided biopsies were not routinely available. Today, surgical mortality and morbidity have decreased dramatically due to more widespread use of minimally invasive surgical techniques and enhanced recovery protocols.[101] Despite the number of trials and large numbers of patients, definitive answers to the optimal management of stage 3A are lacking due to the heterogeneity of patients entered and continuing advances in radiation, surgical, and staging technology.

Other recent clinical trials have attempted to fill the gaps. The Swiss Cooperative Group, SAKK, study compares neoadjuvant chemotherapy and surgery versus neoadjuvant chemoradiation and surgery for stage 3A-N2 NSCLC.[102] No differences were found in overall or event-free survival, suggesting that in future clinical trials, the appropriate control group is neoadjuvant chemotherapy and surgery. Before this study, there was only one completed randomized trial comparing neoadjuvant chemotherapy to neoadjuvant chemoradiation, conducted by the German Lung Cancer Cooperative Group (GLCCG).[103] Although an important study, it had limitations. Many patients were included who would be considered unresectable, including those with T4 tumors, and 44 percent of the patients did not have surgery. No survival difference was observed between the two groups.

A recent excellent review of the surgical management of stage 3A NSCLC summarized the results of five meta-analyses of stage 3A clinical trials to date.[104] In none of the five studies was the surgical arm superior to definitive chemoradiotherapy. The authors concluded that "after neoadjuvant therapy for preoperative N2 involvement, the best surgical results are obtained with proven mediastinal downstaging when a lobectomy is feasible to obtain a microscopic complete resection. However, no definite, universally accepted guidelines exist." These findings emphasize that all patients with stage 3A should undergo multidisciplinary management and treatment.

The emergence of targeted drug therapy and immunotherapy has greatly improved outcomes for patients with stage 4 NSCLC. These include osimertinib, which targets mutations in the epidermal growth factor, and monoclonal antibodies (e.g., nivolumab, pembrolizumab), which block the immune checkpoint protein PD-1, an inhibitory receptor that is expressed by all T cells during activation and stimulates T cells to kill neoantigen-expressing tumor cells. In a recent randomized trial, durvalumab (an anti-PD-L1 monoclonal antibody that binds to the PD-1 ligand) was evaluated as an adjuvant therapy following definitive chemoradiotherapy. Patients with unresectable stage 3 NSCLC who had no evidence of disease progression after two or more cycles of platinum-based chemoradiotherapy received either durvalumab or the placebo.[105] Progression-free survival was significantly longer for durvalumab compared to the placebo. Many investigators are moving these agents into earlier disease settings, including neoadjuvant treatment. In the CheckMate 816 clinical trial, neoadjuvant chemotherapy with nivolumab plus platinum-doublet chemotherapy significantly improved the pathologic complete response rate and event-free survival compared with chemotherapy alone in patients with resectable stage 1B–3A non-small cell lung cancer.[106] This regimen is now FDA-approved based on the data in this clinical trial.

Cascone and coworkers reported the results of the phase 2

randomized NEOSTAR trial (NCT03158129) of neoadjuvant nivolumab or nivolumab plus ipilimumab (a monoclonal antibody that blocks the CTLA4 checkpoint) followed by surgery in forty-four patients with operable NSCLC, using major pathologic response (MPR) as the primary endpoint.[107] The nivolumab plus ipilimumab arm met the prespecified primary endpoint threshold of six MPRs in twenty-one patients, with a 38 percent MPR rate (8/21). In the thirty-seven patients resected on trial, nivolumab plus ipilimumab had an MPR rate of 50 percent. The authors concluded that nivolumab plus ipilimumab resulted in higher pathologic complete response rates (10 percent versus 38 percent), less viable tumor (median 50 percent versus 9 percent), and greater frequencies of effector, tissue-resident memory, and effector memory T cells. They evaluated the gut microbiome and found increased abundance of gut Ruminococcus and Akkermansia spp. was associated with MPR to dual therapy. They concluded that neoadjuvant nivolumab plus ipilimumab-based therapy enhances pathologic responses, as well as tumor-immune infiltrates and immunologic memory, and merits further investigation in operable NSCLC. Multiple randomized clinical trials have now shown a survival benefit with perioperative treatment incorporating immunotherapy.[108,109] The treatment strategy, which we first implemented over thirty-seven years ago, continues to save lives. It has been an honor and privilege for me to participate in clinical trials over the years from the first neoadjuvant chemotherapy trial in lung cancer to the latest studies of neoadjuvant checkpoint blockade.

19
PUBLISHERS PERISH, OR HOW I LEARNED TO STOP WORRYING AND LOVE THE PREPRINT SERVER (WITH APOLOGIES TO STANLEY KUBRICK)

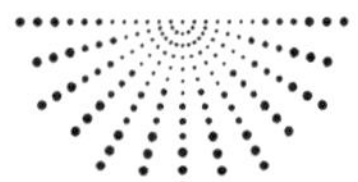

I was appalled to find that the first referee recommended that part A be omitted and B condensed, while the second referee recommended that B should be omitted and A condensed! Perceiving that even referees were not infallible, I decided to persist, and after a lot of bother to myself and to other referees, I got both parts published.

—Sir John Richardson

Now, here, you see, it takes all the running you can do to keep in the same place.

—The Red Queen in Lewis Carroll's Alice through the Looking Glass,

"My paper was accepted by Nature!" The joy and elation expressed by the young scientist were infectious. Nature is considered the most prestigious journal for the publication of new scientific findings. It was founded in London in 1869, and its name came from a line by William Wordsworth, "To the solid ground of nature trusts the Mind that builds for aye." It had the goal to "provide cultivated readers with an accessible forum for reading about advances in scientific knowledge." There is a history of highly cited papers being published in Nature, for example, the Watson and Crick structure of DNA.[110]

Nature is a multidisciplinary journal that also publishes commentary. It has maintained its aura of prestige by rejecting over 90 percent of submissions. Not surprising that our young scientist was so elated. At least until the realization that, because of a stipulation in his NIH grant, he must publish open access, so no paywall existed for his paper. This would cost twelve thousand dollars, an amount not budgeted in his grant—another unfunded NIH mandate. Perhaps he could get his department to come up with the funds, as there would be favorable reflection on the department chair, and publication in such a prestigious journal would greatly aid in his promotion. Unfortunately, after the paper was published, a website focused on detecting scientific errors noted that certain figures had been duplicated and some of the raw data submitted did not agree with the published figures. This has become all too common a story. How did these perverse financial and data manipulation incentives arise, and how can we address the crisis in the scientific publishing industry?

Contemporary scientific publishing is founded on the principle of peer review, which means that a submission to a scientific journal is sent to usually three individuals whom the managing editor deems experts in the subject of the paper. This was not always the case. Only one of Einstein's papers was reviewed by peers. This instance was so offensive to him that he withdrew the paper and submitted it to another journal.[111]

When the NIH began distributing grants, study sections composed of peers were convened to review and select the best submissions for funding. Journals were deluged with papers because publications (especially in prestigious journals), as a measure of productivity, provided justification for grant funding. However, the conduct of peer review has evolved over the past half century to the point where it is detrimental to scientific communication, as described by Eiko.[110] Authors are frequently asked to recommend or disqualify reviewers.[112] "You scratch my back, and I will scratch yours" is common, as in recommending academic friends who may lack impartiality. Journals do not have a system in place to prevent this. Peer reviewers frequently disagree over the same manuscript. This either triggers additional reviewers, adding more time to the process, or falls on the editor to make an arbitrary decision. Poor agreement among reviewers has been documented.[113] Of course, to be accepted by a high-prestige journal, all reviews must be glowing, which is highly unlikely, consistent with their greater than 90 percent rejection rate. There are no standards for peer reviewers. I am frequently asked to review papers in subjects in which I have no expertise. But reviewers continue to provide service because it is felt to be part of the academic mission. There is no reimbursement for this, and the flood of journal articles provides additional stress in an already stressful academic environment. However, the quality of the reviews is not a consideration. Reviewers are kept anonymous. A reviewer could simply reply, "This stinks." It is up to the editor to decide whether to use the reviewer's recommendation. Reviews are confidential, so the reputations of poor reviewers are never shared or publicized. Reviewer performance has been measured in studies where errors are deliberately placed in a sham paper and sent for review. In one such experiment, peer reviewers in this study failed to identify two-thirds of the major errors in such a manuscript.[114] Several years ago, one of my fellows submitted a paper, and it was rejected because of the poor peer reviews. I discussed this with him, and we selected another journal from the same publisher. However, my fellow unintentionally submitted it to the same journal that had rejected it. It was accepted with minor revisions because of the glowing peer reviews.

Rarely is a scientific manuscript accepted without revisions requested by the peer reviewers. These can range anywhere from minor wording changes to the need for new experiments. Revising a paper, resubmitting it, and then waiting for the response can add months of delay to publication. I have seen papers go back and forth for years, only to be finally rejected by the journal. A paper on which I was a co-author was caught in the ping-pong-like back-and-forth for two years. Finally, after submitting a response to the reviewers that exceeded the original paper in length, it was accepted. The process of revisions does little to improve papers and ultimately adds significant publication delays.

The majority of published scientific research is not reproducible.[115] This may appear astonishing to nonscientists and an enormous waste of resources. But the Reproducibility Project in Cancer Biology has definitive data showing this to be true. The peer-review process has had no impact on improving this. In fairness, it would be impossible for reviewers to devote time and resources to assess reproducibility. This is the purview of the scientific process. If a published finding is important, other laboratories will attempt to reproduce it to make advances. Peer review prior to publication is not the answer.

Peer reviewers are not detectives. They are not expected to find evidence of data manipulation. The journal publishers, until recently, have also failed at this. In 2023, more than ten thousand scientific papers were retracted, which is a disturbing record number.[116] This has occurred with Nobel Prize awardees and scientists who have achieved high-level administrative positions at Dana-Farber and Stanford.[31,32,117] Retracting a paper is a professional disaster. It labels the scientist as careless at best, and at worst, there may be fraudulent data. It is difficult to detect fraudulent data. Clearly, reviewers for Nobel Prizes and scientific academy membership were unable to spot the problems. More troubling is their failure to act in addressing them, and I discussed their lack of relevance to contemporary science in Chapter 7. There are businesses that sell bogus work and authorships that are estimated to number in the hundreds of thousands. Once again, peer review has done nothing to reverse this trend. Publishers are closing journals in large numbers because of this problem, as reported by the Wall Street Journal on May 14, 2024. There are websites and investigators who specialize in identifying fraudulent data, and it may be necessary to rely on them, as the skills and software required are highly specialized. Science must be, to a large degree, self-correcting, as the data in these papers will be identified when it cannot be reproduced.

Peer review of publications, as it is currently performed, has failed and should be abolished. It is time-consuming, causes excessive delays in publication, and is ineffective in assessing reproducibility and fraud. The submission of papers to preprint servers, with accompanying commentary and metrics linked to search engines, is a potential solution. This would also eliminate the predatory practices of for-profit scientific publishers. Such a shift would require a change in how publications are evaluated for promotion decisions. However, metrics such as citations, views, commentary, and downloads provide a much better picture of the science than the artificial metric of the journal impact factor. The paper could undergo formal publication in a journal if that were desired, but it would not be required.

What is a preprint server? These are open-access repositories. One such server, called BioRxiv, is hosted by the Cold Spring Harbor Laboratory.[118] Papers hosted on preprint servers are not peer-reviewed. They undergo some basic screening, including for plagiarism. Reviews and comments are posted alongside the paper. The process can be completed in a day. There is no charge. BioRxiv is funded by the Chan Zuckerberg Initiative.

The for-profit scientific publishing industry is one of the most profitable businesses. As McGill has written in an excellent analysis, "The 20–30% profit margins are among the highest in all industries. Pharmaceuticals, computers, and tobacco are really the only other industries that comes close (10–25%), and most other industries fall at 10% or lower."[119] Thus, there is a huge incentive to maintain the status quo. These publishers have established a high-end brand. For Springer, this is Nature, and for Elsevier, it is Cell. These are the Ferraris and Rolexes of journals. What makes them so special? They have developed a cachet as the most difficult journals for acceptance of a scientific manuscript, with rejection rates exceeding 90 percent of submissions. They also boast a high impact factor.

What is an impact factor? The impact factor is the frequency with which the average article in a journal has been cited in a particular year. A good impact factor is above 10. The impact factors for Nature and Cell exceed 60. The problem with an impact factor is that it measures an average for all the articles in the journal but tells nothing about the individual article. Publications with the highest impact factors are generally review articles that do not contain original scientific research. The journal with the highest impact factor is CA: A Cancer Journal for Clinicians, which publishes cancer statistics. Its impact factor is over 250. Promotion and tenure committees pay attention to the journals on curriculum vitae. They should be looking at how often the applicant's papers are cited. As an academic community, we should eliminate this prejudice for high-impact journals and incentivize submission to preprint servers, where individual metrics for a paper can be assessed. One solution is to remove the journal names from curriculum vitae used for promotion reviews and limit the reviews to the candidate's last five or ten scientific research papers.

Promotion and tenure decisions are also based on the number of scientific research publications. Quality would be a better metric. As stated by McGill, "Publishing is growing exponentially.While the number of scientists is also growing exponentially, it is at a slower rate than papers. We are producing more papers per scientist every year. This is a profoundly important fact. Every ecologist knows the power and unsustainability of exponential growth. This also makes it abundantly clear that the publishers only deserve half the blame. Scientists have created a Red Queen situation in which we're aggressively chasing opportunities to publish." .[119]

Scientists are focused on science and not on the business of scientific publication. Thus, the current situation has evolved because we let it evolve. Business saw an opportunity and took over by establishing solid branding. The opportunity was obvious: the costs of scientific publishing are all paid by someone other than the publisher, and the publisher can charge exorbitant fees for publication, subscription, and access. A scientist obtains the funding for the research, pays for the research, writes, and submits the paper, all at no cost to the publisher. Other scientists serve as editors for the journal and peer reviewers, again at no cost to the publisher. The journal publishes the paper, reaping a variety of charges, including subscriptions for individuals (two hundred dollars) and institutions (hundreds of thousands for a publisher package), as well as open access (twelve thousand dollars for one Nature article). None of the researchers gets compensated. Since the original research grant comes from taxpayers, the research is sold back to the taxpayers at an exorbitant price, creating the high profit margin for the publisher.[119]

Scientific publishing is an oligopoly that includes five for-profit publishers (Elsevier, Springer, Wiley, Taylor & Francis, and MDPI) with over 50 percent of all publications. Publishers have realized they can capitalize on the exclusivity of their brand. In the very likely event a manuscript is not accepted by Nature, Springer (the publisher of Nature) has created thirty-four journals with Nature in their titles. The publishers will happily submit your rejected paper to a lower-ranked but highly branded journal with no additional effort on your part. Thus, eventually, every paper will find its journal, with the publishing costs borne by you, the principal investigator. And you can now boast that your paper is in a Nature-something journal.

The concept of making a scientific manuscript immediately available to the scientific community at no cost is laudable and could greatly enhance scientific progress while at the same time reducing the costs and barriers to research. When President Biden's Cancer Moon Shot program was initiated, this became a cornerstone of the program. All papers with research funded by the NCI Moon Shot must be published open access, meaning they are available to anyone online without charge. However, the costs of publication must be covered, and publishers have offloaded these costs to the principal investigator responsible for submitting the paper. The NCI does not cover this in the grant budgets, so it is an unfunded mandate. Publishers recognized this as another great way to extract money. The more prestigious a journal, the higher the cost of publishing open access. Nature charges around twelve thousand dollars to publish one paper open access. NCI does not accept submission to a preprint server as an open-access publication, forcing investigators to pay for publishing in open-access journals or pay for open access at an exorbitant price in subscription journals. Thus, open access in its current form is a disaster. One form of protest to these rising costs and predatory practices has been the mass resignation of editors at a journal.[120] This has occurred sixteen times since 2021 and five times so far in 2024. In many cases, this is due to the publishing charge model, not the concept of open access. The editors may set up their own journal with a nonprofit publisher.

There are solutions to these problems that can be implemented immediately. The problem of erroneous or fraudulent data can be addressed with more sophisticated software and AI. There are individuals who make a career of detecting this, and we must continue to review and publicize their findings. Major scientific societies and academies should be proactive in investigating allegations. Software engineers have offered bounties, either as payment or donations to charity.[119]

The use of preprint services should be accepted as the preferred method for publication. Servers can be financed by universities, institutes, nonprofit organizations, and philanthropy. Revisions can be submitted at any time. Reviews and key metrics, including views, downloads, and citations, are available in real time. The manuscript can be submitted for publication if the author so desires. Submission to journals supporting change in the current system should be encouraged. Currently, NCI does not allow preprint submissions to satisfy open-access requirements because this does not represent the final version. This is, of course, absurd, and the policy must be immediately changed. Search engines should immediately list submissions in their database. The Economist recently reported, "The Bill & Melinda Gates Foundation is set to stop paying article processing charges and will instead require grant recipients to publish preprints on public servers. The Council of the European Union last year called for a new nonprofit publishing model to tackle unsustainable costs." [112,121]

The measures above can be instituted by investigators. For them to be effective, changes in how faculty are evaluated for promotion and tenure are needed, which are more difficult in that they involve institutional changes from the status quo. Faculty should no longer list the journal name but instead focus on the citations and views of their work in their bibliographies. Reviews of their work can be quoted in accompanying letters. The concept that the name of the journal is synonymous with the quality of the science needs to be put to rest. A premium should be placed on openness, transparency, and collaboration in promotion and tenure decisions. Shortening the time to tenure award from the current five to seven years to one or two years also alleviates perverse incentives to publish more in a shorter period. Read and publish agreements with university libraries have multiple benefits. The library pays a sum of money for journal subscriptions. Included in this are benefits to authors publishing in those journals. The article processing charge is eliminated. Every article published through that publisher is open access. Each author has the copyright to their work.[122]These agreements are happening, but the current process is not transparent.

We all helped create and support the existing publication system, which continues to advance, not to the benefit of authors but to the profits of the publishers. We will need to work together persistently to change this system.

20
PROGRESS

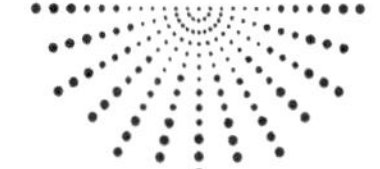

Never regret a day in your life. Good days give happiness, bad days give experiences, worst days give lessons, and best days give memories.

—Richard Feynman

Life continued at an incredible pace. I flew to Bethesda to present our newest gene therapy clinical trial to the RAC on June 10, 1994. In this clinical trial, a new delivery system for the p53 gene was used. It was an adenovirus that had been engineered so it could not cause disease but could still infect cancer cells and deliver a normal p53 gene, which kills the cancer cell. The review went smoothly, and the protocol was passed. My proposal was to perform direct injection of advanced lung cancers with the adenovirus p53 with and without the chemotherapy drug cisplatin. The RAC reviewers rejected including patients with pleural effusions because we did not have toxicity data. However, the rest of the protocol was approved.

The Dusty Miller saga continued. I showed him data with the assay he requested, using spiking experiments to determine the sensitivity of focus-forming assays for the virus. Now he said that he no longer thought this was a good assay for transformation. This exemplified the problems with peer reviewers when they can discredit and delay your research. This applies to any review process, not just journal articles, as I discussed in the previous chapter.

Good news! On Wednesday, June 15, the pharmaceutical company RPR concluded the letter of intent. They decided to invest seventeen million dollars (thirty-five million in today's dollars) into Intron and support the gene therapy clinical trials. We had sealed off a tissue culture room and decontaminated it, cleaning it from top to bottom. We did a double production run for the retroviral supernatant, which was successful. The supernatant was sent to the pharmacy for packaging. The titers, which measure the amount of retrovirus, appeared good. Interestingly, the supernatant we received from Magenta (a new subsidiary of Microbiological Associates devoted to gene therapy production) was active for the first time.

On Father's Day, I was taken to Murder on the Menu at Renata's Restaurant in Houston. A murder mystery was performed while we ate dinner. None of us solved the mystery, but the meal and performance were great. J was off to Camp Olympia, and Liz was attending her last ACS study section as chairperson in Atlanta. K was starting the Vivaldi violin concertos and had made incredible progress.

The next day, my insane travel schedule continued. I left for the International Association for the Study of Lung Cancer (IASLC) meeting in Colorado Springs at the Broadmoor. It is an important responsibility to present your science and educate others. The IASLC meeting was a success. I gave three presentations, including a plenary lecture on gene therapy, a discussion of cancer biology, and a presentation of the lung cancer neoadjuvant trial results that had just been published. On the last day, I participated in a roundtable discussion.

J and Michael Bishop, the 1989 Nobel Prize awardee for discovering oncogenes, at the 1994 Aspen Conference.

While in Colorado, I had a chance to go whitewater rafting on the lower Arkansas River. The rapids were class 2–3, and it was quite a ride, with the kayak close to overturning on several occasions. On our return, Liz and I went to Phantom of the Opera at Jones Hall, and the rest of the week, we were together without the kids. J returned from Camp Olympia on July 10, and as usual, she had a great time, having been selected as Camper of the Day. I immediately left for Aspen to attend the Aspen Cancer Conference, and I took J with me. We both looked forward to some relief from the summer heat and humidity. We flew to Denver and then drove to Aspen. The first night there, we went to the Crystal Palace. During dinner, there was a very clever original satirical musical show, which J enjoyed immensely. We went downhill bicycling, riding from the top of Aspen Highlands, where we could view the magnificent Maroon Bells. We also went horseback riding at Snowmass Stables. Mike Bishop was there, and J and I had a great conversation with him. After the conference was over, we drove to Keystone and went whitewater rafting on the upper Arkansas, which I really enjoyed, with more difficult class-4 rapids. On Friday, we flew to Portland, Maine, via Newark to meet Liz and pick up K at Camp Encore/Coda, which is a music camp in Sweden, Maine. K received a standing ovation for her first solo performance.

She was concertmaster for Eine Kleine Nachtmusik and had a lead role in the musical. From there, we drove to Salem and then to Boston and had dinner with my uncle David, whose neurosurgery practice was flourishing now that he had left Harvard and entered private practice. We then did the Freedom Trail in one day. On returning, I had to spend two solid days with RPR discussing our budget.

The latest word was that RPR would, in addition to the seventeen-million-dollar investment in the company, invest fourteen million dollars in the clinical trials. Yet more problems plagued the production of the retroviral supernatant. Our first lot passed all the quality assurance tests. Then I found out the sterility test failed. Apparently, the supernatant got contaminated either during packaging in the MD Anderson pharmacy or during shipping. This was a complex production process, and problems seemed to occur at every step. Now we needed to repeat the sterility tests and send a second lot for testing. Would we ever be able to start the clinical trials?

Of major concern were the finances of MD Anderson. It was a nonprofit institution but only received 10 percent of its budget from the state. The legislature had stipulated when the institution was established that it would be required to accept indigent patients and that all other patients must be referred by an outside physician, which had severely limited patient referrals. The huge burden of indigent care and the lack of paying patients were sinking the institution financially. A bill was sent to the state legislature to free the institution from all these restrictions and was eventually passed.

On Wednesday, I left for Bethesda for a National Heart, Lung, and Blood Institute conference on gene therapy for lung diseases. The conference was mostly about benign diseases, but I did learn about lung-specific promoters from Jeff Whitsett, which could be useful in limiting gene delivery to the lung. I called Microbiological Associates while in Bethesda and was informed that the third lot of supernatants, produced by our laboratory using cells left after the first production run, passed the sterility test. It appeared that nothing could stop my gene therapy clinical trial from beginning. All protocols had been resubmitted to the RAC for final approval. The end of one of the longest journeys of my life was in sight.

Liz and I had received an invitation to speak in Japan from a former research fellow, Toshi Fujiwara, who was now on the surgical faculty of Okayama University, and it was time to depart. We flew to Los Angeles and then took a direct flight to Osaka, landing at the new Kansai Airport, which had just opened three days earlier. Toshi met us at the airport and escorted us to Okayama by train. We stayed at the Kokusai International Hotel in a large suite with a living room and a kitchen. The accommodations were truly luxurious. The hotel was situated among hills overlooking the city, and the roads provided excellent jogging every day. The weather was somewhat warm and humid but became cool and crisp during the last two days. Toshi and his wife, Keiko, took us on a tour of Okayama the following day. We saw the exquisite gardens surrounding the Crow Castle, which is a medieval castle dating from the fourteenth century. We had lunch at a Japanese steakhouse, Harada, which had delicious Kobe beef. We then toured the castle, which had been destroyed in World War II but was rebuilt as a replica.

Liz, Jack, Keiko, and Toshi Fujiwara in Okayama, October 1994.

That evening, a welcome banquet was given for the speakers at the hotel. The invited speakers included Henry Lynch, Eva Klein, John Healey, Charles Coltman, Charles Boone, and Geoffrey Hanks. The banquet featured a six-course French-style dinner. We donned happi coats and broke a keg of sake, which is a ceremony designed to bring good fortune to the meeting. There was entertainment by a Japanese soprano. The next day, Liz gave her presentation on the results of immune chemotherapy in melanoma, followed by Dr. Klein's presentation. We all had lunch together at a scenic Japanese restaurant called Kohraku in a tatami room. After lunch, we were taken by limousine to a scenic area called Kurashiki. This was the site of a large weaving factory that opened at the beginning of the twentieth century. The factory had been turned into a hotel. We visited the Ohara Art Museum, donated from the private collection of one of the wealthy citizens of the area. The collection was extensive, featuring works by Van Gogh, Monet, Picasso, Chagall, and many contemporary artists. The village was charming and dated back to the Edo period.

I met with the translator at the hotel. I had written out my address, which I usually do not do, and the translator had little difficulty with it. That evening, we had dinner at an excellent sushi restaurant with Toshi and Keiko. Following this, there was a party for the invited speakers, with Dr. Orita in attendance. I presented him with a copy of my thoracic oncology textbook as a remembrance of the meeting. The next day, I gave my lecture at the Okayama Symphony Hall, the largest auditorium in the city. There were at least one thousand people in attendance. My talk on gene replacement for the prevention and therapy of lung cancer was well received. I discussed our preclinical data as well as the future clinical trials. I received an Award of Excellence for the lecture and a beautiful clock. We had been showered with gifts during the meeting, including a Bizen vase and pearls for Liz. The level of Japanese hospitality was extraordinary. After the talk, we had lunch with Dr. Ohashi, the scientific director for the Meiji Milk Co., which is a large biotechnology company in Japan. They were interested in our work, and I told them about Introgen. We then went on a tour of shrines in the Kibisu area. We visited an old Shinto shrine dating from the fourteenth century. We were taken on a tour by the head priest, whose daughter was a friend of Keiko. The driver also took us to a huge shrine primarily for business people. In the evening, we had another superb Japanese dinner at Harnasaku with other surgery faculty members from Okayama University, including the thoracic surgeon Dr. Inoue. The next morning, we slept late and finally went shopping with Keiko and Toshi. We bought some gifts for the girls (pearl earrings) and then had lunch at Gontazushi, which had very tasty shabu-shabu. We then left for the airport on the express trains. We took a United flight to Hawaii and a Hawaiian Air flight to Kauai to the Hyatt Regency to break up the long flight home.

Kauai is perhaps the most beautiful and least developed of the Hawaiian islands. Scenes from Jurassic Park were filmed there, and the Napoli coast is a spectacular, primitive volcanic landscape descending into the ocean. In the evening, we had dinner at a restaurant with grass huts on a large pool filled with tropical fish. The ocean had a high surf, so the next day we hiked to Poipu Beach and went snorkeling. We caught a bus back and had dinner at an Italian restaurant. We played tennis and went to the Anara Spa for massages and facials, helping us relax from the previous hectic travel. Finally, we took a flight back to Los Angeles. At the last minute, as we were leaving the hotel, we received the replacement credit card mailed to us after our card was canceled because of a fraudulent mail-order purchase. In Los Angeles, our Continental flight was delayed for repairs (instead of the option of flying at a low altitude and making a fuel stop). Liz called from an airphone and made a reservation on the next flight. We finally arrived in Houston minus one suitcase.

On Monday, October 3, RPR signed the agreement with Introgen. The agreement specified seventeen million dollars in equity investment with milestones tied to clinical trials, along with five million dollars a year for three years for operating expenses. The day after I returned, there was a development committee meeting with the RPR scientists. Our group had presented in my absence the previous day. Another meeting was held on Friday. My parents, who were caring for J and K, left for Italy on Sunday. On Monday and Tuesday, Houston was hit with torrential rains and flooding, and I was unable to drive to the hospital. This was a premonition of future events. Hurricanes and flooding would become a fixture of life in Houston.

Now that we had the financial backing of a major pharmaceutical company, requests for membership on the Scientific Advisory Board were met with enthusiastic acceptance. Mario Capecchi, Peter Nowell, Carl Barrett, and Michael Imperiale had all accepted. Nowell and Capecchi were National Academy members and GM prize winners. The Introgen/RPR collaboration was written up in the Wall Street Journal and the Houston Chronicle.

Institutional politics was always in the background. I heard that a meeting took place with the president of MD Anderson, Charles LeMaistre, and his executive team of Balch and Hohn to inform us that a formal search was needed for a head of the Division of Surgery. Goepfert was the ad interim head and was doing a good job. All the current chairs endorsed Goepfert, which was interesting since at one point, when Balch arrived, he wanted to eliminate the division because it would demote his authority as a department chair. However, the search would proceed.

On October 27, I left for Cleveland to accept the Ernest Bruell Lectureship Award at the Cleveland Clinic. This was awarded annually to an outstanding oncologist. The evening prior to my lecture, I had dinner with members of the Bruell family. On October 29, after my return to Houston, the whole family saw The Crucible by Arthur Miller, which was appropriate on Halloween eve and after our previous visit to Salem. The play is a partially fictionalized account of the Salem witch trials and was written as an allegory for the anticommunist hysteria of the 1950s. Miller was questioned by the Committee on Un-American Activities and convicted of contempt for not identifying others in meetings he attended. It was a well-acted and chilling production.[123]

I received a fax stating that Schering-Plough and Canji were collaborating on p53-based gene therapy. Apparently, our data impressed them. Imitation is the greatest form of flattery. And Dusty Miller was still hanging on. Even though he was no longer a primary reviewer, he was still responsible for looking at the vector sequences. He wanted more explanations about the SV40 promoters. We sent one reply, and he still asked for more. His efforts to delay our protocol were becoming obvious to all.

The next day, I left for New York to begin the RPR rollout for its new Gencell division, which included fourteen companies. We presented at the Palace Hotel in New York. Other groups involved were AIS and Darwin. The next day, we took the Concorde to Paris. What an incredible experience! There was a screen at the front of the cabin showing the airspeed, which exceeded twice the speed of sound. French cuisine was served. The flight from New York to Paris took three hours. After the presentation in Paris, we went to London for the final presentations. I returned on the eighteenth. I had to give a written copy of my talk to the Introgen CEO because of the close timing of my flight. The other speakers were so long-winded I did not have time to present and still make the flight.

On December 1, I left for Bethesda with Drs. Clayman, a head and neck surgeon, and Zhang to present the head and neck cancer protocol to the RAC. The protocol involved the direct injection of unresectable head and neck cancers with p53 expressed in the adenovirus vector. Additionally, the vector would be instilled in the surgical bed following the resection of high-risk tumors. The protocol passed. However, someone in the audience from France representing a company stood up and stated that the protocol was unsafe because the p53 in the virus could mutate. Finally, it was decided that an assay should be developed to detect the biological activity of mutant p53 if it was present. Canji presented a protocol to inject adenovirus p53 in liver cancer, an obvious knockoff of our own protocol. It was still approved despite concerns over toxicity. The results of other gene therapy studies were presented at the meeting. Considerable toxicity was encountered with the brain thymidine kinase studies, which included meningitis. The tumor-infiltrating lymphocyte studies presented at this meeting from Rosenberg's group did not show preferential tumor localization.

The kids were on holiday break from school, so it was time for another family trip to Keystone, and we left on the eighteenth. The weather was incredibly warm, with the temperature reaching sixty on some days. However, the snow was still in good condition, and the skiing was excellent. One of our family traditions was the Christmas Eve sleigh-ride dinner. A horse-drawn sleigh would take us to one of the original settlement log cabins, where we would be served a Western-style steak dinner. The highlight was walking outside, where the sky was clear and the stars shone brightly because of the absolute darkness and absence of artificial light. This year, we traveled in wagons because of the lack of snow, but it was fun and moving for all our family to be together in this pristine setting. We returned to Houston on New Year's Day.

On January 6, I found out that Harold Varmus, head of the NIH, who had shared a Nobel Prize with Michael Bishop in 1989 for their discovery of the oncogene, had signed off on our gene therapy clinical trial for retroviral p53. Now, at long last, after twenty-seven months of continuing reviews and data submission, the study could begin. I was relieved and excited. I issued an all-points bulletin to the faculty, fellows, and research nurses to find patients and made a presentation at our clinical protocol conference. It would not be long before an eligible patient was identified.

21
CANCER VERSUS P53

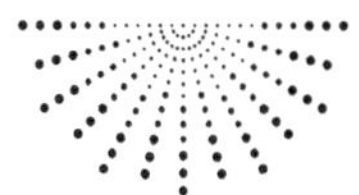

Every great advance in science has issued from a new audacity of imagination.

—John Dewey

On Friday afternoon, January 20, 1995, John Nesbitt and Randi Shea, a radiation oncologist, came into my office to talk about a patient. Joseph had his left lung cancer diagnosed one year ago. It was unresectable and was treated with external beam radiation therapy combined with brachytherapy. Now, some narrowing of the left bronchus was noted on a chest X-ray, and a recurrence was suspected. We all agreed the patient might be a candidate for the protocol and decided to perform bronchoscopy on Monday. The bronchoscopy showed a tumor in the left main bronchus as well as the lower lobe. Joseph was in good shape medically. We biopsied the tumor for p53 analysis. On Friday, a mutation was found by sequencing in exon 5, codon 130. I checked the database and found that the mutation had previously been described in lung cancer. He appeared to be an excellent candidate to be the first patient in our p53 retroviral delivery clinical trial. I scheduled him for an appointment to see me in my clinic to discuss the protocol and see if he would sign the informed consent.

In the middle of all this, it was family time. Liz, our daughters, and I departed for Leisure World, California, where my parents were now living, to celebrate my fiftieth birthday. We had a great lunch at a seafood restaurant near Laguna Beach, followed by dinner at the Ritz-Carlton. The kids had a great time seeing the stables and the beach. We had brunch on Sunday and left.

I returned to a flurry of activity. Now everyone involved with the gene therapy trial was calling at the last minute. The pharmacy wanted to know how to prepare the drug. The OR was concerned about safety issues. The nurses on the floor wanted to know how to handle the isolation procedures. The anesthesiologists were in an uproar as well, as they believed they would be exposed to a toxic virus, which was, of course, not true. My research nurses were preparing all the forms and getting all the specimens.

I saw Joseph in the clinic on Friday. He looked remarkably fit and was very calm during our talk. But he had been through a lot. He was only fifty-nine years old but had been a longtime two-pack-a-day cigarette smoker who had quit ten years ago. He had a history of asthma, high blood pressure, and an abnormal heart rhythm that had just developed the previous week. He was a tough individual who tended to complain only about minor things. He worked as an antique furniture refinisher in New Mexico and was there with his wife and daughter. I carefully explained that what we were proposing had never been done before. Although all our information to date showed the treatment was safe, there were unknowns. Joseph understood that he had no good standard treatment options left and was eager to proceed. We prepared for Monday.

On February 6, the day of the procedure, the atmosphere was charged. Before going down to the operating room, I received yet another telephone call. This was Dr. Bill Putnam, who wondered why his room next to the one used for gene therapy was sealed and what dangers it posed for his patients. I responded that this was a noninfectious agent and that the room to be used for the procedure was sealed.

There were eighteen people in our operating room. The patient had a rigid bronchoscopy performed by Dr. Nesbitt. Two lesions were seen: one in the carina between the upper and lower lobes and one in the lower lobe. The most tedious part of the procedure was debulking the two tumors. The retroviral supernatant arrived from the pharmacy, and the injection went very smoothly. The patient was extubated, but upon returning to his room, he had difficulty breathing and had to be reintubated. This was due to oversedation. I followed the patient carefully and was awake most of the night. The patient also had a fever, probably secondary to the bronchoscopy and laser. We decided to proceed with the procedure the next day. Over the ensuing days, it was clear that the tumor was regressing. Biopsies on the fifth day showed fibrosis and inflammation but no evidence of tumor. The patient was discharged on Monday, feeling well. There was no toxicity associated with the treatment.

My regular operating room schedule resumed. On Tuesday, I had a terrible case. The patient had originally presented with a chest wall tumor involving the ribs. Initially, it was felt that the best treatment was nonoperative, and chemotherapy and radiation were given. The patient then developed what appeared to be a new second primary lung cancer. This would require removing the entire lung. This is a procedure with one of the highest operative mortalities. However, in this case, the lung was already exposed to radiation and chemotherapy, which would increase both the risk to the patient and the difficulty of the operation. The riskiest part of the operation was dissecting the main artery to the lung and cutting it between two staple lines. In this case, the pulmonary artery was like tissue paper, and it tore. When this artery tears, the bleeding is massive, and there is nothing more dreaded than this. The first thing to do is stop the bleeding with pressure and stabilize the patient. This is no time to be the lone hero in the white hat riding in to save the day. I was operating with a resident, and the most prudent course was to call one of my senior colleagues. John Nesbitt answered the call, and together we gained control through the pericardium (the covering of the heart). Postoperatively, the patient did not turn a hair. On Thursday, Michael

Imperiale from the University of Michigan site visited us to review our adenovirus program.

On the nineteenth, we saw K perform with the Houston Youth Symphony at the Galveston Opera House. Spring break arrived for the kids, and so it was time for skiing. On March 17, J and I flew to Keystone. Liz stayed behind so that K would not miss orchestra practice for the fiftieth anniversary gala. We met Uncle David, his wife, and their two sons at Keystone. We had a relaxed and fun week with a sleigh ride, fondue, dinner at the ranch, and tremendous skiing with lots of snow and warmer weather. I won a silver medal in NASTAR (42 handicap) with my best time ever. K won gold, and Liz and J won silver medals.

Our first patient on the p53 protocol, Joseph, developed pneumonia and required hospitalization. He recovered and was discharged home. Joseph had a bronchoscopy to look at the injected sites and obtain a biopsy one month after treatment. The results of the biopsy showed that the treatment worked. The bronchoscopy at one month showed a durable response, with all biopsies negative for tumor.

I organized a party to celebrate entering the first patient on the gene therapy protocol and to thank all those on the team while having some lighthearted fun after the months of trauma getting the trial started. I presented some special humorous awards: Tapas, the molecular biologist who made the gene therapy vector, received the Dusty Miller Award for the most southern blots (to identify the viral DNA) ever required for a single experiment; Nancy, our laboratory supervisor, received the Microbiological Associates Award for producing a reagent no other company could produce; Julie and Faye, our research nurses, received the RPR Award for meticulous protocol preparation; Cynthia, another technician in our laboratory, received the Award for Most Rapid Gene Sequencing Ever; Kathryn, an office assistant, received the Introgen Award for completing the most paperwork ever associated with a sponsored research agreement; Carol, an office assistant, received the Nelson Wivel RAC Communications Award for interpreting and communicating responses to uninterpretable RAC documents.

On April 1, K performed in the Houston Youth Symphony at the Wortham as part of the fiftieth anniversary gala, and John Tesh was also on the program. My travel schedule remained packed. Frequent-flier miles were accumulating at an astonishing rate. I flew to Philadelphia on April 4 to present at Gencell for RPR. On April 6, I attended the American Surgical Association to discuss Larry Kaiser's paper on thymidine kinase gene therapy. Larry was a junior resident at UCLA when I was chief resident. He also became a thoracic surgeon and pursued research. My parents arrived and spent the week. Dad's evaluation for his previously diagnosed prostate did not show any detectable cancer following treatment with androgen deprivation therapy. I was then called on to review grants and programs, an onerous but necessary service. On April 9, I traveled to Bethesda for a site visit to the Navy Oncology Branch. The other site visitors were a distinguished group that included Charles Coltman, David Livingston, Waun Ki Hong, Carlo Croce, and Susan Naylor. Unfortunately, our reviews were not positive. The presentations were very mediocre with lack of focus and a significant number of marginally productive investigators. I continued the work on the SPORE with John Minna, who would step down as cancer center director at UTSWMC although he accepted the position less than five years earlier. He retained a position as head of a program of translational research. I was concerned that this would sink our SPORE, but apparently this was not a problem for NCI.

I had been gifted tickets to the Wagner Festival in Bayreuth, Germany, by Liz for my fiftieth birthday to be held in August, and to improve our understanding of Wagner's operas, we took a course at Rice University taught by a Wagner expert, Nancy Baily. The final lecture was given on Monday. We learned interesting insights into the music, its form, and the history of its composition.

I discovered the RAC had still not forwarded our adenovirus protocol to Varmus. This was hardly a surprise, but my fear was that there would be a repeat of the obstructionist efforts I experienced with the previous p53 retrovirus clinical trial. Apparently, one of the reviewers resigned for personal reasons, and another reviewer forwarded the reviewer's comments to Arnold Levine, one of the scientists who discovered p53. The issue was misunderstood. Levine thought an assay for mutations was needed when what was called for was an assay to confirm the function of the gene. I called Levine and explained this, and he promised to speak to Wivel. I traveled to ASCO to give a Meet the Professor session on lung cancer. I was fortunate to be honored again on June 8 at the University of Minnesota as the Sigurd Professor.

K and Liz were traveling together in Italy. Liz would attend a scientific meeting, and then they would visit Florence and Rome. On June 12, J and I left for Keystone and Aspen for the tenth Aspen Cancer Conference, at which I was a speaker. The runoff into the rivers from the recent snows was so high that we could not go rafting. We went on a cattle drive and had dinner at the Crystal Palace. On June 20, I was a speaker at the GM Cancer Symposium. General Motors played an important role in funding cancer treatment and research. Alfred P. Sloan was the chairman of General Motors, and in 1945, he donated $4 million (equivalent to $67.7 million in 2023) to establish the Sloan Kettering Institute for Cancer Research. Charles F. Kettering, GM's vice president and director of research, would develop a cancer research program.[124] GM established a cancer awards program, but this was later discontinued. The awards ceremony was elegant, with dinner in the Folger Shakespeare Library. Ed Harlow, Li, and Fraumini received prizes.

Our data on p16 as a tumor suppressor gene were published in Cancer Research. The p16 protein is a regulator of the cell cycle, which is the cycle of cell growth and division. Our group made an adenovirus that expressed the p16 protein and found that it greatly inhibited the growth of cancer cells.[125] Thus, this adenovirus vector can be used as a platform to deliver many tumor suppressor genes.

The tortuous saga with the RAC continued. The RAC was dragging its feet on the adenovirus protocols even though our protocol and Clayman's had been approved by the FDA. The issue was the one reviewer who sent the review to Arnold Levine. He apparently did not understand the concept of a functional assay that detects the effect of the protein made by the gene compared to an assay that detects gene mutations. I spoke with Wivel this week, and I may need to return to the RAC. Liz, J, and K returned from West Virginia on August 10. J left for Space Camp in Huntsville, Alabama, on August 12.

The RAC could not resolve the issues of the adenovirus p53 vector. Samulsky, the reviewer, thought safety was still an issue. I now needed to present the new safety data we acquired in Bethesda.

The balcony fanfare preceding the curtain at the Bayreuth Festival.

For my fiftieth birthday, Liz had arranged with one of my former research fellows from Germany, Paul Schneider, to purchase two tickets to the Bayreuth Festival's Wagner Der Ring des Nibelungen four-opera cycle. One of Paul's patients was a singer at Bayreuth who was able to obtain seats that otherwise were impossible to get. Wagner built his own opera house for his works in Bayreuth, subsidized by his patron, King Ludwig II. Wagnerites considered a pilgrimage to Bayreuth essential to hear Wagner's operas as he wanted them to be heard. The day arrived, and on August 19, Liz and I left for Bayreuth. My parents arrived two days earlier to take care of the girls.

We flew to Frankfurt and then rented a Mercedes to drive to Bayreuth. We stayed at the Hotel Rheingold. The festival began on August 22 with Das Rheingold and continued on August 23, 25, and 27 with Die Walkure, Siegfried, and Gotterdammerung. James Levine conducted. The performances were uniformly outstanding. The sets were reminiscent of outer space. However, the voices and acting were superb. Jon Tomlinson (Wotan) and Deborah Polaski (Brunnhilde) were particularly outstanding. In the cast was a young Nina Stemme singing the role of Freia. Of course, I did not realize at the time that she would become one of the great Wagnerian sopranos of the twenty-first century. The audience was interesting as well, with a fight almost breaking out behind us. The schedule was civilized, with the performances beginning at 4 p.m. Between acts, we ate at the Steigenberger Restaurant at the Festspielehaus. The weather was cool. The town itself was interesting, with several parks for jogging and the Wagner Museum in his house, Wahnfried. Altogether, it was an extraordinary experience.

Liz and Jack at the 1995 Bayreuth Festival

More patients had been entered in the retroviral gene therapy clinical trial. One patient died, but there was no evidence of a tumor at the treatment site. A patient who had a chest wall tumor reported major shrinkage (>50 percent) two weeks after treatment.

The RAC review meeting was held at 4 p.m. on September 11. The overall level of discussion at the RAC was very unfocused. They wanted to bring in experts to tell them about assays for p53. Our presentation finally convinced them to give approval. Abbey Meyers, one of the RAC advocates for rare diseases, was doing crossword puzzles during the discussion. Ten days later, Varmus signed off on the protocol.

Introgen had decided to proceed with private placement funding. The kickoff began at the Coronado Club in Houston on September 14, and Denton Cooley had been invited and attended, although he had no connection with cancer treatment. On September 28, I left for Toronto to give the keynote address for a meeting called Lung Cancer: Strategies for the 21st Century. I had a very nice dinner at the hundred-year-old home of Francis Shepherd, a lung cancer medical oncologist who played a major role in the Lung Cancer Study Cooperative Group. Somehow, I could not refuse speaking invitations. This forced me into very untenable travel situations where I went to some lovely locations and then had to immediately travel to the next speaking engagement. For example, I next made a one-day trip to Miami to present our gene therapy data to ASTRO, the largest society for radiation oncologists.

FDA approval was given for new adenovirus vector clinical trials. We now had all our protocols RAC- and FDA-approved for a total of 112 patients, which made this the largest cancer gene therapy program in the world. On October 22, I flew to New Orleans for the ACS meeting. I chaired the Graham Traveling Fellowship meeting and the first Oncology Surgical Forum session. There were many excellent presentations, including that of Dao Nguyen, who presented a novel technique developed in our laboratory to deliver genes to cancer cells by directly linking them to replication defective adenovirus.[126] I was invited to become a member of the Surgical Biology Club II. One of the benefits of membership was dinner at a gourmet restaurant. That year, we had dinner at the Commander's Palace, and alligator pie was a specialty.

There was another fire drill with the retrovirus packaging cell line. The cells grown by Introgen did not express p53. We had to go back to the freezer again to grow old clones. This was critical because production must be scaled up for phase 2 trials, which were under discussion. A meeting was held by RPR with an advisory group to discuss this. Retroviruses are, by nature, unstable. The solution would be to move to our adenovirus vector for future clinical trials.

On Saturday, November 4, I flew to Dallas to give the plenary lecture at the CALGB meeting. I presented our gene therapy data, which was well received. On November 1, I had gone to San Diego to speak at the 4th International Conference on Gene Therapy of Cancer. I presented some of the patient responses seen with the retrovirus study, and these were commented on very favorably. One of our Japanese fellows, Dr. Inoue, had submitted an abstract for a poster session at this conference without telling me. The author was then expected to give an oral presentation. Inoue had received the letter stating this but wrote back to the organizers, saying he could not be present. Finally, about thirty minutes before the session began, I found out about this. I then gave a five-minute presentation of the data without slides.

The next week was the beginning of an extremely hectic travel schedule, even for me. I had previously made a commitment to attend an AACR conference in Ft. Myers, Florida, on drug mechanisms. However, a Gencell Partners meeting came up in San Juan, so I had to fly in and out to give my talks. Although both locations were beautiful, I spent little time at either one. On November 30, I flew to St. Louis to Washington University to deliver a lecture and receive the Roper Award. The thoracic surgery program there, under Dr. Joel Cooper, was extensive, with an emphasis on transplantation and volume-reduction surgery. However, cancer was not a strong point. I discussed the management of stage 3 lung cancer with Cooper, who believed that patients with cancer metastatic to their mediastinal nodes should not have an operation. I informed him of our latest clinical trial results with perioperative chemotherapy and told him in no uncertain terms that he needed to get up to date. The lecture went well, and there was a dinner with the faculty and guests that evening.

Good news! I found out that the lung cancer SPORE prepared in collaboration with John Minna received the best priority score of all the submitted applications, including those from Colorado and Hopkins that had been awarded previously. At last, we had grant funding for our SPORE program, which would continue to be competitively renewed uninterrupted for the next 30 years, up to the time this book was published in 2025.

Martine George, who worked for RPR, had arranged with NCI to begin to develop clinical trials to evaluate adenovirus p53 gene therapy. The NCI wanted to develop five clinical trials for breast, brain, bladder, ovarian, and hepatocellular cancers. Patient entry for the head and neck and lung cancer patients with adenovirus p53 had begun. Meanwhile, we went back to evaluate the clinical supernatant used in the retroviral p53 trials. The titer, biological activity, and p53 gene expression all seemed to be intact. Part of the beta actin promoter region could be lost with growth of the clones, but this was not critical as the actual promoter length was only a few hundred bases.

Finally, at the end of 1995, I had a break from travel. For Christmas, the family stayed home. I spent some time doing activities with the children. Both Liz and I were invited to the Sixth International Congress on Anticancer Treatments, held in Paris in January. We stayed at the Intercontinental Hotel. Snow was falling, and the temperature was frigid. However, the meeting was quite good, with several interesting talks. I gave a talk at the Institut Gustave Roussy. Jean Bernard Lepeq then took us to dinner at a fine restaurant. We also had dinner at one of my favorite French country restaurants, Chez L'ami Louis. On February 22, 1996, I left for Berlin to present at the 22nd National Cancer Congress of the German Cancer Society. After I accepted this, I received an invitation to a meeting in Hawaii at the same time, which I sadly had to turn down. Berlin had wintry weather as well. Dr. Guido Schumacher, who was coming to our laboratory as a fellow, gave me a tour of the city. It was a bit eerie and emotionally unsettling to see the Reichstag and some of the buildings standing from the war, as well as the former East Germany. I could still visualize the scenes of Nazi rallies I had seen in the newsreels of the time in various documentaries. Berlin at that time was not a very picturesque city, and most of the new buildings were nondescript.

New discoveries were taking place in the lab on a regular basis. Tapas had found that an estrogen metabolite, 2-methoxyestradiol, which inhibits angiogenesis, also enhances the expression of the p53 protein. This allows apoptosis to occur in tumor cells with wild-type p53 or in cells with mutant p53 transduced with wild-type, and only a low amount of virus is needed. Bingliang Fang, who had just joined our group, had a new producer cell line for adenovirus vector production. The E4 promoter was replaced with an inducible promoter that worked only in the producer cells but not in the transduced cells. This prevented the expression of adenovirus proteins that are toxic to the cells.

It was spring break again, and on March 15, the whole family left for Keystone. The snow was great, with over a hundred-inch base. I won a silver racing NASTAR with a 32 handicap, my best. I returned to a March 25 special p53 therapeutics meeting held at the Ritz-Carlton in Tysons Corner, Virginia. I was an organizer and chaired a session. Bert Vogelstein was there, and we discussed our protocols. There were several confirmatory talks using the p53 adenovirus. I was beginning to write up the results of the retroviral study. This was a laborious procedure. The data had to be checked and rechecked. Fortunately, all of it had been collected prospectively, so we did not need to dig up old records.

Another busy round of travel had arrived. I went to San Diego to preside at the Evarts Graham Fellowship reception. A dinner was also held for the fellows and recipients of the Thoracic Surgery Foundation grants. Then I flew to Denver to receive the Jack Sadler Memorial Lecture Award at the University of Colorado. This was the most prestigious lecture given during the year at the University School of Medicine. An elegant dinner was held afterward.

On returning, I had a bizarre meeting with Dan Von Hoff, a medical oncologist. Dan apparently spouted off at an RPR Clinical

Advisory Board meeting that local treatment was not useful in cancer and that our strategy would not be approved. I guess he thought removing and controlling the primary cancer were not important, without realizing that unless the primary tumor was controlled, there was no chance for a cure. He also did not consider the bystander effect on uninjected cancer cells. On my way back from Denver, I stopped in San Antonio to meet with him, David Nance, Mary Harper, and J. Merritt. RPR was supposed to have a clinical development meeting, but this was canceled at the last moment. Apparently, they had heard about some responses in the head and neck study and wanted to set doses at 10^9. There were some harsh words between David and Martine. Finally, a meeting was held in Houston, where they audited the data. There had been some responses in Clayman's study, but higher doses were needed. On June 21, I received a fax that the retrovirus study was accepted by Nature Medicine. Although it took over two years to get the trial approved, we completed it and had it accepted for publication in 1.5 years.[87] Over the weekend, I frantically worked to shorten it by about 2,000 words. Some other minor things were changed. In addition, I completed an invited review of all the clinical cancer gene therapy trials in the world.[127] We submitted this massive project for publication.

My paper reporting the results of our p53 retrovirus clinical trial was published in September 1996 in Nature Medicine. Nine patients were treated in this phase 1 study, with the primary endpoint being safety. The drug itself was safe, with no adverse events associated with it. There were minor adverse events associated with the bronchoscopy procedure, but none of them was serious. Three patients had normal tissues available from autopsies. None of the tissues showed the presence of the retroviral vector. Thus, only the injected tumor was infected, and the retrovirus did not spread to any other tissues. In three of the nine patients, the injected lung cancer disappeared, with no live cancer on subsequent biopsies. In another patient, the tumor shrank to half its previous size. Biopsies after treatment showed the presence of the retroviral vector in cells and evidence of the type of cell death associated with normal p53 protein expression in cancer cells. Thus, this was a successful clinical trial and the first to show that the genetics of cancer could be changed in cancer patients. But it was clear that we needed a more efficient and easier-to-produce delivery system, like the adenovirus we had developed. While these drugs were useful in the treatment of local tumors, ultimately, I would need to develop gene therapy that could be delivered to all organs in the body via the bloodstream.

22
DEDICATION

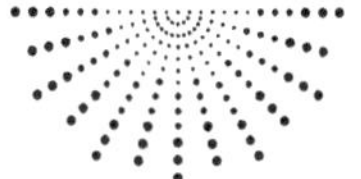

Research is to see what everybody else has seen, and to think what nobody else has thought.

—Albert Szent-Gyorgyi

It was mid-1996, and I departed with J for the Aspen Cancer Conference, first stopping in Keystone. We returned on the eighteenth. K returned from music camp, and J left for Aviation Challenge camp in Huntsville, Alabama. I picked her up there at the end of the week. In early August, the whole family left for Europe. From Frankfurt, we went to Heidelberg by car. There was a conference in Heidelberg, and Liz and I presented talks. We cruised on the Neckar River and attended a reception in Heidelberg Castle. This was an opportunity to see more of Bavaria and drive the Romantic Road (Die Romantische Straße). One of our first stops was the tiny village of Wies. Wieskirche, the pilgrimage church of Wies, is an oval rococo church designed in the late 1740s by Dominikus Zimmermann.[128] It is one of the finest examples of Baroque architecture. The ornate complexity of the interior is breathtaking in its intricacy. From there, we drove to Rothenburg, Augsburg, and then Fussen. Rothenburg is a well-preserved walled medieval town. Although it bears my name, I doubt whether any of my ancestors originated there. We dined at Welser Küche in Augsburg, which was the most unusual dining experience. The restaurant is in a medieval cellar where one dines as Augsburgers did 450 years ago, sitting at large, crude wooden tables. The only utensils are a dagger and fingers. The gargantuan eight-course meals, plus mead in tankards, were served by knaves and wenches in sixteenth-century costumes. The food, which is as genuine as the atmosphere, is prepared strictly according to recipes in the cookbook of Philippine Welser (1527–1580), a daughter of the patrician family who was married to the Habsburg Archduke Ferdinand. If you do not behave, you are placed in medieval irons, as I was, to the delight of my wife and daughters.[129]

In irons at the Welser Küche in Augsburg, 1996.

We took the ferry over beautiful Lake Constance to the conference center in Ermatingen, Switzerland, for the IASLC Lung Tumor Biology Workshop, where I presented my work on gene therapy for lung cancer. We drove back to Frankfurt. On our return to the States, the advance notice of our Nature Medicine paper was circulated by the journal, and I began receiving calls for interviews. An interview was set up with CNN as well as all the local TV stations. There was a blitz of publicity. Over three hundred telephone calls poured into the office from patients. I continued to be besieged with requests for interviews. It is always difficult to impart perspective to the press. You have no control over what ultimately appears. However, I did my best to place the work in perspective and not artificially raise expectations. Based on the resulting articles, this was handled quite well, with the story's perspective kept in balance.

On September 7, the Houston Symphony had an opening-night concert with Midori playing the Beethoven violin concerto, and the whole family attended. It was necessary to bring in extra nurses to answer all the telephone messages. However, we were able to enroll many patients on our new study. The research nurses felt very stressed and needed more help, which I found resources to provide.

On September 18, I flew to Washington, DC, to the patent office to directly present our data on patient responses. This was highly unusual and has never happened to me subsequently, despite over one hundred patent filings. The meeting went well, and it appeared several patents, including the adenovirus p53 and the combination therapy patent, would be issued. I then flew to Durham, North Carolina, for a lung cancer conference at Duke. One week later, I made a day trip to Atlanta for a lung cancer conference chaired by the medical oncologist who was the New England Journal of Medicine reviewer for our rejected lung cancer clinical trial. I had decided that I could do better by presenting our findings rather than holding a vendetta against the reviewer. Of course, it was the responsibility of the journal to determine the validity of the review.

October was an even more chaotic travel month. Ultimately, I would accumulate close to two million frequent flier miles. Bob Ginsberg, the head of thoracic surgery at Memorial Sloan Kettering, had been asking me for over a year to be a visiting professor. I flew up and listened to their research for a day. We enjoyed an excellent dinner at an Italian restaurant with David Skinner, another thoracic surgeon whom I knew from my student days at Johns Hopkins. Bob had trained in the Canadian thoracic surgical program at Toronto General Hospital. He was a founding member of the Lung Cancer Study Group. Tragically, he was a lifelong smoker who died from lung cancer several years later. The following Monday, I flew to San Francisco to give a lecture in an American College of Surgeons postgraduate course on gene therapy. Next, I was talked into going to Tokyo to participate in BioAlliance, a group that tried to set up agreements with Japanese partners. Toshi Fujiwara, Liz's and my former research fellow, was there. We had some good dinners while staying at the New Otani. Two Japanese companies, Chugai and Ono, seemed the most interested. However, gene therapy was new to Japan, and the companies were being very cautious.

Liz and I felt we needed more room for the children and for entertaining. We made a momentous decision to build a new home. We finally found a hundred-by-two-hundred lot in West University on Brompton, which was a quiet neighborhood and near work, and we closed on it. During this time, the roadshow opened for the Introgen public offering underwritten by Paine Webber and Genesis Merchant Securities. I traveled to New York for a meeting with analysts at the 21 Club. The final trip of the month was to London. I attended an IASLC conference on the staging of lung cancer. I flew on Sunday, arrived on Monday, and gave my talk. There was endless discussion on staging systems and lymph node maps. Although staging systems are useful for prognosis and for identifying which patients will benefit from certain treatment regimens, they do not ultimately contribute to increasing survival. During my career, it seems an inordinate amount of time was spent attempting to refine the systems to the point where they became so complex and the subgroups so small that any utility was lost. We had a dinner at Rules, which was the oldest restaurant in London, founded over two hundred years ago and located near Covent Garden. The menu was, of course, traditional English, with an emphasis on beef, game, and puddings. Harvey Pass, my former fellow from NCI, and his wife were there. He was moving to Wayne State, and she would be at Ann Arbor. They now had twins.

The next day, I attended a gene therapy meeting chaired by Karol

Sikora, a medical oncologist and deputy director for the Imperial Cancer Research Campaign. After my talk, I was whisked over to Paine Webber's offices in London and then back to the Royal Brompton Hospital for the last session of the staging conference. That evening, Sikora hosted us for dinner at the Athenaeum, a club near Trafalgar Square. It was unique in that members were elected because of their achievements rather than their background, with both men and women eligible. Charles Dickens and Charles Darwin were both members. Finally, I returned home the next day. Now we were busy working with Charles Ligon, an architect, to draw up plans for the house. On November 9, we attended a moving performance of the Mozart Requiem.

Occasionally, good news comes in bunches. I received notice from NCI that our program project grant Restoration of Apoptosis in Cancer would be funded. This grant was for over five million dollars. The W. M. Keck Foundation donated four million dollars for the establishment of the W. M. Keck Center for Cancer Gene Therapy at MD Anderson, with me as director. Now we would have consistent funding to move our gene therapy program forward.

Remember the dot-com frenzy of 1999? Everyone was setting up website-based businesses where the metric was eyeballs and not profit. Of course, this later collapsed in 2000. However, business associates invited me to New York for a meeting to discuss setting up a website for facilitating patient entry into clinical trials. David Nance, Jim Albrecht, Frank Russo (Noonan-Russo), and Thierry Soussac, among others, met with me for dinner. Soussac and Russo had a company for selling drugs on the internet called iPharm. Discussions on how this might interface with ClinMatch were held. I learned about another web-based company called MyDoctor, which was attempting to do the same thing, although it had not progressed very far since its founding in 1996. Fortunately, I did not invest any money or time in these ventures. I traveled to San Francisco for my presentation to the Surgical Biology Club. I gave my standard lecture on gene therapy, and this was well received. The dinner afterward was decent.

It was 1997 and MD Anderson now had a new president, John

Mendelsohn. Mendelsohn had been the chair of the Department of Medicine at Memorial Sloan Kettering Cancer Center in New York. Charles LeMaistre, the previous president, was retiring. LeMaistre was a prodigious fundraiser, and one of his major achievements was the addition of over two hundred endowed faculty positions to MD Anderson. However, there was considerable discontent among the faculty concerning institutional operations and clinical inefficiencies. A new administration usually sweeps out the old rapidly. Thus, when I saw Charles Balch, a former MD Anderson executive vice president and a candidate for the president position, at the meeting, I found out he was now in private practice in California after leaving MD Anderson.

The clinical trials with the adenovirus p53 were adding patients rapidly. We had found that injecting the adenovirus p53 into cancers in mice, combined with radiation therapy, increased cancer cell death, and greatly slowed tumor growth compared to treatment with radiation or adenovirus p53 alone.[130] This finding stimulated the initiation of another clinical trial in lung cancer patients. Steve Swisher, one of our former thoracic surgery fellows whom I recruited to MD Anderson and was now on our faculty, was the principal investigator for this clinical trial. Patients with lung cancer who were eligible to receive combined radiation and chemotherapy could be enrolled in this clinical trial. The adenovirus p53 would be injected in their tumor as they were receiving radiation treatments. Although one is always optimistic when beginning a clinical trial, I was astonished to find that for the first ten patients completing treatment, seven had negative biopsies, representing complete tumor regression, and eight had major responses that were greater than 50 percent tumor shrinkage. This suggested that the p53 was contributing to an antitumor effect in cells that did not take up the adenovirus. Later, we and other groups would identify the mechanism behind this bystander effect.

I traveled to Santa Ana, California, to give a presentation for the Chao Cancer Center of UC Irvine. From there, it was a short car trip to see Mom and Dad in Laguna Hills, who both looked quite well. Dad had his new computer and was telling me about its DRAM and hard drive. We worked together to set up a video teleconferencing system.

Then it was off to Hilton Head for the Forbeck Foundation meeting on gene therapy. This was a highly selective meeting with only twelve participants, chaired by John Minna and Inder Verma. The discussions were animated and argumentative. Our data was criticized because it was thought the tumor regression was due to an immune response. This was very prescient, as it turned out the immune response did play an important role, although at that time, we did not realize it. Also, they criticized our clinical trials for a lack of vector-only controls. Asking patients with no other treatment options to consider receiving an inactive placebo, at least in early-stage trials, was considered unethical. The final data on the randomized studies would be available with a standard treatment for the control arm.

Introgen had been expanding, and the company decided to open its own production and research facility rather than be dependent on subcontractors and contract research organizations. I was surprised and honored to learn that the research building would bear my name. A ceremony was held for the dedication. My parents, Liz, and my daughters all attended. I gave a short speech, which follows:

> December 2, 1999: Dedication of the Jack A. Roth Research Building at Introgen.
>
> I thank you for this great honor; my father and mother thank you, and my children, who are rarely impressed by anything I do, are even impressed by this. When I first learned from David Nance that my name was being considered for a building, my first reaction was that I was not old enough. Then, upon reflecting on the named buildings in the medical center, I realized that many were named posthumously, and I really became worried. I certainly thank you for this, with the realization that this is the accomplishment of many, not just one. I regard my association with Introgen with great pride, particularly because of its leadership in an entirely new approach to the treatment of disease.
>
> A major shift in the direction of medical research is occurring. The genetic basis of disease is rapidly being elucidated. Now, treatments can be developed to specifically target molecular and cellular pathways

implicated in the disease process. This is happening not only in cancer but in cardiovascular disease, diabetes, and other chronic diseases. Introgen, through its clinical trials and research, has pioneered this approach.

This shift in cancer treatment parallels the evolution of treatments for infectious diseases. In the early part of this century, surgery was the only available treatment for infectious diseases. Subsequently, heavy metals were used, which sometimes cured the disease but frequently poisoned the patient. Of course, now antibiotics specifically target infectious agents with few side effects. The point of this is not that surgeons are obsolete! But in cancer, we are moving from generalized poisons to specifically targeted agents with greater therapeutic effects and few or no side effects.

As physicians, we still do not have all the effective tools we need to win the battle against cancer. This reminds me of another story. A patient was in his physician's office and asked, "Doctor, what can I do to live longer?" His physician replied, "Eat only fruits and vegetables, don't eat fats, exercise every day, don't have sex, and don't smoke." The patient replied, "If I do all that, I really live longer?" "No," the doctor replied, "but it will seem that way!"

Gene therapy represents an unprecedented opportunity to make dramatic changes in the treatment and cure of genetic disease. This cannot be accomplished in solitude. An effort as significant as this requires the collaboration of many institutions and scientists.

It is appropriate now to recognize the partnership between Introgen and MD Anderson that has played a major role in moving gene therapy forward. An editorial last month in Nature, arguably the most prestigious basic science journal, attributes the economic boom "of unprecedented strength and duration" in the United States in part to the efficient transfer of intellectual property from publicly funded institutions to the private sector. I quote from Nature, "Only the private sector is ultimately capable of efficient commercial exploitation of such ideas." In the laboratory, we do well at curing mice, but we need to bring these treatments to patients. I have a poignant story to relate from Karen Antman, head of the Cancer Center at Columbia.

The day after Judah Folkman made the statement, "If you are a mouse with cancer, we can cure you," a patient of hers appeared in the clinic wearing a pair of Mickey Mouse ears.

David Nance, president and chief executive officer of Introgen Therapeutics, recognized the importance of this partnership much earlier than Nature. David, in helping to found Introgen Therapeutics, provided the support and infrastructure to bring tumor suppressor gene replacement to the clinic. He is an individual with the highest ideals and integrity. David realizes the excellence in research and translation to patient care is, in fact, good business. He is also a good friend, and I thank him for this honor.

My association at Introgen has provided an opportunity to collaborate with an outstanding group of individuals and make many new friends. I would like to personally recognize all of you and mention a few who were together in the early days. When the history of all this is written, it will still not be clear who the first Introgen employee was. When I saw Debbie Wilson's curriculum vitae during her application for a position at Introgen and realized she attended Cornell, my alma mater, and graduate school at Purdue in Indiana, where I was born, I knew she had the right credentials. Debbie has been a creative scientific force for Introgen, and I have greatly enjoyed collaborating with her. J. Merritt has added industrial strength to our clinical trials. Jim Albrecht has managed to keep our sponsored research agreements in balance despite the best efforts of the accountants at MD Anderson. Shawn Gallagher has turned a laboratory curiosity into a mass-produced product with great skill. David Enloe keeps things running smoothly. Lou Zumstein and Sunil Chada have been great scientific collaborators. I could go on and on. I personally thank all of you. A company is not an entity but a group of individuals. The individuals at Introgen have a wide range of talents, exceptional skills, ingenuity, and expertise. It has been my privilege to be associated with everyone at Introgen.

The partnership between the University of Texas MD Anderson Cancer Center, the W. M. Keck Foundation, and Introgen Therapeutics has been fundamental in establishing our gene therapy program and moving it at the pace it needs to take full advantage of the incredible inroads that we have forged in the field of gene therapy. I thank Bill Doty, head of technology development at MDACC, who first introduced me to David Nance and helped establish Introgen. I thank Dr. John Mendelsohn, president of the MD Anderson Cancer Center, for providing the leadership, support, and infrastructure that make such collaborations work.

Finally, and most importantly, we must recognize the patients who we all hope will benefit from our endeavors. The patients who have participated in clinical trials of gene replacement are selfless and courageous. Their efforts will benefit all future generations. To all of you at Introgen and to our patients, I in turn, would like to dedicate this building.

As part of our gene therapy program at MD Anderson, I invited a prominent speaker every year. The speaker for 1999 was James Wilson, a world-renowned gene therapy pioneer from the University of Pennsylvania. During a reception for him prior to his talk, one of my colleagues pulled me aside and said that a patient in one of Wilson's gene therapy trials had just died during treatment. I thought this was unexpected, as gene therapy, up to that point, was safe. Our group had never had a serious adverse event from the gene therapy we administered. Wilson gave his speech and never mentioned anything about a death in his program. Shortly thereafter, the details of the first gene therapy death emerged. Jesse Gelsinger was an eighteen-year-old boy who suffered from ornithine transcarbamylase deficiency, a genetic disease of the liver in which the gene for the enzyme is defective. As a result, the body cannot metabolize ammonia, which accumulates from the breakdown of protein. Although this genetic defect is usually fatal at birth, Gelsinger had a milder form and survived on a protein-restricted diet and medications.[131] Gelsinger was enrolled in a clinical trial overseen by Wilson at the University of Pennsylvania, where he was injected with an adenovirus that expressed the normal ornithine transcarbamylase protein, with the primary goal of testing the safety of this procedure. Four days later, he died from a massive immune response caused by the virus. This triggered an investigation by the FDA, which concluded that there were violations of the protocol and the conduct of the clinical trial. These included: 1) entering Gelsinger in the clinical trial even though he had high ammonia levels that were an exclusion in the protocol, 2) two patients who had experienced serious side effects had not been reported to the FDA, and 3) the informed consent did not state that monkeys given the same treatment had died.

Following Gelsinger's death, all gene therapy trials were put on hold. This event caused a furor in the U.S. Congress. Wilson was called to testify. Members of Congress called for a review of all gene therapy programs. It was noted that most of the patients entered in cancer gene therapy clinical trials died. This observation caused an uproar. What was the explanation for this? Why was there no oversight? What they failed to realize was that all the clinical trials were Phase 1 toxicity or early Phase 2 clinical trials, which, because of the untested nature of gene therapy, only enrolled patients who had advanced cancer and who otherwise had no treatment options. Patients were dying from the progression of their cancer, not from the gene therapy treatment. But some members of Congress saw an opportunity for self-promotion and either ignored or failed to understand this while holding press conferences to chastise the gene therapy community. My office was inundated with calls from the press, wanting comments. Although the death was tragic, it was an anomaly. The accusations against all gene therapy investigators were unfounded.

Although I did not want to speak to the press, which I thought would legitimize these false accusations, I was ordered to speak to the press by a senior MD Anderson administrator. Tragically, this episode resulted in the field of gene therapy losing scientific credibility. Funding for gene therapy dried up. No gene therapy grants would be funded by NCI study sections. This lasted for over a decade until dramatic positive results from treating another hereditary condition, adenosine deaminase deficiency, became public. During this time, a small group of gene therapy researchers persisted, with positive results emerging in clinical trials, including long-term remissions using new gene delivery systems. This was one of the most painful episodes in my career.

Wilson and the University of Pennsylvania had financial interests in the outcome of his research. Wilson was a founder and had stock in a company that could sell the gene therapy being tested, and Penn would also benefit. This revelation precipitated a tsunami of calls to prevent abuses of conflict of interest. The concept of conflict of interest was developed to describe a situation where a researcher primarily employed by an academic institution receives financial benefit from an outside company for their research. The term conflict of interest is pejorative and inaccurate. Most researchers are honest individuals who will not falsify clinical trial data to make money. Researchers realize that the only way to get their discoveries to patients is through commercialization, either through pharmaceutical companies or by founding their own company. This is a critical fact; therefore, research and industrial collaborations should be encouraged. Academia and industry have common interests, not conflicts of interest. There are many safeguards as well. Clinical trial data is exhaustively reviewed by regulatory agencies, and attempts are made to reproduce the findings. Falsification will always fail.

Nevertheless, the guardians of academic integrity began to make self-righteous statements that conflict of interest must be eliminated. The critical element that must be present in every financial or company relationship is full, transparent disclosure in all documents, including institutional forms, grants, publications, and informed consents for clinical trials. When full disclosure is present, the reader, reviewer, or patient can make a fully informed decision. Eliminating these relationships or erecting bureaucratic obstacles is counterproductive. Although the research environment became more challenging, I persevered.

23
PERSISTENCE PAYS OFF

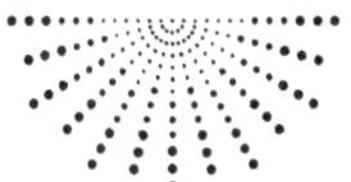

Nothing in the world can take the place of persistence. Talent will not; nothing is more common than unsuccessful men with talent. Genius will not; unrewarded genius is almost a proverb. Education will not; the world is full of educated derelicts. Persistence and determination alone are omnipotent.

—Calvin Coolidge

Despite the fallout from the Wilson affair, an intrepid band of researchers continued to carry the gene therapy torch. We all understood this was a crucial area of research that could not be forgotten. A review article written in 1999 listed over three hundred gene therapy clinical trials. Our initial approvals with the RAC had exploded as other investigators hopped on the bandwagon.[132] Of even greater significance, initial clinical trials began in 1996, with our novel adenovirus p53 gene therapy completed and appearing in high-impact scientific journals. The history of p53 is tortuous.[133] In 1979, three separate groups identified the p53 protein, initially believing that it was an oncogene. However, it was later found that the p53 gene in cancers contained point mutations that caused the p53 protein to lose its normal function, which is to suppress cell proliferation and cancer growth. Our research group found that adding back a normal p53 to the cancer caused cancer cells to die. Delivering the p53 gene with an adenovirus that was altered so it could not cause illness was more efficient than the retrovirus we used in earlier clinical trials.

Our first trial was in lung cancer patients.[134] Advances in interventional radiology allowed the drug to be injected in any tumor site. The target would be visualized by computerized tomographic imaging, allowing precise needle placement for the injection. I collaborated with a skillful radiologist, David Lawrence, who made these injections look simple with minimal discomfort for patients. In this phase 1 clinical trial, we administered adenovirus p53 to 28 patients with non-small cell lung cancer whose cancers had progressed with conventional treatments. Patients received up to six monthly intratumoral injections by use of computed tomography-guided percutaneous fine-needle injection (23 patients) or bronchoscopy (five patients). One of the important aspects of this trial was that biopsies of the tumor were taken before and after injection. The patients were incredibly courageous and generous to consent to this. Fortunately, the risk was very low and discomfort minimal and transient. These biopsies provided valuable information. Close to 90 percent of the patients showed presence of the viral DNA in the tumor cells, and in almost half of the patients there was increased cancer cell death. This gave us confidence that the clinical responses we were seeing were caused by the gene therapy. There were no serious side effects, unlike the experience with chemotherapy. Therapeutic activity in 25 evaluable patients included partial responses in two patients (8 percent) and disease stabilization (range 2–14 months) in 16 patients (64 percent); the remaining 7 patients (28 percent) exhibited disease progression. Thus, over 70 percent of the patients had control of their cancer. We concluded that repeated intratumoral injections of adenovirus p53 appeared to be well tolerated, resulted in transgene expression of wild type p53, and mediated antitumor activity.

The benefit of the gene therapy was exemplified in two patients. Patient K presented with a left upper lobe large-cell carcinoma, which is a very aggressive type of lung cancer. Because of poor results on lung function tests, the patient was not eligible for surgery and was treated with radiation therapy. The primary tumor recurred and was treated with six cycles of chemotherapy, but the tumor continued to grow. The patient was subsequently enrolled in the gene therapy protocol because the tumor had progressed. The tumor shrank with a greater than 50 percent decrease in size. No viable tumor was found when the tumor was biopsied following two treatments with the gene therapy. After the completion of gene therapy in June 1997, the patient was observed without further treatment, and at the time of the last follow-up nine months later, there was no sign of cancer.

In September 1994, patient O had an adenocarcinoma that was partially obstructing the left airway to the upper lobe of the lung. The patient had been treated with two courses of chemotherapy, followed by radiation therapy. In December 1995, the tumor recurred with bronchial obstruction of the left upper lobe and was treated with laser therapy and twenty-one courses of a new chemotherapy. One year later, in December 1996, the patient's left upper lobe airway was found to be reoccluded, and laser therapy was attempted but failed. Direct intratumoral injection of adenovirus p53 was begun in December 1996, resulting in a partial response and reopening of the airway. This response was maintained for six months. At the completion of therapy, a residual tumor remained, and three additional courses of chemotherapy were given, resulting in complete regression of the tumor, which lasted for one year. These were dramatic results in patients who had very advanced cancer with no standard treatment options.

Our team observed in laboratory experiments in mice that injecting the adenovirus p53 along with the intravenous chemotherapy drug, cisplatin, was more effective than either single agent alone. I then began a clinical trial combining adenovirus p53 and cisplatin in lung cancer patients.[135] Twenty-four patients received a total of eighty-three intratumor injections with adenovirus p53, and nineteen (79 percent) of the patients had their tumor stop growing or shrink (two patients). The post-treatment biopsies in 79 percent of the patients showed an increase in cancer cell death of the type that would be caused by an increase in the normal p53 protein. Injection with adenovirus p53 in combination with cisplatin was well tolerated, with no increase in the side effects expected with chemotherapy. Of the seven patients who received injections of adenovirus p53 to endobronchial sites (inside the airway), five achieved substantial reductions in the obstructing tumor mass, which significantly relieved bronchial obstruction. All six patients who showed a significant response had previously progressed with the disease after failure of treatment with either cisplatin or carboplatin. Thus, the gene therapy was able to overcome acquired drug resistance to chemotherapy.

Gary Clayman was a head and neck surgeon at MD Anderson who became interested in our adenovirus p53 gene therapy as a treatment for head and neck cancer. Head and neck cancers can be locally extensive and difficult to treat, making this an ideal application for this gene therapy. Cisplatin chemotherapy and radiation, both of which are synergistic with p53 gene therapy, are commonly used to treat head and neck cancer. Gary started a clinical trial with our adenovirus gene therapy.[136] Patients with incurable recurrent local or regionally metastatic head and neck squamous cell cancer (HNSCC) received multiple intratumoral injections of adenovirus p53, either with or without tumor resection. Tumors of 33 patients were injected. No dose-limiting toxicity or serious adverse events occurred. Once again, p53 expression was detected in tumor biopsies, indicating that the adenovirus-delivered gene was making the normal p53 protein. In 17 patients with tumors that could not be removed surgically, 2 patients showed tumor shrinkage of greater than 50 percent, and 6 patients showed stable disease for up to 3.5 months. In one patient, the tumor completely disappeared. The p53 gene therapy was working in a second tumor type and once again showed no significant side effects.

Our laboratory also showed in mice that adenovirus p53 and radiation therapy worked together synergistically. A clinical trial was begun to test this in lung cancer patients.[137] Nonmetastatic non-small cell lung cancer patients who were not eligible for radiation therapy combined with chemotherapy or surgery were treated as outpatients with radiation therapy to 60 Gy over 6 weeks in conjunction with three intratumoral injections of adenovirus p53. Biopsies after treatment were performed in 15 patients, and 12 showed no cancer (80 percent). The local p53-injected tumor was completely controlled in 15 of the 19 patients (79 percent). These were success rates much higher than would be expected with just radiation therapy alone. However, 11 of the patients ultimately developed the spread of cancer to distant organs. This emphasized to me the need to develop a gene therapy that could be injected into the blood so it could eliminate cancer in every organ. Serendipitously, some ongoing experiments in our laboratory would lead us to such a drug. The synergistic interaction of p53 and radiation would lead to a clinical trial in another part of the world that none of us anticipated and that would revolutionize the gene therapy field.

My team and our collaborators had now published the results of four clinical trials unequivocally showing that adenovirus p53 gene therapy was safe and effective in lung cancer, head and neck cancer, and when combined with chemotherapy and radiation therapy, confirming the many papers we had published on the laboratory experiments. Now it was up to the drug companies to initiate larger clinical trials and the FDA to provide a logical and reasonable pathway for drug approval, a pathway that accounted for the small number of patients who would be able to enter a clinical trial and an endpoint that could be achieved rapidly. Tragically, both the drug companies and the FDA would fail, and patients in the United States would not gain access to p53 gene therapy, while halfway around the world it would be rapidly approved and benefit thousands of patients (Chapter 26).

24
THAT'S FUNNY

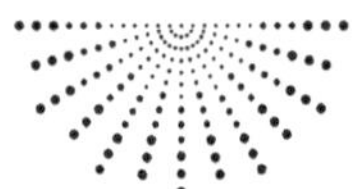

> The most exciting phrase to hear in science, the one that heralds new discoveries, is not "Eureka!" but "That's funny . . ."
>
> —Isaac Asimov

It was early in 2000, and I was sitting in my office after completing some surgical cases when there was a knock. In came one of our recently hired research scientists, Rajagopal Ramesh. Ramesh had received his PhD in molecular biology at the prestigious All India Institute of Medical Sciences in New Delhi and had completed a postdoctoral fellowship at Tulane. He quickly developed a xenograft mouse model of lung metastases (spread) using human lung cancer cells in a mouse whose immune system was altered so the human cells would not be rejected. Three weeks after the human cancer cells were injected in the tail vein of the mouse, we could see many small white nodules on the surface of the lung where the cancer cells were growing. We were trying to figure out a way to deliver genes to cancer cells anywhere in the body. The problem with the adenovirus was that it stimulated an immune response that neutralized the adenovirus vector in patients. Many patients had been previously exposed to adenoviruses, which commonly caused cold-like symptoms. Multiple injections of the adenovirus caused patients to produce high levels of anti-adenovirus antibodies. One of the scientists at Introgen had read about small lipid (composed of fat molecules) vesicles that could encapsulate genes, circulate in the blood to deliver the gene to any organ, and not trigger an immune response to the vesicle. We were using these particles to deliver a novel tumor suppressor gene, TUSC2, to the lung metastases in our mouse model.

When Ramesh walked in, he had two small bottles in his hand and a puzzled look on his face. He said he had done his first experiment with the new gene therapy. But when he euthanized the mice and examined their lungs, none of the mice injected with the gene therapy had visible tumors. He showed me the lung from one of those mice, and it looked perfectly normal. However, he said the lungs from the control mice, who did not receive the gene therapy, had many lung tumors. He showed me a mouse lung covered with white spots. He looked puzzled. I was taken aback also. "Well," I said, "there must be some technical error. Perhaps the technician injecting the tumor cells in some of the mice treated with the gene therapy injected the cells outside the vein. Then they would not go to the lungs." Ramesh countered, "But none of the lungs from the gene therapy-treated mice had tumors. We couldn't have messed up all those mice, especially when all the untreated mice had lots of tumors." Of course, the possibility in the back of both our minds was that the new gene therapy was incredibly effective. "Look," I said, "maybe this really works. Let's repeat the experiment to see if the findings are reproducible." One rule that I have always insisted on is that experiments of this type were blinded. The person counting the nodules and evaluating the final data had no knowledge of the treatment groups. All the specimens were placed in random order, and the treatment group list was sealed and held by a second person in the lab. There was no way the results were manipulated.

In 1982, when John Minna was at the NCI-Navy Medical Oncology Branch, his group had a series of publications on 3p chromosomal deletions in lung cancer.[136] I was in the NCI Surgery Branch at the time and was collaborating with John. At the time, DNA sequencing and functional analysis of genes were primitive or nonexistent. The suspicion was that this region of the chromosome harbored a tumor suppressor gene. Where that gene was located and how it functioned were mysteries. The work continued when we all moved to Texas. Eventually, Mike Lerman and John identified genes in a smaller, frequently deleted region of 3p. One of my first SPORE projects was to functionally characterize the genes in this region. Nine genes were identified in this deleted region. I had previously recruited a molecular biologist following his postdoctoral fellowship at Stanford, Lin Ji. Working with him, we encountered a finding that none of us had expected. Multiple genes in this region had tumor-suppressor properties. Lin took each gene and inserted it in an adenovirus just as had been done for p53. Next, the adenovirus-gene construct was used to deliver the gene into lung cancer cells that were lacking the protein coded for by the gene.[79] Four of the genes caused dramatic slowing of human lung cancer growth or regression in mice and greatly reduced lung metastases.

Putting this together with previously published data showed that five of the nine genes in this small chromosome region were tumor suppressor genes, a remarkable finding. One of the genes, originally called FUS1 and now known by its HUGO name TUSC2, was of great interest. It was the most active in causing cancer cell death and was very active in the mouse experiments. We later observed that the expression of the TUSC2 protein was missing in most human lung cancers and other cancer types as well[138]. The more we studied TUSC2, the more fascinating it became. It must have been a critical tumor suppressor gene because many cancers were found with either low or no levels of detectable TUSC2 protein. We later discovered that there were multiple ways the cancer cell could eliminate TUSC2 expression. Deletion of the gene only occurred in less than 20 percent of the cases in lung cancer, although it was more frequently deleted in other cancers, such as renal cell cancer. The addition of a lipid, myristoylation, was necessary for the TUSC2 protein to be stable.[139] Certain RNA sequences were required for the protein to be made.[140] If the cancer altered any of these RNA sequences, the TUSC2 protein would be reduced or eliminated from the cancer cell. When the TUSC2 protein was expressed in cancer cells where it was previously absent or present in low amounts, the cancer cells died by a process called programmed cell death, or apoptosis (a Greek word meaning falling off). When cells begin to die by this process, parts of the cell membrane detach like petals falling off a flower.

TUSC2 also regulates a critical function of signaling in the cell. Cells have proteins on their surface called receptors. When a molecule binds to a receptor, it may activate that receptor. One of the mechanisms of activation is called phosphorylation, in which a phosphorus molecule is added to an amino acid residue, typically tyrosine. This can activate or, in some cases, inactivate the signaling of the receptor to the cell. There may be a cascade of proteins that need to be activated to trigger a response in the cell nucleus. In cancer cells, molecules that signal cell growth and division are abnormally activated. The TUSC2 protein, surprisingly, can block the activation of these abnormally activated proteins. While drugs such as osimertinib can block a single growth-factor receptor, TUSC2 blocks multiple different activation pathways. This is unique in a cancer drug and extremely valuable. With a drug such as osimertinib, which blocks only the activated epidermal growth factor receptor, resistance to the drug inevitably occurs because of the activation of other bypass pathways. The ability of TUSC2 to block multiple pathways could prevent or delay this drug resistance from developing.[141] We would find out in the future that TUSC2 gene therapy can overcome drug resistance.

But there were more surprises. The protein produced by the TUSC2 gene plays a major role in regulating the immune response, including to cancer. When the TUSC2 protein is expressed in cancer cells, it causes the release of many proteins that increase the immune response to cancer. It is also crucial for activating a type of immune cell called the natural killer cell, which is very potent in killing cancer cells.[84] Classical immune cells (e.g., T lymphocytes) must recognize a specific foreign protein on the cancer cell to kill it. But natural killer cells were developed as the rapid response team of the immune system. They can immediately recognize foreign invaders such as viruses and attack them without needing the helper molecules required by T cells. Now we needed to deliver the potent anticancer gene systemically via the bloodstream so it could engage cancer cells anywhere in the body, thus overcoming the limitations of our previous gene therapy. Any delivery system would also need to protect the gene from being degraded by enzymes in the blood and not stimulate an immune response against it. How would this be possible?

In another fortuitous event, one of the scientists at Introgen mentioned a new type of gene-delivery platform developed by Nancy Templeton, a research scientist at the NCI cancer research facility in Frederick, Maryland.[142] Nancy had developed a formulation of cholesterol with an agent that modifies surface properties, 1,2-Dioleoyl-3-trimethylammonium propane (DOTAP). Mixing these two agents in a certain ratio and then extruding them through a filter would form lipid particles that would be extraordinarily small, in the range of 10^{-9}meters. When these were mixed with the gene, the gene was encapsulated by the fat particles, forming vesicles that protected it from enzymes in the blood and enabled its delivery to every organ in the body. The chemicals in these vesicles were inert to the immune system, so no immune response occurred, and they could be injected intravenously in a patient indefinitely.

Now we needed to test this new gene-delivery system in my lab. I arranged for Ramesh and others in our group to visit Nancy's lab in Frederick and learn the technique for preparing the liposomes and complexes. They were successful and were able to prepare the nanovesicles in our lab. We found that intravenous injection of the TUSC2-containing nanovesicles dramatically reduced human lung cancer metastases and prolonged survival in mice, with some mice surviving over three months, which, in mouse terms, is essentially a cure.[143] TUSC2 nanovesicles worked not only in non-small cell lung cancer but also the very aggressive, difficult-to-treat small-cell lung cancer.[144] All these findings were so compelling that I wanted to take our new TUSC2 gene therapy into a clinical trial. But this would mean overcoming some major hurdles even more daunting than I faced with our previous gene therapy clinical trials.

25
SYSTEMIC GENE THERAPY FOR CANCER—A FIRST

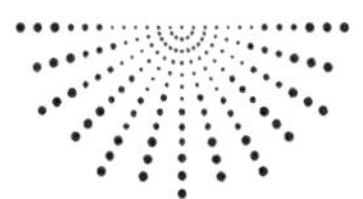

To achieve great things, two things are needed: a plan and not quite enough time.

—Leonard Bernstein

I cannot think of a more poignant moment than taking your child to college. There is the joy experienced in seeing someone you love, who has matured under your gaze, begin a stimulating new chapter in their life, reliving your own intellectual and personal discoveries. J had loved Mount Holyoke at first sight. It turned out to be her first choice, and she would go on to thrive in the academic and leadership programs on campus. We had shipped boxes, which had all arrived, and then helped her set up her room and computer. Then we left, a bittersweet moment.

Fortuitously, Nancy Templeton had moved to the Baylor College of Medicine which is located across the street from MD Anderson. In April, we published a paper showing that intravenous delivery of nanovesicle-encapsulated p53 could cure mice with disseminated human xenograft tumors.[145] Now I wanted to rapidly move forward with a TUSC2 clinical trial. But first, we needed to produce the nanovesicle TUSC2 DNA complex for clinical use, which had never been done before; however, our choices were limited. We tried to get the DNA produced for the clinical trial by Selective Genetics, a company in California. However, because of liability issues, they would not produce it for human use.

The TUSC2 phase 1 gene therapy protocol for the clinical trial was written over two years earlier, with Charles Lu, a faculty member in thoracic medical oncology, as the principal investigator. Charles had limited clinical trial experience and had never dealt with the FDA. This inexperience would come back to haunt me. The protocol had passed the MD Anderson gauntlet of regulatory and compliance committees and was approved by the MD Anderson Biosafety Committee, the Clinical Research Committee, and the Surveillance Committee. However, to produce the plasmid DNA, we had to set up a clinical-grade facility at Baylor with Nancy Templeton. Nancy agreed. I also talked with her boss, another gene therapy researcher, Malcolm Brenner. He expressed interest. We agreed that the cost would be in the fifty-thousand-dollar range. I trusted him and did not insist on a contract, which turned out to be a huge and costly mistake. I then toured the facility and confirmed it was able to produce clinical-grade material.

Next, we called the FDA to discuss the protocol. The conversation was punctuated with abrasive comments from one of our collaborators, who insisted that liposome-alone controls were not necessary. One thing I learned from earlier experience is that if you are too confrontational with the bureaucracy, it will make you pay, but now it was too late. This antagonized the FDA, and they insisted on a two-species toxicology study, which would include primates, an extremely expensive and time-consuming endeavor. We set up the toxicology study with the veterinary group at Bastrop. They could conduct the studies under good laboratory practice (GLP), which was adequate for the FDA. However, they needed a lot of hand-holding. I received daily emails with questions about the protocol. The clinical trial required RAC approval as well, but this went more smoothly and rapidly than our earlier clinical trials.

While the TUSC2 clinical trial was developing, Rhône-Poulenc, the

French pharmaceutical company that was sponsoring our adenovirus p53 clinical trials, merged with the German firm Hoechst to form a new pharmaceutical company called Aventis in 1999. This merger resulted in major consolidation, with the resulting discontinuation of the adenovirus p53 clinical trials; they were returned to Introgen, which was now the sponsor in 2000. Aventis ultimately merged with Sanofi in 2004.

Now we had to set up a production facility for the TUSC2 gene therapy from scratch at Baylor under Nancy Templeton's direction. There are guidelines for the manufacture of materials to be used in patients, called good manufacturing practices (GMP), and we needed to ensure any manufacturing at Baylor followed these guidelines. A major part of GMP procedure is documentation, which includes protocols that describe in exquisite detail everything that is done in a procedure and forms that document all the steps and results. Quality assurance procedures were needed. All of this needed to be written without any preexisting material to help. I asked Nancy and a science writer who had worked with me previously to work together to develop this. At one point, I found ten emails on my computer between Susan Grammer and Nancy Templeton about writing GLP protocols. In addition, there were institutional compliance issues between MD Anderson and Baylor. For example, a production conference call with the Baylor group revealed that the material transfer agreement between the two institutions was not signed. These agreements often took months as the attorneys for each institution resolved their differences.

Liz and I visited J at Mount Holyoke for parents' weekend. She looked great and was thriving in the college environment. She was selected for the community service board of the college. I heard Vincent Ferraro, chair of international relations, discuss strategies for dealing with September 11; a psychology professor discuss conditioning; and Eva Paus, an economics professor, expound on globalization. We had dinner in J's dorm.

I received frequent invitations to speak at conferences on both clinical and scientific topics. I refused many because of clinical responsibilities and family events. One that caught my attention was the Albert B. Sabin Vaccine Institute's Colloquium on cancer vaccines and cancer immunotherapy held on March 8–12, 2000, at Walker's Cay that lies fifty-three miles to the northeast of West End, Grand Bahama, in the northern Bahamas.[146] Liz was invited as well, and since neither of us had visited the Bahamas, this seemed like a fantastic opportunity. Walker's Cay is a very small island with a surface area of less than one hundred acres. It was primarily known as a deep-sea fishing resort. The conference had arranged for us to arrive at the resort by seaplane. This was a gripping experience, as when the plane landed, the windows were submerged. We stayed at the only hotel on the island, which had a small building attached for the conference. There was a port for the fishing boats, and during that Saturday night, as we finished dinner, the scene became rowdy. Then a fight broke out between two men, not from our conference. It was a scene out of a bad motion picture. A beer bottle was broken, and one of the men sustained a deep cut on his cheek. As the blood flowed, the fight suddenly stopped. Hotel staff rushed to the scene, and a call went out for a doctor. I was the only surgeon on the island, so I aided the staff in moving him to a small room stocked for emergencies. Although he was bleeding profusely, the man's high blood alcohol level had rendered him beyond pain. We stretched him out on an exam table. The first thing was to stop the bleeding, so pressure was applied with some of the sterile gauze on hand. The only hospital was on Grand Bahama Island, an hour away by air, and no planes were available. I asked about surgical supplies, and there were some sterile silk sutures and a clamp, which could function as a needle holder. I ignored the expiration date on the sutures. I decided the best course of action would be to suture the cut and then evacuate him to a plastic surgeon on Grand Bahama in the morning. I used some injectable lidocaine to numb the edges of the cut, although at this point, my patient was not experiencing pain. I sutured the cut closed, and in the morning, he was on a flight to the hospital in Grand Bahama. That was a memorable conference.

During our struggles with the gene therapy trials, another unexpected institutional drama unfolded. John Mendelsohn became the president of MD Anderson in 1996, succeeding Charles LeMaistre. He came from Memorial Sloan Kettering Cancer Center in New York, where he chaired the Department of Medicine. He had attended Harvard as an undergraduate, where he took a course with James D. Watson, the co-discoverer of the structure of DNA. Mendelsohn always emphasized his relationship with Watson as his scientific mentor, and despite Watson's biased statements on race and his misogynistic behavior, Mendelsohn continued his close association and invited him to speak at a scientific seminar held to celebrate his retirement.

Kenneth Lay was the founder, CEO, and chairman of the energy company Enron. He was a major donor to MD Anderson and on the board of visitors. One of my first patients when I arrived at MD Anderson was a member of Lay's family. LeMaistre personally escorted me to the patient's room, where I met Lay. Lay continued his relationship with MD Anderson under the new president, John Mendelsohn. Mendelsohn was remarkably effective in raising money for the institution. In the previous five years, the cancer center's research budget had grown by 71 percent, and the number of patients had increased by 49 percent.[147] MD Anderson also went on a building spree. One of the buildings was entirely dedicated to housing administrators. It was in the shape of a ship. The rationale was that many of the administrators were currently housed in leased space, so this would be a money saver. The alternative of reducing the number of administrators was not considered. New research buildings sprouted as well. Some faculty diagnosed Mendelsohn as having an edifice complex.

Our group applied for a $4,000,000 grant to support cancer gene therapy research from the W. M. Keck Foundation, which supported outstanding science, engineering, and medical research and, in Southern California, arts and culture, education, health, and community service projects. Our group received the award contingent on MD Anderson providing matching funds, to which Mendelsohn agreed. I quickly found out that Mendelsohn's interpretation of matching meant that I was to match the funding, not the institution. Fortunately, our grant record had been stellar, with my involvement with over $100,000,000 in extramural funding to MD Anderson. The following year, I met with Mendelsohn to discuss our progress with the Keck funding and presented him with a large binder of publications and progress reports. He waved it off with the comment that he did not have time for details. Another Mendelsohn characteristic was his ability to sleep at any given time. I recall a program presentation from epidemiology where he was awake for perhaps five minutes. Finally, one of his assistants tapped him on the shoulder to wake him at the end of the presentations.

One of the perks of being president of MD Anderson is the high level of visibility in Houston and the desire of companies and organizations to have your involvement, which can serve as an imprimatur of integrity and excellence. In 1999, Mendelson joined the board of Enron and became chair of its audit committee, overseeing the company's relationship with its auditor, Arthur Andersen, and the accuracy of financial statements.[147] After the Enron collapse, questions and concerns about Mendelsohn's involvement emerged in the press. Mendelsohn did not have the expertise to serve on the audit committee, and he and the committee failed to recognize the sleight of hand that went into disguising the Enron losses. How could he voice concerns to Lay, who was a generous contributor to MD Anderson?

But then the second shoe dropped loudly. When Mendelsohn was head of the cancer center at the University of California, San Diego, he had discovered work in Gordon Sato's laboratory on an antibody to block the epidermal growth factor receptor, which played a role in stimulating cancer cell growth.[148] The creator of the antibody was Gordon H. Sato, a cell biologist at UC San Diego. An article in the New York Times stated, "Erbitux is most closely linked with Dr. John Mendelsohn, president of the M. D. Anderson Cancer Center in Houston. Dr. Mendelsohn's reputation rests largely on the development of the drug and related work in controlling cancer cell growth. But the creation of what became Erbitux occurred in Dr. Sato's laboratory at the University of California at San Diego, where both he and Dr. Mendelsohn were professors."[148]

"The thing is, he was a member of my team," Dr. Sato said. "It was my team that developed the antibody and had the idea." Dr. Mendelsohn, he said, "came by the lab, got interested, and joined in." I tried to collaborate with Mendelsohn, and the antibody was used in our laboratory in several experiments to see its effect on lung cancers that expressed the epidermal growth factor. I did not see any therapeutic effects of the antibody and gave up testing it. It was not a good drug, and although it eventually received FDA approval, its use was very limited. A recent study showed that cetuximab (Erbitux) was inferior to the chemotherapy drug cisplatin when combined with radiation therapy for the treatment of oral cancer.[149] It is currently combined with chemotherapy to treat metastatic colon cancer with a nonmutated KRAS gene. The breakthrough in targeting the epidermal growth factor came with small molecules that bound the receptor, blocking its function, such as gefitinib and osimertinib. These drugs only worked in a small proportion of cancers that had an activating mutation in the epidermal growth factor receptor.

Mendelsohn eventually found a company called ImClone to continue clinical trials with cetuximab. The ImClone CEO was Sam Waksal, whose checkered past was well documented.[150] It was surprising that Bristol-Myers Squibb signed a two-billion-dollar agreement to market the drug when, shortly thereafter, the FDA did not accept ImClone's drug application. The stock price cratered, triggering an insider selling scandal that entrapped Waksal and Martha Stewart, among others. Mendelsohn was not implicated in insider trading but did benefit from a previous sale of his ImClone stock to Bristol-Myers. These events resulted in a review of the conflict-of-interest (COI) policies at MD Anderson. The COI police once again pointed to the evils of scientists being involved with pharmaceutical companies and managed to enact draconian COI policies that further impeded research progress. Mendelsohn had not done anything illegal and had disclosed all his financial relationships, which is the essential requirement for COI compliance. But the optics of the situation were poor, and it was unfortunate that these scandals were associated, even if peripherally, with MD Anderson.

Now, after two years of gaining approvals and setting up our production facility at Baylor, the first patient was entered into our TUSC2 nanovesicle systemic gene therapy clinical trial on May 5, 2003, three years after the initial approval of the clinical trial. The GMP documentation was prepared by a company called Integrity for a cost of about fifty thousand dollars. The first patient had metastases from lung cancer that grew after surgery, chemotherapy, and treatment with another investigational drug. His cancer stopped growing after treatment with the TUSC2 gene therapy and did not grow for another seven months until after the gene therapy was stopped since the protocol limited patients to six doses.

26
AN UNEXPECTED EVENT

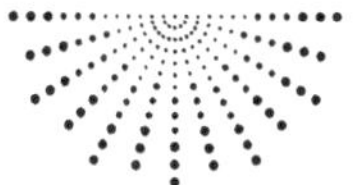

No one is so brave that he is not disturbed by something unexpected.
—Julius Caesar

John Cameron, the director of surgery at the Johns Hopkins School of Medicine, was stepping down. I had received a call asking if I would be interested in being considered for his position. Events had come full circle from my days as a Hopkins medical student. I was honored to be considered for a position previously occupied by William Halstead and Alfred Blalock, two of the founding fathers of modern surgical practice. I decided to accept the invitation. On April 14, 2002, I flew to Baltimore. During the following day, I interviewed with seventeen faculty members, including Ronald Peterson, the president of the Johns Hopkins Hospital and Health System. I ended the day with an hour-long meeting with the search committee. The position and resources were impressive, but I realized that taking such a position would involve a significant increase in administrative responsibilities while markedly reducing my ability to continue with research. I declined. The position was eventually taken by Julie Freischlag, a vascular surgeon from UCLA and the first woman to hold that title.

MD Anderson 2003 with Roy Herbst, Ritsuko Komaki, Ki Hong, visiting professor Everett Vokes, and the author.

Perusing the medical news during breakfast, my usual routine, I was astounded to see that on October 16, 2003, Shenzhen SiBiono GenTech (Shenzhen, China) obtained a drug license from the State Food and Drug Administration of China (SFDA; Beijing, China) for its recombinant adenovirus p53 gene therapy for head and neck squamous cell cancer (HNSCC), which accounts for about 10 percent of the 2.5 million annual new cancer cases in China.[151] What would unfold was a colossal intellectual property theft and an abysmal failure by Introgen and the FDA in the drug development process. In 1998, Zhaohui Peng, a Chinese researcher, set up a company called SiBiono to commercialize adenovirus p53 gene therapy which was named Gendicine. Although the patents for this were held by the US biotechnology company Introgen, no attempts were made to license the drug, acknowledge the intellectual property, or give credit to the scientists who developed the drug.[151]

SiBiono began randomized clinical trials in head and neck cancer patients in 2000. Adenovirus p53 combined with radiation therapy was compared to radiation therapy alone. When the trials were completed in 2003, the results showed that overall response rates and complete responses were statistically significantly higher in the group receiving adenovirus p53. The control of the local tumor was tenfold higher in the gene therapy group. The results of these clinical trials resulted in the China FDA drug approval. SiBiono never recognized the U.S. patents nor acknowledged the research our group had done. Introgen was considerably behind China in getting FDA approval, but this treatment approach received further validation in January 2004, when adenovirus p53 gene therapy was granted fast track designation by the FDA for the treatment of refractory head and neck cancers. Side effects were minimal. The International Society for Cell and Gene Therapy of Cancer organized a meeting in Shenzhen, China, where SiBiono was located, on December 9 to 11, 2005. The theme of the meeting was Gene Therapy in the 21st Century. I was invited to give a plenary lecture, which was titled P53 Gene Therapy—Concept to Clinic." Earlier, I flew to Hong Kong to visit a thoracic surgery colleague. Then I was driven to Shenzhen. The pollution was so dense that it was difficult to make out any of the surroundings. Our hotel was in a resort that was restricted for the use of Communist Party members only. When I checked in, I found the toilet in my room was not working, and finally, a maintenance man arrived to fix it.

The next day, I was introduced to Zhaohui Peng, the founder of SiBiono, the company that had pirated our technology. He looked embarrassed and would not look me in the eye. During my presentation, I mentioned that although p53 gene therapy was developed first in the United States, it was ultimately the Chinese who first gained drug approval, a comment met with stony silence in the mostly Chinese audience. A frequent response to the drug approval in China is "Well, that's China, and that would not be accepted by the US FDA." But this was refuted by Peng Shang, vice director of the cell engineering research center at the Fourth Military Medical University (Xi'an, China) in a commentary in Nature: "In fact, the SFDA had a routine practice not to approve any new kind of medicine if the kind of drug was not authorized by the US FDA," Peng Shang says. [151] Peng Shang had been lobbying the SFDA for years, and the agency gradually changed its approach, as shown by the approval of the new gene therapy and, on November 22, by giving a green light to clinical trials for a new SARS vaccine developed by Sinovac (Beijing).[151] Subsequent clinical trial data confirmed the efficacy of adenovirus p53 gene therapy. The results of these clinical trials were published in peer-reviewed high-impact English-language journals, further confirming their validity. Thirty clinical trials have been reported, to date, in addition to those conducted in the United States.

Adenovirus p53 gene therapy has benefited thousands of cancer patients over the past twenty years. More than thirty thousand patients, 10 percent of whom resided in one of more than fifty countries other than China, have been treated with Gendicine alone or in combination with chemotherapy and/or radiation therapies, and various other regimens. Overall, Gendicine treatment has produced 30 to 40 percent complete responses and 50 to 60 percent partial responses, with total response rates ranging from 90 percent to 96 percent in various clinical applications or studies, consistent with the results of the phase 2 and phase 3 clinical trials on Gendicine that formed the basis for approval.[152,153]Three additional randomized clinical trials in hepatocellular carcinoma, oral squamous cell carcinoma, and nasopharyngeal cancer have shown a statistically significant survival benefit when adenovirus p53 was added to standard treatment.[154-156] Positive clinical trials have been reported for cancers of the lung, breast, female reproductive system, liver and pancreas, esophagus, and colon.

On May 28, 2008, Introgen reported the results of the phase 3 clinical trial of adenovirus p53 in refractory head and neck cancer patients. In this clinical trial, HNSCC patients who had previously been exposed to platinum or taxane therapy in the recurrent disease setting were randomly allocated to receive either adenoviral p53 gene therapy (Advexin) or methotrexate (the control agent). Eligible patients in the phase 3 trial had histologically confirmed HNSCC with cytologically confirmed recurrence after first-line therapy administered with curative intent (at least 50 Gy of radiotherapy and/or surgery with or without initial chemotherapy). All patients were required to have had at least one prior platinum or taxane chemotherapy regimen. Thus, the patients had exhausted standard treatment and were heavily pretreated. The median survival of the adenovirus p53 gene therapy-treated patients was 6.1 months compared to 4.4 months for the chemotherapy patients, a 37 percent increase. This was a small clinical trial of only 123 patients total, so this difference in survival, although very large for a clinical trial, did not achieve statistical significance. It would take a trial of 200 patients or more for this difference to be statistically significant. This trial had been in progress for 7 years with multinational sites, but the patients who met the criteria for enrollment were scarce, and with Introgen running out of money, the only hope was to submit the results to the FDA.

A major finding of the clinical trial was the identification of biomarkers that could predict patients who would respond to p53 gene therapy. Biomarkers are useful in that, by testing, one can identify patients who will or will not have a probability of benefiting from a treatment. The biomarkers used in the study were simple: the presence or absence of p53 mutations and high or low levels of the p53 protein.[157]A statistically significant increase in tumor responses was observed for patients with favorable p53 efficacy profiles compared with those with unfavorable p53 inhibitor profiles in patients from the phase 1/2 trials—favorable (34 of 46, 74 percent) versus unfavorable (1 of 5, 20 percent)—which was validated in the patients from the phase 3 trial: favorable (17 of 24, 71 percent) versus unfavorable (2 of 11, 18 percent). In the phase 3 trial, there was a statistically significant increase in time to progression and survival following p53 gene therapy in patients with favorable p53 profiles compared with unfavorable p53 inhibitor profiles (median time to progression: 2.7 months versus 1.4 months; median survival: 7.2 months versus 2.7 months). This almost threefold increase in survival was exceptionally high for a clinical trial. In contrast, the biomarker profiles predictive of p53 gene therapy efficacy did not, as expected, predict methotrexate responses.

One of the most important findings was that the gene therapy had minimal side effects compared to the multiple side effects from the chemotherapy. In this phase 3 clinical trial, adenovirus p53 gene therapy had a superior safety profile compared to methotrexate. Methotrexate side effects can be life-threatening and more dangerous than the self-limiting side effects from gene therapy, including fever, chills, and injection site discomfort or pain. Common side effects from the study in methotrexate patients versus adenovirus p53 gene therapy patients are, respectively, as follows:

- Lymphopenia (abnormally low levels of lymphocytes): 25.6 percent versus 4.9 percent.
- Stomatitis (inflammation of the mouth lining): 12.7 percent versus 0 percent.
- Leukopenia (decrease in white blood cells): 12.1 percent versus 0 percent.
- Neutropenia (abnormally low level of neutrophils): 12.1 percent versus 3.1 percent.
- Pneumonia: 10.9 percent versus 1.6 percent

A patient death associated with methotrexate was reported, while no patient deaths were associated with gene therapy. The FDA notified the company that its biologics license application for Advexin (adenovirus p53) for the treatment of recurrent, refractory squamous cell carcinoma of the head and neck, submitted on June 30, 2008, was not sufficiently complete and would not be filed at that time. The company intended to appeal the refuse-to-file decision.[158] As the Introgen CEO was headed to New York to discuss a funding round with Lehman Brothers, the 2008 financial crisis unfolded. Introgen had run out of money, and with Lehman filing for bankruptcy, the former had no choice but to follow.

The tragic failure of adenovirus p53 to be approved in the United States, thus effectively denying its use to patients, can be attributed to the propensity of pharmaceutical companies such as Aventis to develop copycat drugs rather than innovate; the poor design of the registration clinical trial, where adenovirus p53 should have been combined with chemotherapy in the experimental arm and compared against a control of chemotherapy alone; Introgen's inability to enroll patients; the FDA for not providing a reasonable drug development pathway and ignoring data showing drug safety and efficacy; and the financial crash of 2008, which prevented Introgen from funding additional clinical trials. Ultimately, the patent issues with China and the lack of scientific recognition were of no consequence as, most importantly, the drug was ultimately approved in a country where thousands of patients had their lives prolonged by adenovirus p53 gene therapy.

A fascinating observation from the clinical trials was that some patients had dramatic responses, in some cases complete regression of their cancer, that must have exceeded the ability of the virus to enter every cancer cell. The answer to this conundrum was finally obtained by a Japanese surgical scientist who was one of our first postdoctoral researchers, working jointly with Liz and me, Toshiyoshi Fujiwara, now the chief of surgery at the Okayama University Hospital. His research group found that p53 gene therapy induced a long-lasting immune response to the cancer.[159] This theme would recur with our future TUSC2 gene therapy studies.

Adenovirus p53 was the first gene therapy approved for human use. Recently, an expert consensus panel for head and neck cancers stated, "At present, adenovirus p53, a novel gene therapy reagent, has been widely applied to treat HNSCC, and been proved safe and effective in clinical practice."[160] Despite the setbacks for gene therapy from the Gelsinger/Wilson event, gene therapy would make remarkable progress and become a fixture of medical care for cancer and many other diseases. As summarized by Zhang et al.:

> "In July 2012, nine years after adenovirus p53 approval, the second commercial gene therapy product, Glybera (AAV-lipoprotein lipase, alipogene tiparvovec), was approved by the European Medicines Agency. The third commercial gene therapy product, approved by the U.S. FDA on October 27, 2015, was Imlygic (talimogene laherparepvec), a recombinant herpes simplex virus type 1 carrying the effector gene of granulocyte-macrophage colony-stimulating factor for the treatment of melanoma. On August 30, 2017, the U.S. FDA approved two chimeric antigen receptor (CAR) T-cell therapies (ex vivo gene therapy). The first of these was Kymriah (CTL019, tisagenlecleucel) for the treatment of relapsed or refractory B-cell acute lymphoblastic leukemia in pediatric and young adult patients. The other, Yescarta (axicabtagene ciloleucel), was approved on October 18,

> 2017, for the treatment of adult patients with certain types of large B-cell lymphoma who did not respond to or who relapsed after at least two other kinds of treatment. Most recently, on December 19, 2017, the U.S. FDA approved Luxturna (voretigene neparvovec), an adeno-associated virus (AAV)-based gene therapy for patients with vision loss due to confirmed biallelic RPE65-mediated inherited retinal disease."[152]

Based on this activity in the international medical research community, it is apparent that adenovirus p53 gene therapy ushered in a new era.[152] But the use of viruses to deliver genes remained problematic. The virus based drugs were difficult to reliably produce for clinical use. They caused immune reactions that could be severe. It was difficult to deliver repeated doses because of the immune response neutralizing the virus. There was a critical need to develop an entirely new way to deliver genes to cancer cells. And now a clinical trial of the nonviral lipid nanovesicle TUSC2 gene therapy for lung cancer was about to begin.

27
BEYOND

One coincidence is just a coincidence, two coincidences are a clue, three coincidences are a proof.

—attributed to Agatha Christie

I need to backtrack a bit, as I have gotten ahead of myself with all the events surrounding adenovirus p53 gene therapy. I thought it best to present the entire sequence of events and all the resulting advances, as they could be confusing and fragmentary if written chronologically, interspersed with other events. The year 2004 was unusual, as there were several major international trips for Liz and me together, and our younger daughter was graduating from upper school and would be off to college soon. I received word that I would be honored by my alma mater, Johns Hopkins University School of Medicine. A renowned philanthropist, Evelyn Glick, was establishing an honorary lectureship. I was selected as the inaugural Evelyn Grollman Glick Lecturer in Thoracic Surgery. I lectured on Targeting Thoracic Cancers. Afterward, I attended a dinner with Hopkins faculty hosted by one of my first research fellows, Steve Yang, who was now chief of thoracic surgery at Hopkins.

Once again, there was an upper school graduation to celebrate. As

K was both a violinist and pianist, there were musical events to attend. K had a longtime friend who was a violist. They decided to give a farewell recital featuring solos and duets. Writing this and opening the video of their recital, I am struck by how accomplished they both were. K would matriculate at Wellesley College, where, surprisingly, she would major in violin performance, although, ultimately, she would not become a professional musician but pursue a career in oncology.

Liz planned to attend an International Nitric Oxide meeting in Nara, Japan, in May, so I arranged a special one-day symposium to celebrate the opening of the Center for Cell and Gene Therapy in Okayama, which Toshi Fujiwara, our previous joint research fellow who is now Chief of Surgery at Okayama University, was supervising. This turned out to be an international symposium attended by the dean of the university and the head of the prefecture. I also presented a lecture at Kyoto University on our gene therapy research. Both of our daughters traveled with us, which provided an exceptional opportunity to see three beautiful and historical Japanese cities: Nara, Okayama, and Kyoto. We had a splendid visit with Toshi, his wife, Keiko, and their two daughters. Toshi was an exceptional host, providing tours of historic sites and multicourse Japanese feasts. We recovered from all this by spending three days in Maui when returning from the meetings.

Liz and I received invitations to attend the 5th Princess Chulabhorn International Science Congress in Bangkok, Thailand, Evolving Genetics and Its Global Impact, August 16 to 20, 2004. This was an exciting opportunity, as neither of us had traveled to Thailand previously. The program included a lengthy list of prominent scientists, including Harold Varmus, Inder Verma, and Harald zur Hausen. Princess Chulabhorn of Thailand, the Princess Srisavangavadhana, is a princess of Thailand, the youngest daughter of King Bhumibol Adulyadej and Queen Sirikit, and the younger sister of King Vajiralongkorn, the current king of Thailand.[161] She has a doctorate in chemistry, is involved in the promotion of scientific research, and regularly gives awards and prizes. She held the position of guest lecturer in chemistry at Mahidol University. She also serves as president of the Chulabhorn Research Institute. She had been a postdoctoral fellow with Fred Becker, a former MD Anderson vice president for research, and it was Fred who recommended us as speakers.

This also provided an opportunity to see one of the great archaeological treasures of the world, the Angkor Wat Temple complex in Cambodia. We stayed at the Raffles Hotel, a beautiful and elegant hotel from the colonial period. We had a private tour guide and spent several days touring the Hindu-Buddhist temple complex, built in the twelfth century, which is the largest religious structure in the world according to Guinness World Records.[162] Then it was on to Bangkok for the congress. Bangkok was vibrant and teeming with people. The congress had many interesting talks and provided an opportunity to network with other scientists. We toured the impressive temple district and had a dinner cruise on the Chao Phraya River. I had heard of a men's bespoke tailor in Bangkok whose prices were very reasonable. I read that President George W. Bush and his Secret Service agents frequented Jesse and Victor Rajawongse. The secret agents were pleased that inside pockets could be tailored to fit their firearms. I visited the store and had some suits made for an incredible price. Jesse helped me and was meticulous in taking measurements and tailoring. The suits would be shipped to Houston.

The final trip for the year would be to Taiwan to speak at a meeting on pulmonary and critical care medicine. I spoke about our research on the genetic lesions in lung cancer and our treatment of esophageal cancer. All the international travel I had done in a relatively short time finally caught up with me. The evening before my first talk, my hosts took me to a traditional Taiwanese dinner, which included some strange dishes and too much alcohol. The following morning, I was ill. Fortunately, I had packed Imodium, which I took in large amounts, and by the time of my presentation, I was able to get through the hourlong talk without having a restroom break. I returned to Houston in time for the Houston Grand Opera production of Turandot, which I had never seen in a live performance. I wanted to spend more time with K before she left for Wellesley, so I took her to dinner, and then we both attended a performance.

In May 2003, the first patient was entered on the TUSC2 nanovesicle phase 1 clinical trial protocol. After six patients, it was discovered that there was a twenty-four-hour decrease in the absolute lymphocyte count, which was listed as a grade 3 adverse event. It turned out that some patients developed a fever immediately after receiving the intravenous infusion of the gene therapy. The medical oncologist Charles Lu, who was supervising the clinical trial, decided to pretreat patients with a steroid (Decadron) and Benadryl, which was a standard combination used to treat similar reactions in chemotherapy patients. He was inexperienced in phase 1 clinical trials and dealing with the FDA and had assumed that because this was standard for other drugs, he did not need to report the change in protocol to the FDA. This was a major lapse in judgment, which I should have picked up. Because this was not immediately reported to the FDA, as soon as they found out about it, the protocol was placed on clinical hold. This lasted for almost six months. There was no medical reason for this, but the FDA reviewer wanted to punish the investigators in some way.

Then in March, when the FDA finally allowed us to reopen the protocol, we were hit with another shock. Malcolm Brenner and the Baylor Cell and Gene Therapy Core informed me that I had a bill for $250,000, some three years after the original agreement to produce the first lot of drugs, for our share of the fermenter in producing the plasmid DNA. When I first discussed this with him, he was enthusiastic and collaborative and quoted a price of $50,000. I trusted him and sealed the agreement with a handshake rather than go through the process of drawing up a contract. I learned a valuable and expensive lesson. This resulted in a dispute that further delayed patient entry until August 2004. There was some good news: two of our patients in the lung cancer adenovirus p53 clinical trial had reached the five-year point for survival. Andy von Eschenbach, a urologist who had been chair of the department at MD Anderson, was appointed as the head of the National Cancer Institute by President George W.

Bush. Andy was a good friend and maintained an optimistic outlook on cancer research. Introgen wanted to keep him informed of the ongoing clinical trials, so I traveled to the NCI to visit Andy to discuss the impending approval of Advexin, along with David Nance and Bob Sobel from Introgen.

The International Association for the Study of Lung Cancer, which my predecessor, Cliff Mountain, played a major role in founding, had a world congress every two years (now annual) to showcase the results of clinical trials and progress in lung cancer research. On July 3–6, 2005, the IASLC World Conference was held in beautiful Barcelona. I was presenting several talks and, as a member of the board of directors, also attended planning sessions. I had heard rumors about a technique called stereotactic body radiation therapy that was curing early-stage lung cancer in clinical trials in Japan. My colleagues and I were skeptical, as radiation therapy up to that time was not very effective in curing lung cancer. However, the technology behind stereotactic radiation therapy was novel and very compelling.[163]

Stereotactic ablative radiotherapy (SABR), also called stereotactic body radiotherapy (SBRT), delivers high doses of radiation to a tumor in five or fewer fractions. The critical novel design is that multiple low-dose radiation fields are delivered from varying angles, which converge on the tumor. The dose distribution of radiation is fine-tuned so that the dose steeply falls a few millimeters beyond the tumor, thus sparing nearby normal structures from radiation damage. The five or fewer doses of radiation with SABR represent a dramatic change from traditional radiation therapy. Conventional radiotherapy may last up to six weeks. If the number of fractions is reduced so that the tumor receives a few large doses instead of many small ones, the tumor cells cannot repair the DNA damage, and the cancer cells die. In these cases, the radiation dose is said to be ablative. With the development of four-dimensional CT imaging, the tumor and adjacent tissues could be visualized across an entire respiratory cycle to avoid normal structures during all phases of breathing.

There were two presentations on SABR at the Barcelona meeting: one from Japan and the other given by Robert Timmerman, a radiation oncologist at UT Southwestern, both showing survival of early-stage non-small cell lung cancer comparable to what would be expected from surgery. These were astonishing results. Five or fewer radiation treatments given to an outpatient over a week could cure early-stage lung cancer without the risks, pain, discomfort, weeks-long recovery, and loss of lung function associated with surgery, which was the standard at that time. Progress had also been made in developing what was called minimally invasive surgery, where the surgery was done through very small incisions using a video camera and special instruments. However, a large portion of the lung was removed, and, in my experience, postoperative pain was still present. Overall, the differences in patient outcomes between standard thoracic surgery using an incision between the ribs and minimally invasive approaches were very small. Stereotactic radiation was noninvasive and preserved the patient's normal lung function, an important consideration as lung cancer patients frequently had reduced lung function due to smoking and the resultant emphysema. But the clinical trials reported were small and did not have a randomized control group treated with surgery. Was stereotactic radiation equivalent to surgical resection of early-stage lung cancer when compared in a rigorous randomized clinical trial? Ritsuko Komaki, a radiation oncologist and colleague at MD Anderson, was attending the presidential reception. We discussed initiating a randomized clinical trial to test this, and she was enthusiastic. Now we just needed to figure out how to fund this clinical trial and enroll enough patients. I did not anticipate how difficult this would be, nor the radiation therapy cooperative group politics that would obstruct our trial. It would be another three years before the trial began.

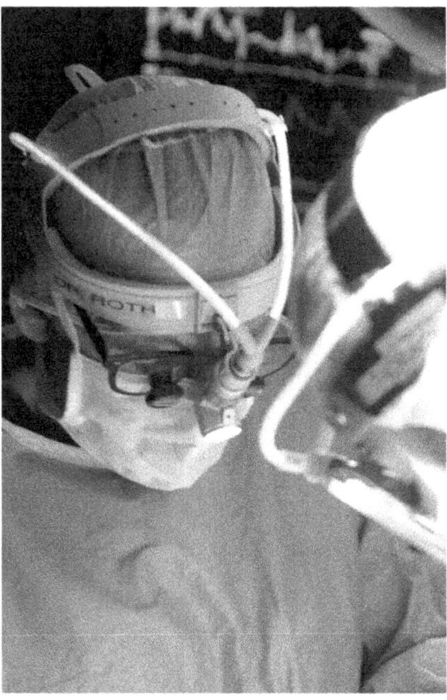

The author in the operating room.

Suddenly, it had been twenty years since I became chair of thoracic surgery at MD Anderson. This is an unusually long time in academic medicine for an administrator, but it did provide enough time to develop the premier department in thoracic surgical oncology. I had recruited and trained a group of thoracic surgeons who were outstanding and innovative, with technical excellence, compassion, empathy toward patients, and a focus on improving outcomes and the patient care experience. I had developed a training program with the new thoracic track that was developing thoracic surgeons, who were now assuming leadership positions in other institutions. Our research program had an unparalleled record of discovery, publication, and funding. Administratively, I had set up a smoothly running organization. Now, other interests that I had pursued throughout my life began to expand and take on more meaning and excitement. Research from my laboratory had developed an entirely new class of gene therapy drugs to treat cancer, which needed extensive development for production, clinical trials, and commercialization. Obtaining funding for our laboratory was becoming increasingly time-consuming. The stereotactic radiation therapy clinical trial could lead to a new standard of care for lung cancer patients that dramatically reduced side effects. However, that trial needed to be funded and completed.

Of all my activities, administration was one that I enjoyed least. Although building a department and mentoring trainees and faculty were enormously rewarding, there were many aspects of administration that were not enjoyable and could be stressful. The department chair position evolved into one where a person bore responsibility but had little authority. If a faculty member's professional or personal life was not going well, the department chair needed to provide guidance and sometimes was singled out as the responsible party for poor outcomes or decisions. Although most faculty members were personally and professionally a joy to work with, there were occasional instances of someone placing their personal goals above those of the department and employing backstabbing to advance themselves. Disloyalty was very disappointing to me, and I did not want to deal with these issues going forward. Oftentimes, this behavior was triggered by a life-altering event: divorce, alcoholism, professional disappointment, or life-threatening illness. These individuals would leave MD Anderson, but the process of dealing with them and the associated administrative issues took their toll.

Then there was the institutional administration. MD Anderson, although having the University of Texas in its name, was not a university. It did not have the depth and diversity of science departments that many universities possess, nor did it have a primary academic educational function. It was fundamentally a cancer center for treating cancer patients. Thus, clinical and laboratory research struggled to coexist with the overarching demands of clinical care. The need for financial stability had always been a priority. MD Anderson was a nonprofit institution, but operating losses threatened its ability to expand or even to exist. Mendelsohn recruited a chief financial officer from, as he stated, "the dark side," which referred to his background in for-profit hospital systems. Thus, the focus became seeing more patients, doing more procedures, all with fewer resources to reduce operating costs. This put pressure on the faculty and left little time for research. MD Anderson also took a risk-elimination approach to compliance issues rather than the more practical and less intrusive risk-management approach. This resulted in an ever-increasing number of mandates and training programs run by a cadre of over fifty attorneys. This was top-down administration, which I found antithetical to my academic mission and entrepreneurial spirit.

I had been chair of thoracic surgery for twenty years, which is a long time to be in an academic administrative position. It was important to bring in a new generation of leaders. It was also important to give me a break from the stress of administration so that I could pursue the clinical and laboratory research I loved. Now I had personal pursuits I wanted to explore in depth. Spending more time with my family was a priority. Liz and I had several travel destinations on our list. My passion for music was unabated, and I yearned to hear more live performances by both the symphony and opera in Houston and great performances around the world. I was a fitness buff and wanted to have time for my fitness routine and tennis. I had gotten into fitness when one of my college roommates commented on my lack of a physique and a need to start weightlifting. I began a regular routine of running, weight training, and stretching. I eventually began working with trainers and tennis coaches. I was in good shape and playing singles tennis three times a week and wanted to ensure I could continue. But most importantly, I could now spend more time on lung cancer research.

One year earlier, my father was diagnosed with a glioblastoma, a highly malignant brain tumor. He had stopped at a gas station to fill up the car, and my mother noticed he had difficulty computing and paying the bill. He had surgery to remove the tumor. He recovered well; however, because of his age, eighty-eight, no further treatment was given. He stayed with my mother and a caregiver in their apartment in Laguna Hills. He died on January 27, 2006. His work ethic, business savvy, and generosity enabled my career and those of his younger brothers and sisters. I could not have had a better role model.

28
MY NEXT ACT

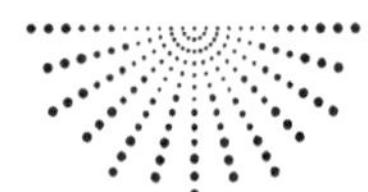

> The test of a first-rate intelligence is the ability to hold two opposing ideas in mind at the same time and still retain the ability to function.
>
> —F. Scott Fitzgerald

Like many preceding department chair searches, the search of the Department of Thoracic and Cardiovascular Surgery Chair was filled with sturm und drang. Searches seemed to go on for years, and this one was no different. Two of the final candidates, one from the University of Maryland and another from the Medical College of South Carolina, were clearly not good fits. One candidate alienated Mendelsohn by declaring he would show him how to run a multidisciplinary program and asked for twenty million dollars in startup funds. He either could not have been serious or was incredibly naive. A second candidate, frustrated by the length of time it took to put together an offer, pulled out because the final offer was too low. There was a vice president who oversaw these searches, but that individual had no understanding of clinicians, clinical affairs, or translational research. That vice president resigned shortly thereafter.

The above events were fortuitous, as they resulted in Steve Swisher being appointed chair of our Department of Thoracic and Cardiovascular Surgery in February 2007 after a search of almost two years, while I remained chair during this time, as it was felt an interim chair would not be appropriate. Steve was the right choice. I had recruited him as one of our first thoracic surgery track fellows, and because of his stellar performance, he remained a faculty member. He had trained at UCLA in general surgery and had taken two years for a surgical oncology research fellowship, which paralleled my career path. Steve was a superb surgeon, teacher, and researcher. Importantly, he possessed a high degree of emotional intelligence and was able to solve problems in a way that satisfied both parties. As soon as Steve took over, it felt as if a great weight I had been carrying was lifted. Now I could focus on patient care and research and leave the administrative problems to others. To celebrate, Liz and I flew to Athens and attended the 12th World Oncology Congress on the legendary island of Crete. We then returned to Athens to board a ship for a cruise to the Greek isles and Istanbul. It was a spectacular trip, visiting Santorini, Mykonos, Patmos, and Ephesus, where we had a candlelight dinner and concert in the ancient ruins of the library. Our trip concluded in Istanbul with visits to the Hagia Sophia and the underground Roman cisterns.

I favor predictability and routine in my daily life. I was totally unprepared for a telephone call I received one day in May 2007. It was from the Assistant Secretary in the United States Department of Defense. He wanted me to evaluate a high-value patient who had a lung tumor. I agreed, and he told me to expect more details in the future. Later that week I was instructed that I would be escorted to Hobby Airport to meet the patient. The day arrived. Several men in dark suits wearing dark glasses and earpieces arrived at my office. I was escorted to a car that whisked me off to the private aircraft terminal at Hobby. When I arrived, I saw a 747 with the U.S. Government logo parked close to the terminal. I entered a room with a large table and waited. After some time, the patient entered dressed in Arab garb with a small entourage and several agents. We exchanged cordialities, and then he proceeded to relate his story. He had developed a new cough and being a long-time cigarette smoker was concerned enough to see his physician who noted a nodule on his chest x-ray. We discussed what needed to be done and that I would schedule the tests required for his evaluation at MD Anderson including a biopsy. We were in for a shock. The biopsy returned with a diagnosis of small cell lung cancer. This is an uncommon subtype of lung cancer but highly aggressive and usually fatal within one or two years. Patients are treated with radiation and chemotherapy, but surgery is not usually recommended. I discussed this with the patient and his family and referred him to our medical oncology and radiation therapy team for treatment. He later decided to return to Tehran for further treatment. Although I did not know his identity at the time, I later found out he was the Head of the Supreme Islamic Iraqi Council in Iraq and a US ally. Unfortunately, he died on August 26, 2009. I received a personal letter from the Assistant Secretary of Defense expressing gratitude for my service.

The author was inducted as a Fellow of the American Association for the Advancement of Science (AAAS) in 2007 by Nobel Prize awardee David Baltimore

Now the unexpected occurred, but in a good way. I was never motivated by awards or prizes for scientific work. Saving lives was always the goal. But sometimes, recognition from peers is a welcome validation that other knowledgeable and esteemed scientists think you are on the right track. While traveling, I received an email that I was elected a Fellow of the American Association for the Advancement of

Science (AAAS). The notice was sent as a letter. I was inducted in the Section on Biological Sciences, and the list appeared in October 26, 2007, in the journal Science. The award letter cited my gene therapy work. I had joined this organization many years before because it strongly advocated for science in the United States and published one of the highest-level scientific journals. The fellows' program is described on the AAAS website:[164]

AAAS Fellows are a distinguished cadre of scientists, engineers, and innovators who have been recognized for their achievements across disciplines, from research, teaching, and technology to administration in academia, industry, and government, to excellence in communicating and interpreting science to the public. In a tradition stretching back to 1874, these individuals are elected annually by the AAAS Council. Newly elected Fellows are recognized for their extraordinary achievements at the ceremonial Fellows Forum, a time-honored event at the AAAS Annual Meeting where they are presented with a certificate and a blue and gold rosette. Eligible nominees are members whose efforts on behalf of the advancement of science or its applications are scientifically or socially distinguished and who have been continuous AAAS members for at least four years leading up to the year of nomination. Fellows have included Thomas Edison, W. E. B. Du Bois, Maria Mitchell, Steven Chu, Ellen Ochoa, and Irwin M. Jacobs.

Liz and the author at her induction as a Fellow in the AAAS in 2012.

Our eleventh-year SPORE competitive renewal was submitted before I left. News of a recent study section was not encouraging, with Hopkins, Colorado, and Dana-Farber all receiving unfundable scores. However, we would continue to receive SPORE funding and become the longest-funded SPORE. I needed to find a sponsor for our stereotactic radiosurgery versus surgery for stage 1 NSCLC trial, for which I had an acronym: STARS. Ritsuko Komaki and I had organized a symposium on stereotactic radiation therapy for lung cancer with both U.S. and Japanese clinicians to determine if a randomized clinical trial could and should be done. The symposium was affiliated with the International Association for the Study of Lung Cancer and was entitled Workshop on Stereotactic Radiation Therapy and Surgery for Stage I Non-Small Cell Lung Cancer, held in Maui in February 2006. The consensus was that a clinical trial was appropriate. Later that year, I had just finished speaking at a lung cancer meeting when I was approached by Omar Dawood, the head of clinical research for a company called Accuray, which manufactured units to deliver stereotactic radiation therapy. He was excited about the possibility of a clinical trial and would bring the concept back to his company.

Another positive event was that the FDA finally let us continue entering patients in the DOTAP: Chol TUSC2/FUS1 clinical trial. This gene therapy was given systemically by intravenous injection, unlike our adenovirus p53 gene therapy, which was directly injected into the tumor. The nanovesicle carriers for the gene were not targeted with antibodies or other proteins that could selectively bind to the tumor. Our group and others had shown in mice that the particles selectively trafficked to the cancer cells most likely because the blood vessels around the cancer were leaky. Also, we had shown that this specific type of lipid mixture was selectively ingested by cancer cells but not normal cells.[164] But did this happen in cancer patients? This was one of the critical questions I was attempting to answer. To answer this question, biopsies needed to be taken before and after treatment. This was not easy for patients, but fortunately many generously agreed to consent. Biopsies of the tumors were now available, and the important finding that TUSC2 gene expression was detected in the post-treatment specimen but not pretreatment was reported at that year's American Association for Cancer Research meeting, the first time anyone had shown gene transfer following intravenous injection.

The problems with this clinical trial seemed never-ending. All GMP manufacturing was successfully exported to MDACC. A vice president for clinical research met with our group to inform us that the gene therapy product now produced at Baylor did not meet his definition of GMP-grade, which the FDA required, even though I had paid fifty thousand dollars to develop this documentation. I was informed the clinical trial must stop, and no path forward was presented. I was taken aback by this and requested that an audit be done so that any deficiencies could be corrected. He agreed. They retained a reviewer, but it became obvious that this was a setup. The reviewer was primed to do a hatchet job, with so many perceived deficiencies that they could not be corrected. This entire scenario was representative of the risk-avoidance policies of MD Anderson as opposed to managing risk. Their goal was to stop the trial despite the potential for patient benefit. What could I do now?

I recalled that there was a GMP facility at MD Anderson that produced the stem cells given to patients with leukemias who needed a bone marrow transplant to treat their disease. But the facility had never produced a gene therapy drug. I met with Elizabeth Shpall, who was the head of the facility. She was interested in the clinical trial and offered to do everything possible to help restart it. Elizabeth became one of my most valuable collaborators. She worked with Nancy Templeton to train technicians and set up the documentation. On completion of a successful lot production meeting all specifications, this was presented to the administrators, who had no choice but to reopen the clinical trial, as everything was now produced in their GMP facility.

Accuray was a Silicon Valley startup founded by a neurosurgeon, John Adler, to develop a platform for delivering stereotactic radiation therapy. Stereotactic radiation had been primarily used for brain tumors, but adding imaging technology and the ability to correct for motion allowed it to be applied anywhere in the body. Accuray was eager to expand applications in lung cancer and announced our clinical trial. Varian, one of the largest companies making equipment for the delivery of radiation therapy, and the Radiation Therapy Oncology Group (RTOG), a cooperative group overseeing many clinical trials, were upset. However, I had previously contacted both groups, and they had declined to participate.

I traveled to Boston to see K. She was majoring in violin performance and writing her senior thesis on Alban Berg, a composer of the Second Viennese School; she was also preparing his violin concerto for performance. The Boston Symphony Orchestra was performing the Berg concerto with James Levine conducting and the incredible violinist Christian Tetzlaff, whom I had heard in recordings but had never seen live in performance. The performance was beautiful and passionate, and Tetzlaff played an unaccompanied Bach piece for an encore. This was followed by an inspired reading of Mahler's ninth symphony. K had contacted Tetzlaff, and he graciously met her for lunch. We then attended his master class at the New England Conservatory. We visited J for Thanksgiving, and Liz left for Paris for a scientific presentation.

It was December, and 2007 was ending. Introgen completed its European filing for approval of Advexin in Li-Fraumeni, which was accepted. I located nine head and neck specimens for immunostaining for p53, which is crucial for biomarker determination and eventual drug approval, despite Clayman saying they did not exist. They were hidden away in a secret tissue bank. Once again, I would need to be involved in what seemed to be interminable negotiations with the NIH. I had submitted an SBIR grant with Introgen over a year and a half ago. This started out as a small business technology transfer program. It scored well, but we were advised by Min Song, the NCI program administrator, to convert it to a small business innovation research grant. We encountered a bureaucrat named Ted Williams. He wrote endless emails over eighteen months asking for countless changes and documents, resulting in an audit of Introgen by the Small Business Administration, eventually confirming that it was a small business, which should have been obvious merely by looking at its financial statement. After all of this, we had a conference call scheduled. Min Song wrote an email that the aims changed and too many months had passed since the grant was submitted. Finally, we persuaded them to remove their objections for this $150,000 grant, and it was awarded. The MD Anderson bureaucracy was equally cumbersome and just setting up a simple sponsored research agreement, which would bring millions of dollars into the institution coffers, was finally completed after eighteen months of back-and-forth.

As our research gained more notoriety, offers for collaboration became commonplace. Dr. Naomi Halas, the Stanley C. Moore Professor in electrical and computer engineering, professor of biomedical engineering, chemistry, and physics at Rice University, and the founding director of the Rice University Laboratory for Nanophotonics and the Smalley-Curl Institute, was working with gold nanoparticles, which had some unusual properties. These could be targeted to cancer cells with monoclonal antibodies. In collaboration with Naomi Halas, we linked small interfering RNAs (siRNA), which can stop the expression of specific proteins coded by the RNA to the particles and then released the RNA with near infrared laser pulses.[165]

On December 20, 2007, Introgen sent out a press release stating that it would not be filing a biologics license application (BLA) with the FDA for Advexin. The stock price immediately plunged over 30 percent. Unfortunately, Introgen had only one year of operating funds remaining. The reason for the delay was that additional histologic sections from the cancers of head and neck patients treated with Advexin needed to be located for further analysis of the clinical trial results. This could improve the odds of a significant survival difference by including biomarker analysis. It was time for a break from this bad news, and so, with both girls home, we were off to Telluride for ten days of skiing.

Introgen stock had been on a downward spiral since the release of the phase 3 clinical trial results for adenovirus p53 in head and neck cancer patients (the clinical trial and results are described in Chapter 26). The FDA betrayed the company by not accepting the BLA and sending it back as incomplete. Although all the conditions for data analysis were approved by the FDA and the data met the prespecified conditions, it still rejected the application. Bob Sobol, John Nemunaitis, and I worked for several months on a manuscript summarizing the data. This was reviewed by the best investigators in the field, including Arlene Forestiere, Everett Vokes, Carol Prives, David Sidransky, and Bert Vogelstein, all of whom were excited by the data.[157] David Nance was in New York to discuss another funding round with Lehman Brothers. The stock market had crashed, and with the financial crisis, Lehman Brothers filed for bankruptcy. The application was accepted by the EMEA (the EU equivalent of the FDA), but Introgen could not continue because of its inability to raise capital during the financial crisis.

The good news was that I completed two new major contracts. Over three years ago, at the IASLC World Congress, I had the idea for a randomized clinical trial to compare stereotactic radiation therapy to surgery for stage 1 lung cancer. I worked with Drs. Ritsuko Komaki and Joe Chang but could not convince the cooperative groups to sponsor this trial. Finally, Accuray, which made the CyberKnife, agreed to fund the trial. The contract took a year for MD Anderson to approve. This involved six administrators who did not communicate with me or with each other. Every time the contract neared completion, some objection would be raised. Finally, after numerous calls, the contract was signed.

Our nanoparticle-FUS1 clinical trial continued with doses so high that we exhausted the supply of DNA with the gene (plasmid). Our GMP facility at MD Anderson could mix the lipid and gene together but could not produce the gene DNA. I arranged for Larry Couture at City of Hope to produce this, as they had a GMP facility that had FDA approval. However, once again, the contract required lawyers from both institutions to negotiate. Then one of the MD Anderson administrators became involved with some regulatory issues and almost torpedoed the contract at the last minute, requiring an urgent call to the Institutional Review Board chair Ralph Friedman, who fortunately was helpful and approached issues with common sense so the production moved forward.

I was honored to be elected to the board of directors of the International Association for the Study of Lung Cancer (IASLC). There were several meetings each year, some at international locations, which required extensive travel. One weekend, fortunately, was a short flight to the IASLC BOD meeting in Chicago. The previous weekend was spent at the NCI Translational Research meeting, which presented pathways for translational research and poster presentations by senior investigators.

29
A NEW BEGINNING

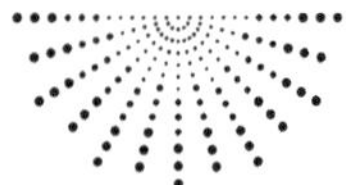

Success is not final. Failure is not fatal. It's the courage to continue that counts.

—Winston Churchill

A surprise—each year, MD Anderson had a series of endowed awards for excellence. I was notified that I received the Faculty Achievement Award in Clinical Research, which would be presented at the Faculty Honors Convocation. I needed to write an acceptance speech, and as I thought about my approach, I realized that whatever I was receiving the award for needed a large team of dedicated individuals committed to a common goal of vanquishing cancer. Many researchers in the laboratory contributed to the mechanistic studies that formed the scientific basis for the clinical trials. Clinical trials required a large staff, including nurses to consent and treat patients and those who obtain and process tissue for research. Our clinical trials were multidisciplinary, and my speech acknowledging contributions of many department faculty and support staff was well received. The presentation was on November 20, 2008. Bob Bast, who was then vice president for translational research, presented me with the award. He gave a very kind introduction, listing our clinical trial accomplishments. Later he apologized as he never mentioned I was a surgeon.

Following the collapse of Lehman Brothers, it was announced that Introgen was restructuring, retaining only fifteen of forty-five employees and focusing on Introgen Technical Services. Some of the intellectual property was sold, and this presented an opportunity to form a new company.

J was now in law school at Tulane, and K had a research fellowship at the Tulane School of Medicine. They were sharing a rented condominium in New Orleans. November 24 was Liz's birthday, and November 25 would be our thirtieth wedding anniversary, so Liz and I visited them and celebrated Thanksgiving. We went to some excellent restaurants, including August, played golf, and had dinner at J and K's condominium.

A technology that Introgen sold but had never developed was the TUSC2 nanovesicle gene therapy, which had appeared to be very promising in experiments in mice with human lung cancer. In early 2009, David Nance, who helped found Introgen, met with me to see if I had any interest in establishing a new company to develop TUSC2 gene therapy. The state of Texas had a fund called the Texas Emerging Technology Fund (ETF) that provided seed funding for startup companies. The application was prepared and submitted with David Nance. On April 30, we went to meet with the Life Sciences Committee in Austin to give a presentation called a quick pitch. We asked for $3.5 million. The committee approved us for further consideration.

There were reviews by the Texas Life Science Center, along with due diligence. Projects could be eliminated at any time; ours remained in the running. Next, we presented to a section of the Life Sciences Board in June for about two hours. Their initial disapproval was rescinded because of some conflicts of the board members who were with competing companies. We survived these reviews and then presented to the entire Life Science Board on July 15, 2009, in Austin. Progressing past Life Science Day, we presented on the Statewide Presentation Day on July 23, 2009, in Austin. At that time, all the life science and non-life science companies from across the state presented to members of the governor's committee. Decisions were made that day, but it was not over yet. The entire committee of seventeen met on August 6, 2009, and came to a consensus on which deals to fund. We just needed to be available by phone on that day. The committee approved our company to go into due diligence, with the governor's office providing us the opportunity to complete all the due diligence documents required. The next step was for the governor (Rick Perry), lieutenant governor, and speaker to review and sign off on all deals. Our company, called Convergen at that time but later renamed Genprex, was approved for the full $3.5 million. Finally, a contracting procedure needed to be completed, and the funds were partially released.

J completed her final law school exams and graduated on May 18. She had a steady boyfriend whom she met when they were vacationing in Telluride. He was a graduate of the University of Florida and thought he would go into construction and development like his father, who was a civil engineer. They both decided to apply to law school, and they both spent the summer working in D.C. He was now graduating from law school at Emory and had a position with Shutts and Bowen in Miami, which is the oldest law firm in Florida and had been attorneys for Flagler and Vanderbilt as they constructed the first railroad to Florida. J graduated from law school at Tulane at the same time.

I was at my desk on the final day of June 2009, deep in thought reviewing some data from the laboratory, when my office telephone buzzed (landlines were still common). "Have you ever seen a complete metabolic response for patients on your gene therapy clinical trial?" I was speechless for a moment. It was Dr. Faye Johnson, a lung cancer medical oncologist, who had entered several patients in our clinical trials. "No," I replied, although we had entered fewer than thirty patients in this clinical trial. "Well, I have one," she said. The patient, M, was a fifty-four-year-old female with large-cell neuroendocrine cancer of the lung, one of the most aggressive lung cancers. She had received six prior chemotherapy regimens. She had liver and pancreas metastases. The liver metastases began growing while she was receiving a drug called gemcitabine. She was the twenty-seventh patient to receive the TUSC2 gene therapy, and now all her metastases had disappeared on the PET scan. M lived with her husband in Venezuela. She was initially reluctant to enroll in the gene therapy trial because of the need for injecting the drug at three-week intervals. “When the chemotherapy quit working, I was ready to do whatever was needed to beat the cancer,” she said, as reported in the MD Anderson Conquest magazine (vol. 24, pp. 16–19, 2010). Now, a year later, she commented, “They call me their miracle patient. I’m very grateful to the scientists whose research led to this drug. It has stopped the cancer, giving me precious time to travel with my husband, play with my granddaughter and enjoy life.” The concept of an effective anticancer drug that did not interfere with quality of life now seemed attainable. Thirty patients were entered in the phase 1 TUSC2 gene therapy clinical trial. The investigators met with our biostatistician, Jack Lee, and determined the maximum tolerated dose to be 0.06 mg/kg. We were now able to enroll patients on an expansion cohort. The overall toxicity was minimal. We had to accept the grade 3 hypophosphatemia (low serum phosphorus) as dose-limiting, even though this was easily correctable.

The year 2009 was ending. For Thanksgiving, Liz and I visited J and her now-fiancé in Miami and had dinner in their condo. They had both passed the Florida Bar exam in October. We stayed on Fisher Island, which was only accessible by ferry. The island was very secluded, with a pristine beach and harbor. We stayed at the inn, which was formerly the Vanderbilt estate, and had the opportunity to play tennis at the local club. I helped shop for J’s wedding gown. Liz and I welcomed New Year 2010. The next day, we met with J, her fiancé, and his mother to begin plans for the wedding, which would be held in Fort Lauderdale. Now that I had jettisoned much of my administrative responsibilities, I could take a little more personal time. Liz and I decided to take another cruise on January 5 to 21, from Ft. Lauderdale to Cartagena, Colombia; Puerto Caldera, Costa Rica; Puerto Quetzal, Guatemala; Acapulco, Mexico; Cabo San Lucas, Mexico; and Los Angeles, sailing through the Panama Canal. The Panama Canal locks are an engineering marvel. There are electric towing locomotives that operate on cog tracks on the lock walls, which kept our ship centered in the lock. It was an amazing journey. After debarking in Los Angeles, we flew to Ft. Lauderdale for the Society of Thoracic Surgeons meeting. Once ski season was upon us, we were off to Telluride. One of my professors from UCLA Surgical Oncology who mentored me as both a research fellow and resident, Fred Eilber, had built a house in Telluride. Liz and I skied with him each year. This year, my thoracic surgery colleague from MD Anderson, Wayne Hofstetter, and his wife, Rosa, joined us for some great skiing, including some black diamonds.

On May 3, our fellow, Min Kim, had a presentation at the American Association for Thoracic Surgery, the most prestigious annual meeting for our specialty. He observed that a protein called AP2, which regulates endocytosis, the taking up of external matter by the cell, is a predictor of poor survival in lung cancer in early-stage patients.[166] I was a member of the Scientific and Government Affairs Committee meeting, where we discussed the new NCI director Harold Varmus and his potential impact on funding for lung cancer research.

Then it was off to Shanghai because I was invited to speak at the Chinese Conference of Oncology, the largest oncology meeting in

China, from May 19 to 24. I stayed at the Regal International East Asia, which was a very comfortable hotel. I met with representatives from Ruikang, Tianjin, and Nanjing about the STARS protocol to encourage them to become part of the study and enroll patients. We needed many sites to enroll patients, but it turned out that Chinese surgeons were not enthusiastic about participating in this study. Dr. Haiquen Chen, chief of thoracic surgery at Fudan Cancer Center, was a colleague and friend. He graciously took me on an extensive sightseeing tour in Shanghai. I saw EXPO, a large world fair-like exhibition, and went on a river cruise, to a museum, and to the tallest building, the Shanghai World Financial Center. The return trip involved a nineteen-hour flight in one direction with a stop in Newark. On my return, I received an email on June 23 from David Nance that the Emerging Technology Fund Grant was funded for $4.5 million. Now we only needed to resolve conflict of interest guidelines, set up milestones and deliverables for the second segment of funding, and put a monitoring plan in place to finally get the funding. Fortunately, this was all completed expeditiously.

There was no happier occasion than the wedding of my older daughter on November 6. She and her husband were practicing law in Miami. They chose Bonnet House Museum and Gardens in Fort Lauderdale as their wedding venue:[167] "Chicago-born artist Frederic Clay Bartlett created Bonnet House in 1920 on South Florida oceanfront land given to him and his second wife, Helen Louise Birch, by her father, Hugh Taylor Birch, a prominent Chicago attorney, real estate investor, and naturalist." The house was preserved as it was originally built on beautiful grounds and was filled with art. The rehearsal dinner was at the Ritz-Carlton. Many of my family could attend, including my mother and cousin Maury Levine, my father's business partner, and a cousin I grew up with in La Porte, Mark Jacobi. Our paper on combination therapy with AZD6244 and MEK2206 was published in PLoS One showing synergistic effects of the two drugs on lung cancer cell death when the MEK and AKT pathways are both inhibited.[168]

Mendelsohn announced he would step down as president of MD

Anderson. He and Gordon Mills were taking over the newly created Institute for Personalized Cancer Therapy after a long search process. Ki Hong was initially chosen to head this institute, but he gave an ultimatum that he would not be involved unless more financial resources materialized. They did not, and Mendelsohn stepped in to fill the void. The first half of Mendelsohn's tenure as president was productive, primarily due to an increase in building activity, record fundraising, and stability in the financial status of the institution. The second half of his presidency began with the Enron and ImClone scandals, which brought unfavorable publicity. Mendelsohn was never charged with any wrongdoing, although incompetence in recognizing the problems at Enron was evident. Although he did not pay any money personally in the settlements with shareholders, he was covered by a thirteen-million-dollar payment, to which another former MD Anderson president, Charles LeMaistre, personally contributed. These events created a diversion and cast a long shadow on the second half of his presidency.

Interaction with the faculty became more confrontational. The University of Texas Regents' Rules specified that institutions required a faculty governance body. Under LeMaistre's presidency, the faculty senate was created. However, this group of faculty elected by their peers had no real administrative authority. It functioned more like a faculty conscience and seemed to be in perpetual conflict with MD Anderson administrators. An example of this occurred in early 2002 when The Institutional Review Board (IRB) routinely conducted audits of ongoing clinical trials. Two clinical trials had been audited in the leukemia department because of complaints, and then sanctions were made without the investigators having the opportunity to defend themselves. The executive committee of the science faculty and the faculty senate then asked for clarification of the policies and procedures in place related to the IRB and the Office of Research Administration for clinical trial audits. The committee members met with Mendelsohn, who was supported by his management committee. The meeting began with Mendelsohn calling the name of each individual member of the executive committee and handing them a confidential letter addressed to them, indicating how important the IRB was and that they could not interfere with it. The letter reprimanded each individual member of the executive committee for attempting to "initiate an inappropriate and illegal investigation." The conclusion of the letter stated, "Any future participation by you in an activity of the ECFS that is illegal or inappropriate will force me to take disciplinary action." Nothing ever came of this, but it was a prime example of the top-down administrative structure and the adversarial relations between faculty and administration. We hoped that a new president would institute a more enlightened approach, but the situation was going to get much worse.

30
ENTROPY—INCREASING DISORDER

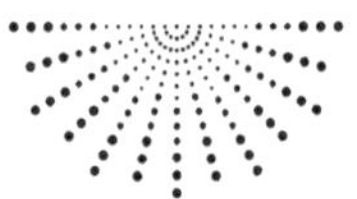

There is nothing supernatural about the process of self-organization to states of higher entropy; it is a general property of systems, regardless of their materials and origin. It does not violate the Second Law of thermodynamics since the decrease in entropy within an open system is always offset by the increase of entropy in its surroundings.
—Ervin László

The year 2011 was off to a challenging start. I was a member of the NCI review panel for the SPOREs, and the review was scheduled for January 27 to February 3 in Bethesda, Maryland. Although I had been tasked with being a primary reviewer, the chair of the session, Paul Bunn, a medical oncologist from the University of Colorado, had not made it in, so I was asked to chair the session. However, there was some wonderful news. Early that morning, as I was awakening from a noisy night in the local Marriott, I saw a text message on my phone to call K. She was accepted in the University of Texas Health Sciences Medical School in Houston. I congratulated her on all the hard work she had put in to achieve this milestone. The SPORE reviews had finally ended, but a snowstorm was coming into Washington, and there were storms in Houston. Miraculously, I got the last plane out of D.C.

The selection of a new president for MD Anderson required an extensive search process. Kenneth Shine, the University of Texas executive vice chancellor for health affairs, oversaw this search. There was a perception that although the cancer care at MD Anderson was first-rate, the science was not up to par. Of course, nothing could be further from the truth, as evidenced by the fact that MD Anderson had more highly competitive NCI SPOREs in translational research than any other institution. Nevertheless, it was rumored that Shine wanted a high-profile scientist to lead the institution instead of a physician with expertise in cancer care and administration. I was walking with Ki Hong, the head of the Division of Medicine, and we were chatting about possible candidates. Ki had an inside track when it came to information, and he said the leading candidate was Ron DePinho. I did a double take. He was a well-known basic scientist on aging but was not known for cancer research and had no experience running a complex cancer center.

In May 2011, DePinho was named the sole finalist for president, meaning that he would be offered the position, which he accepted.[169] DePinho had spent fourteen years at the Dana-Farber Cancer Institute in Boston. He served as founding director of the Belfer Institute for Applied Cancer Science and was an American Cancer Society Research Professor in the Department of Medicine (Genetics) at Harvard Medical School, as reported in the *Houston Chronicle* on March 27, 2016 (pp. A1, A20–21). In interviews during the search, DePinho told the University of Texas regents that he could create a drug discovery pipeline at MD Anderson that would provide a constant stream of revenue. He could attract top academic and research talent from New York and Boston and turn MD Anderson into a "top-notch scientific research institution." On his arrival at MD Anderson, he must have felt he needed to speak in terms understandable to Texans, so he declared, "We will kick cancer's butt!" But events spiraled out of control quickly. [170]

DePinho's wife, Lynda Chin, was appointed chair of a new department of genomic medicine. But a political bomb exploded when a biotech incubator that Chin codirected received a twenty-million-dollar, single-year grant from the Texas state funding agency for cancer research, CPRIT. That grant, which was the largest in the state agency's history up to that time, was awarded based on a six-and-a-half-page proposal that was submitted without review by MD Anderson provost Dubois (Cancer Letter, May 25): "This controversy triggered the resignation of Alfred Gilman from the position of CPRIT's chief scientific officer. Gilman, a Nobel laureate, said that Texas politics trumped science in the handling of the grant." Clinical departments at MD Anderson were required to increase their revenue targets by 5 to 10 percent, causing doctors to complain about increasing a grueling clinical workload to support basic research. But things were about to get worse.

As reported in the Cancer Letter (vol. 39, no. 34, Sept. 13, 2013), "'Buy AVEO Pharmaceuticals,' DePinho said during an appearance on 'Closing Bell with Maria Bartiromo' on May 18, 2012, plugging the company he and his wife, Lynda Chin, co-founded. Records obtained by The Cancer Letter show that on May 7—exactly 11 days before DePinho offered this ill-advised stock tip—Chin traveled to the Boston area to take part in a meeting of the AVEO Scientific Advisory Board as it prepared to present clinical data to FDA." But the FDA declined to approve AVEO's drug TIVO-1 because survival in the drug arm was lower than in the control arm of the clinical trial, and the stock price collapsed. DePinho's comment was a flagrant violation of conflict-of-interest guidelines and a colossal unforced error. There were more painful episodes to come. In 2014, DePinho went against the recommendations of the Promotion and Tenure Committee and denied tenure to three faculty members. Ultimately, the American Association of University Professors censured MD Anderson for its tenure policies. The work environment was described as toxic, and there was a pervasive fear about voicing any dissatisfaction or disagreement with the administration.

My primary interaction with DePinho was in the Moon Shot program. This was a positive development, as research funds from institutional philanthropy were channeled directly into translational research. Steve Swisher, John Heymach (Chair of Thoracic/Head and Neck Medical Oncology), and I organized the lung cancer Moon Shot program. Originally, the program was organized around organ disease sites (lung, colon, pancreas, ovarian, etc.). Each program proposal was presented to a review group made up of reviewers outside of MD Anderson. I suggested that for lung cancer, we needed to include prevention with our smoking-cessation program, targeted therapeutics, and target and drug discovery. This was eventually accepted as the program design. The Lung Cancer Moon Shot was favorably reviewed and became one of the initial MD Anderson Moon Shot programs. As I write this twelve years later, the Lung Cancer Moon Shot is still going strong. Important contributions include a smoking cessation program using pharmacologic interventions to improve quit rates and the development of a library of patient-derived xenografts (PDXs) numbering over two hundred, with extensive molecular characterization. PDXs are a valuable resource for identifying new drug targets and testing the drugs themselves. When a lung tumor is surgically removed, part of it is brought to the laboratory and implanted under the skin of mice with a defective immune system that allows human cancers to grow. Ultimately, about 40 percent of the tumors will grow, and these can be transplanted to other mice or frozen for future use. PDXs are excellent models for drug testing because they have not changed from the original lung cancer in the patient, unlike cancer cell lines, which may undergo changes over time as they are repeatedly passaged. Liz was asked to help oversee the science of the Moon Shot program. She was appointed chief scientific officer and director ad interim in the Moon Shot Office of Strategic Initiatives as a search for the permanent director was begun.

It is possible that DePinho would have survived these events, but under his watch, the institution began incurring large budget deficits, which were unforgivable to the University of Texas System. Chin continued to play a role in MD Anderson's collaboration with IBM Watson. An audit of that abandoned megaproject found that MD Anderson skirted the UT system's procurement regulations as it spent

$62.1 million on an ill-fated artificial intelligence system that never functioned as promised (Cancer Letter, Feb. 17, 2018). This, combined with deficits in the tens of millions each month, sealed DePinho's fate. He resigned on March 8, 2016. DePinho had only supervised a small research group, had no significant clinical experience in cancer care, and the behavior he exhibited was well known to all who worked with him at Harvard. Due diligence in vetting him simply ignored these obvious facts. Kenneth Shine resigned as well. Another presidential search was underway. This time, the outcome would be positive for the institution, leading to better faculty communication and engagement and the elimination of the budget deficits. The new search would culminate in Dr. Peter Pisters being named the new president. Peter was a good friend and surgical colleague. He was Canadian by birth and had interrupted his career at MD Anderson in surgical oncology to lead the University Health Network in Toronto, Canada. He now returned to emphasize clinical care and a servant leadership style. The financial condition and morale of MD Anderson dramatically improved under his leadership.

Despite the administrative turmoil, my day-to-day functioning at MD Anderson was relatively unchanged. Liz and I attended the annual AACR 2011 meeting, which was held in Orlando. The poster on the results from the TUSC2 gene therapy clinical trial from my laboratory received a highest score award at the meeting. Liz was reading the Harry Potter books, and this provided an opportunity to visit the World of Harry Potter in Universal Studios, which had just opened. The rides were entertaining. J's husband is a Jimmy Buffet fan, so we then had dinner with them at Jimmy Buffet's Margaritaville.

On May 12–14, 2011, we were in Nashville for the graduation of my uncle David's oldest son from Vanderbilt. K, J and many other family members were there. After graduation, he would be accepted to medical school and ultimately become an orthopedic surgeon specializing in hand surgery after a fellowship at Harvard.

The invitations to speak continued at an unrelenting rate. On May 27–29, a festschrift was held for Charles Balch in Baltimore. After his unsuccessful bid for the MD Anderson presidency, he served as president and CEO of the City of Hope National Medical Center (1996–99) and then as executive vice president and CEO of the American Society of Clinical Oncology (2000–05). He next went to Johns Hopkins School of Medicine, where he directed clinical trials and translational research. There were scientific presentations followed by a dinner and testimonials. Some of the after-dinner speeches were more roast than toast, with comments on his inability to stay at one job for very long. Currently, he has an appointment at MD Anderson in the Division of Surgery. Liz and I remain grateful to him for recruiting us to MD Anderson.

The IASLC World Lung Cancer Congress was held in Amsterdam on July 2–7. I discussed our experience with salvage surgery following radiation therapy as the primary treatment for lung cancer. I also discussed papers in a plenary session on centralizing thoracic surgery to centers in England. Next, on August 11–16 was a Lung Cancer Congress in Carlsbad, California, where I discussed mediastinal staging and difficult case presentations.

The family needed a break from the heat and humidity of Houston, so we were off to Telluride from August 19 to September 5. November was always filled with activities, especially around Thanksgiving, when we also celebrate Liz's birthday and our wedding anniversary. That year, we were joined by J and her husband, as well as Liz's sister and her husband, and their son. Liz and I capped off the year with a trip to Hawaii. We were invited to participate in a BAP1 symposium in Honolulu from December 1 to 10, hosted by Michele Carbone. There was an interesting association of BAP1 mutations with uveal melanoma and mesothelioma. Michele Carbone, in addition to being a distinguished physician-scientist, was an accomplished chef. He served homemade caponata, an eggplant-based classic Sicilian appetizer. It was so tasty that Liz wrote to him for the recipe when she returned home. We had a reunion with Paul Morris, our first thoracic surgery fellow at MD Anderson, who is now chief of surgery at Queen's Hospital.

The new year, 2012, began with another cancer conference. This one, held on January 6 to 8, was the AACR Lung Cancer meeting in

San Diego at the rather incongruous venue of the Hard Rock Hotel. Next was the Society of Thoracic Surgeons meeting, held on January 28 to 31 in Fort Lauderdale. J and her husband arrived to help celebrate my birthday at the East Asia Restaurant. I was surprised by singing waiters bearing a cake.

The more our laboratory studied the tumor suppressor gene TUSC2, the more surprises we uncovered. We reported that TUSC2 restoration in non-small cell lung cancer cells that had lost the expression of TUSC2 suppressed tumor growth by the induction of programmed cell death (apoptosis) and alteration of cell growth kinetics in vitro and in vivo through a regulatory protein, Apaf-1. In addition, evidence indicated that TUSC2 downregulated the activation of numerous tyrosine kinases, which convey important signals to the cell regarding cell division, including the epidermal growth factor receptor (EGFR).[171] Now a new class of small molecule targeted drugs had emerged that specifically bound to the EGFR. In the first large-scale clinical trials, the drugs had some marginal effect in unselected patients. Groups at the Massachusetts General Hospital, as Dana-Farber noted, found that one of this class of drugs (erlotinib) was only active in patients who had specific types of mutations in the EGFR, which represented only about 10 percent of lung cancers. When TUSC2 gene therapy was combined with erlotinib, which inhibited EGFR signaling, the lung cancers that were resistant with no mutations became sensitive. We restored TUSC2 gene expression in several non-small cell lung cancer cell lines with no mutation in EGFR that were resistant to erlotinib. A significant inhibition of cell growth was observed with TUSC2 transient and stable expression. TUSC2-erlotinib cooperativity in vitro could be reproduced in subcutaneous tumor growth and lung metastasis formation in lung cancer xenograft mouse models. Combination treatment with intravenous TUSC2 nanovesicles and erlotinib synergistically inhibited tumor growth and metastasis and increased cancer cell death in mice. For the first time, we showed that gene therapy could overcome resistance to a targeted drug.

These findings were so striking that the next step for me was the initiation of a clinical trial. A protocol was written, and then the long, arduous, and complex process of clinical trial protocol approval began. On February 13, our clinical trials group had a teleconference with the FDA. Only minor changes were required, including the addition of a lower-dose group to the initial Phase 1 dose-finding cohort. Because of my participation in the discovery and relationship with Genprex, the sponsor of the clinical trial, as a scientific adviser, I could not be the principal investigator nor have anything to do with managing patients in the clinical trial or determining their response to the drug.

Suddenly, I was blindsided by an unpleasant surprise. In my calls to Genprex as a scientific adviser, I had learned that MD Anderson was demanding a payment of five million dollars before it allowed our clinical trial to open. I was stunned, as I had never heard of such conditions being forced on a company or investigator. No one, however, seemed to know the details of where this mandate came from or how it was initiated. I spoke to Ki Hong, now the division head of medical oncology, who was very supportive of the trial. He had not heard anything about this and said he would try to obtain more information. Genprex was a small biotechnology company with very limited resources and could not afford to pay five million dollars to fund the clinical trial. Ki helped organize meetings with the clinical trials regulatory group, but again, no one took responsibility. One afternoon, Ki called me to his office and said, "Look at this." It was a letter to both of us from the provost, Raymond Dubois. The letter said we should cease and desist all inquiries into the five-million-dollar payment. Furthermore, because I was involved with Genprex, the administration could not determine whether I was advocating for Genprex or MD Anderson. This was the usual conflict-of-interest doublespeak. I, of course, was advocating for patients and trying to begin a clinical trial with a potentially life-saving therapy. Others, such as attorneys who dealt with MD Anderson, also dealt with companies associated with MD Anderson and acknowledged they wore two hats and could easily switch them. The real conflict was an institution trying to extract money and potentially sinking an important clinical trial. But Dubois went on to admonish Ki and me that any further inquiries would result in disciplinary action.

Dubois had lost to DePinho in the MD Anderson presidential race. Losing candidates were quickly decapitated, figuratively speaking, and exited the institution rapidly. The new president wanted to put their own team in place and did not want an unhappy rival lurking in the wings. I knew Dubois personally and called him to ask if I could meet to discuss the situation and offer my perspective. He said no. Understandably, Dubois was planning his exit, which likely triggered this excessive, intimidating, and unwarranted response. I tore up the letter and threw it in the trash receptacle. After that, the five-million-dollar payment demand mysteriously and completely disappeared and was never heard about again. These events had always been instructive to me, which is why I relate them in detail, hoping that future administrators will learn from them. This provided another example of how not to handle this type of situation administratively. I believe that subsequent MD Anderson administrators, from my observation of their reactions to similar issues, have learned this lesson.

Finally, the long process of thoracic medical oncology, IRB, biosafety committee, COIC, NIH RAC, and FDA approval for our TUSC2 combined with erlotinib clinical trial was complete. Although the complexity of the process had not lessened, this seemed to occur more rapidly than prior approvals. It appeared that our clinical trial would open smoothly after resolving these issues, but that was an illusion. Events were unfolding now that sent my laboratory research and clinical trials program descending into chaos. In October, I was informed that Genprex had used all the $4.5 million Emerging Technology Funds, and nothing was available to fund the clinical trial. I was shocked, as the clinical trial should have been the focus for Genprex. I immediately called David Nance, the Genprex CEO, and Rodney Varner, who handled the legal affairs for the company. It turned out that financial records documenting the detailed use of these funds could not be found. David Nance then had medical issues and ultimately completely disappeared. Rodney Varner assumed leadership of Genprex. Without funds from the sponsored research agreement, our laboratory could not continue our gene therapy research, and the clinical trial could not begin.

Then, with the beginning of the New Year, I was informed by Accuray in a letter dated January 28, 2013, that their support for the STARS clinical trial comparing stereotactic radiation therapy with surgery in early-stage lung cancer was ending. I was not surprised, as the entry of patients in this clinical trial was slow. Nevertheless, I could not think of a clinical trial more important for lung cancer patients, offering them a potentially curative nonsurgical treatment.

31
A WAY FORWARD

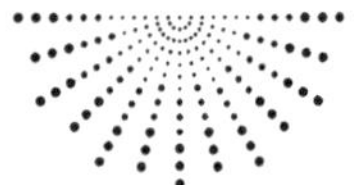

The true worth of an experimenter consists in his pursuing not only what he seeks in his experiment, but also what he did not seek.
—Claude Bernard

It was clear from my experience, and that of others, that a trial that randomly assigned patients to surgery versus the nonsurgical option of stereotactic radiation would not be readily accepted by patients or surgeons. Thus, my radiation oncology colleague Joe Chang and I decided to plan a trial where we treated enough patients with stereotactic radiation prospectively so that we would have a statistically meaningful estimate of the effectiveness and complications of the treatment and could compare this to a contemporaneous series of patients treated with minimally invasive surgery. But we needed funding for this trial. We began discussions with one of the largest companies manufacturing equipment for radiation therapy, Varian. The single-arm trial was approved by our Institutional Review Board. Varian agreed to provide the funding. Our dire situation with clinical trials was slowly improving.

The American Society of Clinical Oncology (ASCO) is the largest assembly of research and clinical oncologists in the world, with over forty thousand attending in 2024. K had done considerable research prior to her acceptance in medical school. On May 31, 2013, she had her first presentation at ASCO, as a second-year medical student, held in Chicago. K presented a poster on c-kit mutations in melanoma. These are relatively uncommon but potentially targetable by drugs.

Happy events continued. Two of our close friends and colleagues at MD Anderson, Anne Tsao and Mark Clemens, were married at the St. Regis Hotel in Princeville on the North Shore of Kauai, Hawaii, on August 30. Liz and I were invited and were thrilled to attend, as Kauai is one of the most beautiful places on the planet. Much of it is undeveloped, and some of the volcanic shoreline descending into the ocean is so primitive and dramatic that it has been the setting for motion pictures, including Jurassic Park. It was a lovely ceremony, and we had an opportunity to spend some leisure time with our MD Anderson colleagues. We snorkeled in the bay, played golf, and explored the island.

Once again, it was time to renew our Lung Cancer SPORE grant. It took over a year to prepare for this, and the final document was over one thousand pages. It was submitted in September, just in time for the federal government shutdown. The review process was delayed indefinitely.

Genprex was a privately held company in the process of attracting investment capital to fund the clinical trial. An investment group agreed to obtain funding for Genprex. The group promised a total of two million dollars. This was a small amount, but at least we could get the clinical trial up and running. Once again, the standard operating procedure (SOP) forms needed to be finalized by the MD Anderson production group to maintain GMP conditions for the production of the gene therapy drug. The SOPs for the production of nanovesicles and complexes under reproducible conditions were completed. We were prepared to enter the first patient.

The IASLC World Lung Cancer Congress was in Sydney, Australia. This provided an opportunity to see another part of the world. Liz and I talked with a group of colleagues attending the meeting, including newlyweds Anne Tsao and Mark Clemens, surgeons Steve Swisher and his wife, surgical breast oncologist Kelly Hunt, medical oncologist David Stewart and his wife, and radiation oncologists Jim Cox and his wife, Ritsuko Komaki. We all decided to extend the trip to New Zealand. On October 25, Liz and I boarded a flight to Los Angeles with a connecting flight to Sydney. Our group had four presentations, including two on stereotactic radiation therapy for lung cancer, and I chaired several sessions. Sydney was beautiful as we sailed toward the harbor with the backdrop of the iconic Opera House and toured the zoo to see native wildlife in a realistic habitat. After the meeting, our group boarded a flight to New Zealand. We landed in Wellington on the North Island and flew into Blenheim on the South Island.

The Brennan Vineyard, Gibbston sub-region of Central Otago, New Zealand. From left to right: Jim Cox, Ritsuko Komaki, the author, Anne Tsao, Mark Clemens, Sean Brennan, Kelly Hunt, Liz, Steve Swisher, Leslie Stewart, David Stewart.

The day after checking into our hotel, we boarded a bus for the trip to Milford Sound. On arrival, we boarded a ship for an overnight cruise through the sound. The views were spectacular, with massive fjords and tall, breathtaking waterfalls. Fur seals populated the rocks. The next day, when we returned to port, we were scheduled to fly back to our hotel on a fixed-wing plane, but the weather had turned cloudy, and the flight was canceled due to poor visibility. However, there was another option—helicopters. We all agreed, and soon we were airborne. We made an intermediate stop, landing on a glacier for more spectacular views of the mountains. We all landed safely with audible sighs of relief. The remainder of our time was spent exploring the vineyards of the South Island. The North Island is known primarily for its white wines, notably the sauvignon blanc varietal, which in their version has a dry citrus flavor. The South Island had gained recent notoriety for red wines, including Pinot Noir varietals. Our group traveled to several beautiful vineyards. Before departing, I had spoken with a friend and colleague of mine from my NIH surgery branch years, Murray Brennan, who was then the chair of the Department of Surgery at Memorial Sloan Kettering Cancer Center, about the best way to see New Zealand on a short trip. He mentioned that his son, Sean, was operating a vineyard and winery on the South Island and encouraged us to visit. In 2009, their pinot noirs won gold medals at a prestigious international competition in London. We stopped at Brennan Wines and met Sean, who was very gracious. I ordered several cases of the pinot noir to be shipped to our home. It was outstanding.

A private dinner on the island of Moto, Bora Bora.

Liz and I felt that the return flight was so long that we should take a break. We boarded a flight to French Polynesia, landed in Tahiti, and then traveled by boat to the Four Seasons Hotel on Bora Bora, where we unpacked in an overwater bungalow and took in the pristine beauty of the island and the surrounding lagoon formed by the barrier islands surrounding the main island. Liz and I had been certified in scuba diving and so availed ourselves of the opportunity to dive in the glass-clear waters of the lagoon with large schools of radiantly colored fish. I surprised Liz with a private dinner on the island of Moto. Our guide took us to the island in a small boat. There, a table was set up on the beach. We were served a spectacular feast while the sun set. Our guide, a very muscular and talented Polynesian, entertained us with native song and dance.

Our entertainment during the private dinner on Motu.

Scuba diving in the lagoon at Bora Bora.

Back to Houston and cancer research. The new year of 2014 began on a positive note as patients were entered into our new gene therapy clinical trial combining TUSC2 gene therapy with erlotinib. All scientists recognize that their published research is immortal. If the clinical trial is instrumental in changing the standard of care, the data will continue to be analyzed over the years. Because I had initiated several important randomized trials, I was contacted by the Meta-Analysis Collaborative Group, Medical Research Council Clinical Trials Unit at University College London. The term meta-analysis was first used in 1976 by the statistician Gene Glass, who stated, "Meta-analysis refers to the analysis of analyses." Meta-analysis statistically combines the results of multiple studies that attempt to answer the same research question. This is a very powerful technique because if multiple studies give the same answer when their data is combined, it increases confidence with larger numbers of patients that the result is correct. The original data from our landmark 1994 clinical trial showing that neoadjuvant chemotherapy followed by surgery and postoperative chemotherapy was superior to surgery alone was requested.[92] Since our original publication, many other studies have reproduced our results. Now the meta-analysis analyzed and combined the results of 15 randomized controlled trials (2,385 patients), which together showed a significant benefit of preoperative chemotherapy on survival, with a 13 percent reduction in the relative risk of death.[172] The results were published in the prestigious journal Lancet. There are few things more rewarding to a scientist than the confirmation of their original findings by independent investigators. Reproducibility is the arbiter of scientific truth. Our clinical trial was criticized as too small when it was first published. But it was carefully designed and meticulously executed so that, even with a smaller number of patients, the results were accurate and reproducible.

Then a sad event occurred. My mother had been slowly deteriorating and was in an assisted living home cared for by the wife of my uncle Manny of Cafe Wha? fame. On July 28, 2014, Bernice Roth died peacefully at age ninety-six, surrounded by loving family. Her influence on my career and especially her early training in public speaking were invaluable. Then I received some good news. A multidisciplinary R01 grant submitted with Xifeng Wu, chair of epidemiology, and Lin Ji, a molecular biologist in our group, would be funded at the seventh percentile. Additionally, we received more good news that our SPORE resubmission would be funded for the fourth time. In 2015, I would be turning seventy, an age that forces one to reflect on the past and future. Chronologically, you are old, with most of your life already lived. Scientifically, there were still many things I hoped to accomplish. Our gene therapy and stereotactic radiation therapy clinical trials were unfinished. Important scientific questions remained unanswered about TUSC2 gene therapy.

Jack and Liz on their expedition to Antarctica.

There were also other places on the planet I wanted to visit. My goal was to set foot on every continent. Two big ones, Antarctica and Africa, were still not checked off my list. I decided to remedy this in my seventieth year. Liz and I chose to travel on a National Geographic expedition to Antarctica. The trip began with a flight to Buenos Aires, Argentina, a beautiful city neither of us had toured before. Next, on January 19, was a flight to Ushuaia, Argentina, the southernmost point in South America. Docked there was the National Geographic Explorer, an ice-rated vessel that accommodated ninety-six passengers and seventy crew members. National Geographic was commemorating the Antarctic expedition led by Ernest Shackleton:[173] "Endurance was the three-masted ship in which Sir Ernest Shackleton and a crew of 27 men sailed for the Antarctic on the 1914 to 1917 Imperial Trans-Antarctic Expedition. A year later, she became trapped in pack ice and finally sank in the Weddell Sea off Antarctica on 21 November 1915. All of the crew survived the ship's sinking and were eventually rescued in 1916 after using the ship's boats to travel to Elephant Island, and Shackleton, the ship's captain Frank Worsley, and four others made a voyage to the South Atlantic island of South Georgia to seek help."

The parkas given to us by National Geographic bore a patch honoring the Shackleton expedition. The ship's course was first to cross the Drake Passage to reach Elephant Island. The Drake Passage is the place where the Atlantic and Pacific Oceans meet, named after Sir Francis Drake, the English explorer and buccaneer. It is one of the most turbulent regions of water on the planet. Our ship would cross the Drake Passage at night. We had just unpacked in our cabin when the boat began encountering big waves. Fortunately, there was plenty of Dramamine on board to control the seasickness. It was impossible to sleep with the constant motion. Another problem became evident: the sliding glass doors to our balcony were not secured. They were constantly opening and closing, and, of course, when they were open, ocean spray would cover us. Even with the lights, it was difficult to see how the locks worked. Finally, I managed to wedge a chair into the door handle to keep it closed. The light of day revealed the simple locking mechanism. It had been a rocky night.

The next day, we saw our first icebergs as we approached Elephant Island. Shackleton and his crew of 28, after living on the Antarctic ice for 281 days, used lifeboats to make their way to land. Three months later, they landed on Elephant Island. Shackleton and five others then set out for South Georgia and returned five months later to rescue his crew, which had survived on penguins and seal blubber. We boarded a Zodiac cruise to Elephant Island and saw chinstrap penguins, sea lions, and fin whales. We also passed the site of the Shackleton camp. The extraordinary revelation of this voyage was the astonishing number of life forms in this hostile environment, including Adélie and gentoo penguins, humpback whales, crabeater and leopard seals, and many birds.

The next day, our ship began breaking through ice and made a landing at a subglacial volcano named Brown Bluff. The landing was populated by huge rookeries of gentoo and Adélie penguins and had a distinctive odor, but the penguins were highly entertaining. The following day, we traversed the Gerlache Strait, named for the nineteenth-century Belgian explorer whose chief officer was Roald Amundsen. Crabeaters, leopard seals, and gentoo penguins populated the icebergs. The next day, the ship entered the Lemaire Channel, seven miles long and one mile wide, with spectacular peaks on both sides. The weather permitted a Zodiac cruise among the icebergs and a landing on Booth Island, filled with penguin colonies. The ship crossed the Antarctic Circle at 10:15 p.m.

The next day was permeated with snow and wind. The seas were too rough for landing. On January 26, we anchored at Port Lockroy, established as a base by the British in 1944 to monitor German shipping or possibly as a decoy. From there, the ship anchored off Danco Island. The seas were calm enough that Liz and I set off in a kayak to explore the icebergs. We had some up-close encounters with multiple ice floes and icebergs. When it was time to return to the ship, I noticed the current was flowing in the opposite direction. We were paddling frantically but not making forward progress. Fortunately, the crew spotted our dilemma. A Zodiac was dispatched and towed us back to the ship. The next day, the ship was at sea, bound for Ushuaia. The return crossing was less harrowing than the previous one.

After returning home, the family joined me for a seventieth birthday celebration with a dinner in our home, capped by opening a bottle of 1945 Chateau Haut-Brion that I had located in France. The postwar vintage of 1945 has been called the best of the twentieth century, and after tasting it, I would not argue. Our group published that TUSC2 gene therapy can overcome resistance to targeted therapy with the epidermal growth factor receptor-inhibitor erlotinib. We then published a paper describing the mechanism of TUSC2 in overcoming this drug resistance.[171] One of the most important characteristics of the TUSC2 gene and its protein product is that it is multifunctional. Whereas targeted drugs inhibit a single protein, TUSC2 gene therapy restores the ability to alter multiple pathways, equivalent to giving multiple targeted drugs. In this case, the ability to restore responsiveness to erlotinib was linked to the inhibition of two proteins and their pathways by TUSC2: fibroblast growth factor receptor 2 and mTOR. Both proteins are critical for cancer cell growth and survival.

Participating in K's medical school graduation ceremony.

March 20 was Match Day. Medical students all over the country found out where they would spend their residency. The residency programs submitted their preferred candidates in rank order, and the medical students submitted their rankings of the programs where they had interviewed. K was elated. She matched with her first choice of USC Internal Medicine. Liz and I were there to congratulate her. She was California-bound, just as I had been forty-three years earlier. This was turning into an intense year.

Liz and the author hosted a dinner on April 23, 2015, for soprano Christine Goerke, who sang the role of Brunnhilde in the Houston Grand Opera Ring Cycle.

Houston Grand Opera had taken on the challenge of staging Richard Wagner's epic four-opera cycle, Der Ring des Nibelungen. The four operas recapitulate the beginning and end of a mythical world populated by gods, demigods, humans, dragons, and an enslaved race of dwarfs living below the earth. Wagner wrote his own librettos in addition to composing the music for voice and orchestra. He was a musical genius of the highest order, although he behaved reprehensibly in his personal life. The music is so beautiful and compelling that most listeners focus solely on it and compartmentalize the objectionable aspects of Wagner. I am spellbound by the beauty, power, originality, and inevitability of Wagner's music. I am such a fan that I named one of our dogs after a character in Wagner's Ring Cycle. I named the dog Siegfried after a character in the Ring who is very big and very stupid, like our dog. Houston Grand Opera, because of budget and rehearsal constraints, presented one opera each year for four consecutive years rather than performing them within a two-week festival period as Wagner intended. The last year, Das Rheingold was performed, and now the next opera in cycle Die Walkure opened on April 18. The performance was intense, compelling, dramatic, and passionately lyrical as conducted by Patrick Summers. Christine Goerke, a soprano who had performed often for Houston Grand Opera early in her career, sang the role of Brunnhilde, the daughter of the chief god, Wotan, who defies him and is forced to sleep surrounded by fire until a hero awakens her. Christine sang powerfully and emotionally. In the following years, she would sing the same role at the Metropolitan Opera in their revival of the Ring Cycle. Liz and I were fortunate to host her at a dinner in our home on April 23 with Patrick Summers and other guests. Christine has a delightful, irreverent personality. She is a great artist but does not take herself too seriously. I also accepted a position on the Houston Grand Opera board of directors, which enabled me to gain insight into the inner workings of this great opera company.

When Accuray pulled their funding from the early lung cancer stereotactic radiation therapy trial, no additional patients could be entered. A total of thirty-six patients were entered in the STARS trial, which was not enough to draw conclusions. Joe Chang and I were attending a meeting when we were contacted by Suresh Senan, a Dutch radiation oncologist who had also attempted to conduct a randomized trial but had only randomized twenty-two patients. Suresh suggested that we pool our data and write it up. We did, and the results were surprising. [174]

Of the fifty-eight patients enrolled with early-stage non-small cell lung cancer, thirty-one had stereotactic body radiation (SABR) therapy, and twenty-seven had undergone surgery. Unexpectedly, six patients in the surgery group died compared with one patient in the SABR group. The estimated overall survival at three years was 95 percent in the SABR group compared with 79 percent in the surgery group, which was statistically significant. Thus, more patients in the SABR group survived than the surgery group. There were no serious treatment-related side effects in the SABR group. The paper was published online on May 14 in Lancet Oncology, one of the most prestigious cancer journals. This was a small clinical trial, but patients were randomly allocated, which is the highest level of reliability. It showed that patients with early-stage non-small cell lung cancer had a nonoperative, noninvasive treatment option. This is especially important for lung cancer patients who are elderly or have other chronic illnesses that increase the risk of surgery.

Liz received an invitation to speak at the International Microenvironment Society, held that year in Tel Aviv, Israel. I was interested in this field of research and decided to attend as well. This provided an opportunity to check off the one remaining continent on our list—Africa. Flying there from Israel would be a relatively short jaunt. The conference was excellent, with several well-known experts speaking on various components of the cancer microenvironment. This was my first visit to Israel, and so Liz, who had been there before, arranged for tours. We toured Jerusalem and visited the sites considered holy by three of the world's major religions, astonishing in their proximity. The next day, we traveled to Masada, an isolated rock plateau where Jewish rebels hid and eventually either committed suicide or were killed during a Roman siege. [175] We then drove to the Dead Sea, where I took a dip. After the meeting, we flew from Tel Aviv to Nairobi, Kenya, to begin our safari.

Hot air balloon ride over the Masai Mara

The next morning, we flew to the Masai Mara, which has the greatest concentration of species in Kenya, including the largest lion population. We camped at the Sanctuary Olonana. The variety of species we saw that day was astounding, including Thompson's gazelles, roan antelopes, topi antelopes, hyenas, impalas, elephants, crocodiles, giraffes, zebras, storks, and wildebeest. The next day, we were awakened before dawn and taken to an isolated site where the major feature was a very large multicolored cloth. This was a hot air balloon. The air in the balloon expanded when heated by a flame in the basket. We climbed in the basket with several other couples and a guide. The restraining ropes were released, and we were up, up, and away. We were airborne just before sunrise. We drifted high above the Mara, and the views of the plains, forests, and rivers were spectacular. We saw herds of wildebeest, antelopes, and hippopotamuses in a river below. When we landed, tables were set for a hearty breakfast. We returned to camp in an open Land Cruiser. We then toured a Masai village, planted a tree, and visited a school. At the Masai village, we toured their mud huts and were shown how to build a fire using a stick to create sparks from the friction. The Masai had a variety of trinkets we could bargain for. I purchased, among other things, a large club symbolic of the power held by the leader of the group, only later to have this confiscated by airport security on our departure.

The following day, we had a sighting of a white rhinoceros, which had been saved from extinction, and a lion feeding on its kill. On the morning of October 20, we were awakened by the sounds of hippopotamuses. At breakfast, we were joined by a monkey who leapt on the table, grabbed a breakfast pastry, and then made a hasty disappearance. We were driven to an airstrip where we boarded a plane for Nairobi to make a connecting flight to Arusha, Tanzania, where we were driven to the manor at Ngorongoro, reminiscent of a country farmhouse with guest cottages. The planes depart from airstrips and are generally single-engine with two bush pilots. The following day, we drove into the Ngorongoro Crater, a large volcanic caldera that is now a conservation area. In addition to Thompson and Grant's gazelles and many species of birds, we saw a black rhinoceros, which is considered endangered. We had a picnic lunch by the hippopotamus pool.

Our guide prepares for our walking safari.

Next, we were taken to another airstrip to board our flight to the Serengeti National Park, covering ten thousand acres. On landing, we were driven to the Migration Camp located on the Grumeti River. The camp was somewhat in disarray, as the previous week a herd of elephants had stampeded through it, causing some damage. Fortunately, our tents were still standing. The sleeping quarters in the tent were comfortable, but sounds from the hippopotamuses and other animals often awakened us. The next day, after a hearty breakfast, we embarked on a game drive in an open Land Rover. I was armed with a digital single-lens reflex camera with a 400mm telephoto lens. Sightings included impalas, topi, hartebeest antelopes, vultures, steenbok antelopes, and a pride of lions. In the afternoon, we opted for a walking safari. Our guides carried high-powered rifles, as they did not know what we might encounter. As we were walking along the river, they suddenly motioned for us to stop and be quiet. About 50 feet from us was a small herd of eight Cape buffalo. These are large bovines with sharp horns. They are highly unpredictable and, therefore, very dangerous. They stared at us and began to move forward. Our guides approached them cautiously, rifles at the ready, and finally got them to leave the area with gestures and vocal sounds without firing a shot. We all breathed a great sigh of relief.

A herd of Cape buffalo was encountered on our walking safari.

One of the goals of our safari was to witness the great migration. Each year, the Serengeti is the scene of the spectacular wildebeest and zebra migration, when millions of these animals make their annual circuit in search of fresh grasses and water. The time of year predicts the greatest concentration of migrating species. I had selected this camp in October because it was likely we would be near migrating herds. The next day, we headed out on a drive that would take us to a river crossing of wildebeest and zebras. The drive was long, and pavement was nonexistent, so we were constantly jostled. Finally, we reached the Mara River crossing. The sighting was spectacular. Hundreds of wildebeest rushed toward the river, jumped in, and swam to the opposite bank. It was a nonstop parade until all were across. The zebras followed, being very clever to let the wildebeests test the water and satisfy any predators on the opposite bank. The next day was our final game drive. Besides the omnipresent antelopes, we saw baboons, a lion pride with twenty-two members, including their young, and cheetahs racing across the plains. The variety and number of different species were astonishing. Evolution clearly moved in bizarre and unpredictable pathways.

Wildebeest crossing the Mara River during the Great Migration

Our last day, the bush pilots flew us to Kilimanjaro Airport, with an incredible view of Mount Kilimanjaro, to connect to Nairobi. From Nairobi, we flew to Schiphol and then on to Houston, concluding one of the most memorable adventures of a lifetime.

32
ACT THREE

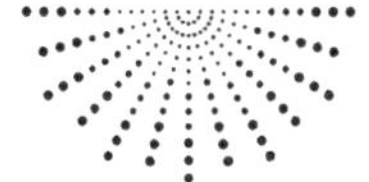

Vollendet das ewige Werk!
—Wotan, Das Rheingold, composed by Richard Wagner

Auf geb' ich mein Werk; nur Eines will ich noch: das Ende, das Ende!
—Wotan, Die Walkure, composed by Richard Wagner

The year 2016 was one of Wagnerian proportions. Houston Grand Opera presented the third opera in Wagner's Ring Cycle, Siegfried. Jay Hunter Morris sang the title role, with Christine Goerke again as Brunnhilde. It was a spectacular and well-sung production, which Liz and I saw twice, the second time with J and her husband. In May, we traveled to Washington, DC, to the Washington National Opera production of the entire four operas of Der Ring des Nibelungen. The greatest Wagnerian soprano of my generation, Nina Stemme, sang the role of Brunnhilde. Francesca Zambello created the production with the concept of an American Ring. Wotan, the principal god, was portrayed as a real estate tycoon with an office in a Manhattan penthouse. The Valkyries parachuted onto the battlefield to take the dead to Valhalla. Siegfried and Mime lived in a trailer park, and the Norns spun computer cables. It was a well-sung and creative production.

The Lung Cancer SPOREs had an annual meeting to present their latest findings and plan for new collaborations. This year, it was held in Bethesda, Maryland, at the NIH campus. I usually check my phone when I awaken, and on June 19, I noticed a text message from K, which was unusual. She had been chosen as Intern of the Year by USC Internal Medicine, a great honor.

The next step for Genprex was to become a public company so that it could obtain sufficient funds to complete the gene therapy clinical trials necessary for approval by the FDA. Plans were moving forward to take Genprex public. Our group was constantly looking for ways to improve the results of TUSC2 gene therapy with additional laboratory studies. When cancer cells were treated with a combination of erlotinib and TUSC2 gene therapy, they became less viable when exposed to factors that stress the cells.[176] We identified an old drug, auranofin, that was used to treat arthritis and inhibited a certain protein, resulting in increased stress and more cancer cell death. This was an approved drug and very inexpensive. When it was added to the erlotinib/TUSC2 combination, cancer cell death increased greatly. The three-drug combination greatly inhibited tumor growth and prolonged survival in mouse cancer models. This showed us that it was not always necessary to invent new anticancer drugs; existing drugs can be repurposed when critical targets are identified.

January 2017 began with a report released by Genprex of the preliminary results of the clinical trial combining TUSC2 gene therapy (now called Reqorsa®) with the epidermal growth factor receptor-blocking drug erlotinib. Patients had tumor progression while they were being treated with standard-of-care drugs. The interim results showed a high level of anticancer activity with minimal side effects. The clinical trial results on nine patients showed an overall disease control rate (stable disease, partial response, and complete response) of 78 percent. Seven patients had stable disease, characterized by a lack of disease progression after at least two treatments, each twenty-one days apart. One patient with multiple targeted lesions experienced a durable complete response that lasted over seven months. One EGFR-negative patient experienced regression of targeted lesions by 24 percent. A third patient achieved stable disease, tumor regression, and decreased metabolic activity by PET scan in multiple tumors. The side effects from the drug were minimal. Two years later, erlotinib would be superseded by another EGFR inhibitor, osimertinib, which targeted the same EGFR mutations as erlotinib, plus a mutation that caused resistance to erlotinib. A new clinical trial would be initiated, combining TUSC2 gene therapy (Reqorsa®) with osimertinib.

Lung cancer research had become dependent on models that had only a remote resemblance to the cancers that developed in patients. These included lung cancers developing in mice, which were not caused by tobacco consumption; cell lines that may evolve over time with thousands of passages; and genetically engineered mouse models, which had only a fraction of the genetic abnormalities in human lung cancer. Previously, it had been shown that a human cancer removed with surgery could be implanted in a special mouse strain with a defective immune system and would grow into a tumor that could then be implanted in more mice. Bingliang Fang, in our laboratory, was able to develop over two hundred lung patient–derived xenografts (PDXs) and showed they had close similarity to the original patient tumor; it was the largest repository of lung cancer PDXs in the world.[177] We could now test new drugs and identify potential drug targets with confidence that they would be active and relevant in human lung cancer. Because of this extensive work with PDXs, we were awarded a four-million-dollar NIH grant for further PDX research and development, one of only five in the United States.

Then, our group made another surprising and startling discovery. Some patients receiving gene therapy had a complete disappearance of their cancers, a goal we were constantly pursuing. I was still puzzled as to how gene therapy could destroy every cancer cell, as we knew the gene did not enter every cancer cell. The answer became obvious when Ismail Meraz, in our group, discovered that TUSC2 gene therapy stimulated an immune response against the cancer.[84] TUSC2 gene therapy was effective against KRAS mutant tumors, which were resistant to current immunotherapy with anti-PD-1 antibodies. TUSC2 gene therapy mobilized natural killer cells, which are another arm of the immune response, distinct from the T cells activated by anti-PD-1 antibodies.

Perryn Leech, Managing Director, the author, Liz, and Patrick Summers, Artistic and Music Director, Houston Grand Opera Ball 2018.

A scene from the Opera Ball

It turned out that 2018 was a year filled with memorable events. In March, our first grandchild was born. J gave birth to a boy, and we all celebrated the joyous occasion. Every year, the Houston Grand Opera (HGO) holds an Opera Ball as a fundraising event in the foyer of the Wortham Center, the majestic theater where HGO performs. The previous year, Hurricane Harvey caused devastating flooding, which was so severe that it flooded the basement of the Wortham, and the theater was closed for repairs. Liz and I were the chairs of the HGO Opera Ball for 2018, and the location was now uncertain. Fortuitously, Tilman Fertitta was opening a new five-star hotel in the Galleria area, the Post Oak, which had a large ballroom, and HGO was able to secure this venue for the Opera Ball. Brooke Rogers, the director of special events at HGO, was an invaluable help in planning the event. She came up with the theme, A Night in Old Hollywood, because one of HGO's operas that year, Guilio Cesare by Handel, was staged in Hollywood of the '30s, and Liz and I loved the idea. I had mentioned to Brooke that my first cousin was David Lee Roth of Van Halen, and she became very excited as she was a fan in her youth, with a large poster of David Lee on the wall of her room. I said I would float the idea of David Lee performing at the ball to his agent. I called the agent, and she said David would often perform at charitable events, and she would ask. Several days later, I received a call that David would be there with his entourage, as he regarded this as a family event and always wanted to help family. We were all ecstatic, although we wondered how the mostly elderly, conservative, classical-music-loving attendees of the Opera Ball would react. They reacted wildly. Diamond Dave gave a spectacular performance, and the audience was standing and cheering. Many told us afterward it was one of the most memorable Opera Balls ever.

The author, K, David Lee Roth, and Liz at the Opera Ball

In June, Liz and I attended K's graduation ceremony for the USC internal medicine residency program. She was accepted in a medical oncology fellowship at the City of Hope Cancer Center. Liz was an invited speaker at the Society of Immunotherapy of Cancer meeting held in Manchester, England. This provided an opportunity to visit the Royal Opera House in London, which was performing the complete four-opera cycle of Der Ring des Nibelungen. I managed to secure two tickets to the sold-out performances. We were not disappointed, as this was the best performance of the Ring we had ever seen, including those at the Metropolitan Opera, Bayreuth, and the Vienna State Opera. Nina Stemme, the finest Wagnerian soprano of our generation at the peak of her career, was Brunnhilde, singing with overwhelming beauty and power. She imparted a vulnerability to the role that touched an emotional chord. Stefan Vinke was a superb and indefatigable Siegfried, who portrayed the complexities of an orphan distraught at losing his parents and who assumed the role of a hero only to be brought down by his arrogance. In the cast was a young soprano whose career I had been following since she won the Operalia competition, Lise Davidsen, who sang the minor roles of Freia in Das Rheingold and the third Norn in Götterdämmerung. Her voice, heard by me live for the first time, had incredible range, power, and beauty. I would hear her again in many future live performances. Keith Warner's direction emphasized the personal interactions of the characters, and Antonio Pappano's conducting was passionate, powerful, and insightful. During the summer, we spent more time in Telluride, savoring the cool temperatures and low humidity. We were visited by K and her boyfriend, L. We decided to drive around the area to see Silverton and Ouray, two former mining towns. On the way back, K said she knew a shortcut over the Ophir Pass. I looked on my phone, but the GPS did not show it. By then, it was too late, and we had turned onto a poorly marked, unpaved single-lane path. L was driving and asked if the vehicle we were in was four-wheel drive. I was not sure and started thumbing frantically through the manual. I did notice that there was a bold warning about a tipping hazard. As we advanced, the road became narrower, and all signs of a road disappeared. The trail was covered with scree, which is a mass of small rock fragments and stones resulting from multiple freeze-thaw cycles. As we approached the summit, the fragments were larger and piled higher. They began to loudly scrape on the undercarriage of the car and the transmission. The car was beginning to tilt. It reached a 45-degree angle, and the outside wheel began to slip. I heard a scream from the backseat. L fortunately was an excellent driver and managed to get over this area and return the vehicle to vertical. The blood returned to my face, and I loosened my grip on the dashboard. We made it back down without incident and encountered some motorcyclists on their way up who were stalled. I still have PTSD from this.

I returned to Houston and focused on the next step in our laboratory research. Now that the immune system was involved in gene therapy, a better mouse model was needed to accurately determine how the human PDX tumors would respond to treatment. Ismail Meraz, in our group, was an expert immunologist and suggested developing a mouse with a human immune system—a humanized mouse. Thus, we could implant human tumors such as the PDXs into humanized mice and test the effects of treatments on the immune response to the tumor. The results should replicate what would occur in patients, thus speeding up drug development and reducing the failure of drug candidates.[83] The technique for producing humanized mice was relatively simple. Mice with a defective immune system were given a sublethal dose of radiation. They were then transplanted with fresh human stem cells. Over several weeks, the stem cells developed in all the major lineages of human immune cells. Now we could forge ahead with experiments to test immunogene therapy harnessing the immune response against the cancer in addition to the direct effect of gene restoration.

Next year I would be turning seventy-five and had been caring for patients for forty-eight years. Treating patients with complex cancer problems and prolonging their lives with surgery was challenging and rewarding. But every surgeon has their "sell by" date. Surgery requires long hours standing in the operating room, and the specter of a major intraoperative complication and difficult postoperative management is always present. The technical aspects of thoracic surgery have changed. Procedures were now being performed through tiny incisions using video cameras and special instruments or using a robot with the surgeon at a console, removed from direct contact with the patient. The outcomes were not substantially different with the new techniques, but there was considerable hype, which drove patient demand. All these factors convinced me it was time to give up my clinical surgical practice. I retired on August 31, 2019, not realizing how fortuitous this would be as the COVID-19 pandemic was about to strike.

As I looked back on my thirty-three-year career at MD Anderson, I could list many satisfying accomplishments. I, along with my superb thoracic surgery colleagues, created the top thoracic oncologic surgery department in the number-one cancer center, as ranked annually in U.S. News and World Report, with our department consistently designated as a high-performing group.[178] I created one of the first and now —under the leadership of the program director, Dr. Mara Antonoff, and department chair, Dr. Ara Vaporciyan—one of the best training programs and board certification tracks for noncardiac thoracic surgeons. I completed the first clinical trial of neoadjuvant therapy in lung cancer, showing that it is more effective than surgery alone. Now, neoadjuvant therapy is a standard of care with immunotherapy and chemotherapy in lung cancer. I, along with my laboratory colleagues, developed the first gene therapy approved for human use. Now there are twenty-one FDA-approved gene therapies, including gene therapies injected directly in tumors, as we originally developed. Along with many collaborators, I developed the first systemic gene therapy for cancer and showed that it was safe and effective for lung cancer patients in clinical trials. Along with Joe Chang and others, we demonstrated that noninvasive stereotactic radiation therapy could treat early lung cancer as effectively as surgery and have the additional benefit of preserving lung function and reducing treatment-associated adverse events. Ismail Meraz and I developed a new model system to study human cancer using humanized mice with PDXs and a large bank of lung cancer PDXs, which are molecularly characterized and will be an invaluable resource for future lung cancer research. These were the most significant and lifesaving achievements of my career. There are over seven hundred peer-reviewed published research papers I authored or coauthored that contributed to scientific discourse, which included over eighty thousand citations by other scientists and clinicians. None of this would have been possible without the collaboration and help of innumerable individuals. We all worked together for a common goal of vanquishing cancer, and this would not have been possible without the spirit of discovery and teamwork. I have been fortunate to have been surrounded by many outstanding researchers and assistants. There is not enough space to name them all, but many are listed as co-authors on my publications.

Writing a memoir near the end of my career, of course, encourages a great deal of self-reflection. The great philosophical questions that have sparked endless debate come to mind: What is the meaning of life? What is happiness? What is truth? And so on. I do not have the answers, but there are some things I have gained from experience. What is most important in my life? Not material gain or achievements. It is the people closest to me whom I love—my wife of forty-six years, my daughters and their partners, my grandchildren, and close friends. Life would be meaningless without them. Richard Wagner, the composer, knew it was love that gave meaning to human existence. He expressed this at the highest level in his operatic works. When I hear his operas, it brings this message home every time.

Although I would no longer personally treat patients, my research was unfinished. I was able to return to MD Anderson as a part-time researcher, and now I could focus completely on the remaining research questions. One of my first tasks was to help analyze the data from our second clinical trial of stereotactic radiation therapy in early lung cancer.[179] Joe Chang and I had tried to do a randomized comparison of stereotactic radiation and surgery for early-stage lung cancer, but the trial had not accrued sufficient patients. So, we developed a clinical trial that would prospectively enter early-stage lung patients to receive only stereotactic radiation without randomization. We would follow the patients for five years and thus obtain an accurate assessment of the overall survival following treatment. Overall survival was 91 percent at three years and 87 percent at five years. We identified a contemporary group of patients who had minimally invasive surgery. Their survival was no different compared to the stereotactic radiation group, thus confirming the results from our first clinical trial and publication.[174] This confirmed that stereotactic radiation was a safe and effective treatment for early-stage lung cancer that had a major advantage in preserving the patient's lung function and quality of life. Only three to five treatments over one or two weeks were required.

Department of Thoracic and Cardiovascular Surgery faculty dinner honoring David Harpole (head of table), the recipient of the 2022 Roth Lectureship.

Now our research was moving along at a rapid pace. One of the major unsolved problems in oncology is acquired drug resistance. That is, when patients are treated with a drug, they may respond with tumor shrinkage, but in all cases, the tumor, after some time, begins to grow again, having developed resistance to the current drug treatment. We must understand the underlying molecular mechanisms of this process if we are to overcome it. Our group was awarded a new grant from the NCI. The NIH Moon Shot program, called the Acquired Resistance to Therapy Network, focused on identifying and overcoming the pathways that cause cancer cells to become resistant to treatment. Only five grants were awarded. Our department had generously established a Roth Lectureship to honor a thoracic surgeon-scientist. For 2022, the honoree was an old friend, David Harpole from Duke University. He presented an informative lecture, and we had an enjoyable dinner at Brennan's afterward. The American Association for Thoracic Surgery had established the Jack A. Roth Fellowship in Thoracic Surgical Oncology, enabling thoracic surgeons from around the world to participate in our programs at MD Anderson. I once again thank my colleagues who donated to this fund. I am grateful to Reza Mehran, who led this effort. I recruited Reza from the University of New Mexico, where he developed the only thoracic surgery oncology program in that state. He had served as the commanding officer of the Advanced Surgical Team for the UN Peace-keeping Forces in Sarajevo in 1993.

The author and Chimaobi Ikechukwu Nwagboso from Aba, Nigeria, recipient of the 2024 Jack A. Roth Fellowship in Thoracic Surgical Oncology.

Our group wanted to further study the novel concept of immunogene therapy. Our initial observations indicated that a single drug could attack the cancer by restoring tumor suppressor gene function and stimulating the anticancer immune response. Current immune therapy with anti-PD-1 antibodies is also very toxic, as it can cause autoimmune responses that may lead to conditions like diabetes or hypothyroidism. These conditions have not yet occurred with the TUSC2 immunogene therapy. Lung cancers with mutations in KRAS/LKB1 (STK11) are intrinsically resistant to immunotherapy with anti-PD-1 or PD-L1. We used a humanized mouse model to show that while carboplatin chemotherapy plus pembrolizumab immunotherapy can reduce tumor growth moderately and transiently, the addition of the tumor suppressor gene TUSC2, delivered systemically in nanovesicles, to this combination eradicates tumors in most mice.[180] We showed that it was TUSC2 immunogene therapy that caused multiple types of anticancer immune cells to infiltrate the cancers.

We also developed osimertinib-sensitive and -resistant cancer cells to model osimertinib-acquired resistance in humanized and nonhumanized mice and delineate potential resistance mechanisms.[181] We found that a master protein that controls many signaling pathways in the cancer cell was responsible for acquired drug resistance to osimertinib. This is an important finding, as there are drugs in development that can inhibit this protein and potentially eliminate or delay the drug resistance. Most recently, we identified another tumor suppressor gene, NPRL2, that can induce anticancer immunity through immunogene therapy.[4] NPRL2 immunogene therapy provided another drug that can be added to our cancer treatment armamentarium. This was exciting progress in our research program, but I was completely unaware and unprepared for what was about to happen.

33
THE DOCTOR BECOMES THE PATIENT

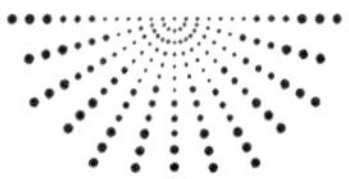

It's taken me over 20 years to appreciate just how little attention is paid in medical education to what it's like to be a patient.

—Professor Keiran Sweeny

I have always been interested in the concept of a healthy lifestyle. Most of the research in this area is observational. That is, the researcher studies a large population and looks for behaviors that are associated with a certain outcome. Of course, there are so many variables that cannot all be known and can affect the result, so these types of studies have limited reliability. Nevertheless, most studies identify diet and exercise as the major components of a healthy lifestyle. The Mediterranean diet is most often associated with a long, healthy lifespan, and I have integrated that into my routine. Even as a surgical resident, I started my day with some exercise. Aerobic exercise is important for cardiovascular fitness, so I run with both a high-intensity interval training routine and an elliptical trainer, which is easier on the joints. This is followed by free weights. I worked for many years with a trainer who was also a bodybuilder. His appearance showed that he knew what he was doing, and although I no longer work with him, I have appropriated his routines. I finish with an abdominal muscle series, isometrics, and stretches. I now do these exercises four days a week. Three days a week, I play singles tennis, and I swim laps every day.

I remember the morning of June 16, 2022, vividly. I was on the treadmill, running at a 5.5-minute mile pace when suddenly I could not breathe. I stopped and still could not catch my breath. I sat down, gasping for air. This was unprecedented. I had never experienced such air hunger in years of running. After a few minutes, my respirations returned to normal. My pulse was elevated, but checking the electrocardiogram on my Apple Watch, there was no arrhythmia, and my oxygen saturation was in the normal range. I had no chest pain or pleuritic pain, so a heart attack or pulmonary embolism seemed unlikely. Perhaps my age had caught up with me, and I could not tolerate the pace. Throughout the day, I noted that activities like stair climbing caused me to become shorter of breath than I had previously experienced. I played tennis in the evening, but once again, I was out of breath just serving. I emailed my primary care physician, Dr. Holly Holmes, with my symptoms, normal electrocardiogram, and normal vital signs. She advised me to see her first thing in the morning.

On physical exam, she noted that my left calf was larger than my right, something I had not realized. There was no pain or inflammation, but she immediately ordered a Doppler ultrasound to look for a blood clot in the veins. There was a blood clot in my left popliteal vein behind the knee. With my level of physical activity, I thought blood clots were highly unlikely. But there it was. This raised a more ominous possibility. The clots may have broken off and lodged in the vessels feeding blood to my lungs, a condition called pulmonary emboli. This is a life-threatening condition requiring immediate treatment. Patients with cancer frequently develop blood clots in the lungs because both the cancers and the treatments they receive predispose them to this condition. I elected to go to the emergency center at MD Anderson. There, I was met by a friend and colleague, Dr. Cezar Iliescu. He made sure I immediately received an injection of low-molecular-weight heparin (Lovenox) to initiate the dissolution of the clots and prevent further clotting. I was admitted to MD Anderson, and for the first time, I had become a patient in the institution where I had been a faculty member for the past thirty-six years.

I was scheduled for a CT scan to detect the emboli and see if there was a cancer that might have caused this. The CT scan was dramatic. There were multiple blood clots blocking the blood vessels to my lungs. I felt fine and did not need oxygen. Although there was some heart strain on my admission echocardiogram, a repeat study was normal. I was fortunate because any additional or larger clots would have been fatal. Perhaps it was my physical conditioning that saved me. It was decided that no further intervention was needed. I was told that the CT scan did not show any cancer that might have caused this condition. I was prescribed a blood-thinning medication called Eliquis, which I would need to take for three months, and was then discharged from the hospital. The next day, I received a call from Dr. Holmes wanting to know how I was doing. I said, "Fine," and then came an unwelcome surprise. "What do you plan to do about the nodule that showed up on your prostate on the CT scan?" she queried. My heart sank. I thought I was in the clear. I had not seen the scan or a written report, and the MD Anderson physicians had not mentioned this. I asked her to send a report to me. There was a small, dense area in the prostate that was indeterminate on the CT but could represent prostate cancer.

I had an extensive family history of prostate cancer. My father, at age seventy-three, was diagnosed with prostate cancer that had spread to a pelvic lymph node. The only treatment he received was medical castration with a drug that blocks testosterone. He was on the drug for the remaining fifteen years of his life, but the cancer disappeared and never returned. Another of my father's brothers had localized prostate cancer removed with surgery and was cured. He lived to age ninety-five. A third brother was diagnosed with metastatic prostate cancer in his mid-eighties and died from it five years later. I was very aware of my risk and began to have annual prostate-specific antigen tests (PSAs) in my early fifties. PSA tests can become elevated for a variety of reasons besides prostate cancer, and PSA levels increase with age. The standard treatments for localized prostate cancer, surgery and radiation therapy, have a significant risk of adverse effects, the most serious of which are incontinence and impotence. Physicians have been concerned for many years that prostate cancer was overtreated, leading to unnecessary surgeries and increased complications without a survival benefit. Some varieties of prostate cancer detected by biopsy are very indolent and would not alter a patient's lifespan. Because of these controversies, large clinical trials were performed randomly, allocating men to PSA screening or routine follow-up. These studies could not detect any survival benefit with PSA screening. Recommendations were made to stop PSA screening after age seventy to avoid the harm of unnecessary treatments.

However, a family history of prostate cancer is a major risk factor. I began taking a drug called finasteride, which decreases the production of dihydrotestosterone and, in randomized clinical trials, reduces the risk of prostate cancer. It also reduces the size of the prostate and increases hair growth, all beneficial effects in the aging male. My PSA at age seventy had risen slightly, and I was referred to a urologist in the Methodist Hospital system in Houston. My prostate exam was normal. He was very aggressive and wanted to go straight to a biopsy, which he would do transrectally, meaning placing a probe in the rectum and then sticking needles through the rectal wall into the prostate. This type of biopsy had a significant risk of sepsis, so I refused. Now, prostate biopsies are done through the skin between the genitals and the rectum, which is much safer. We compromised on obtaining an MRI, which was negative for prostate cancer. Now, eight years later, there was a radiographic abnormality in my prostate.

The next step was to see a urologist at MD Anderson. He found a nodule on my prostate, and my PSA was elevated. An MRI showed a nodule in the prostate that was highly suspicious for cancer. The nodule was very small but, according to the hematologists treating my pulmonary emboli, was likely the cause of the blood clots. Thus, a 1 cm asymptomatic prostate cancer almost killed me. Now I faced a conundrum: I needed to be on the blood thinner for a total of three months. The next step was a biopsy of the prostate nodule, but this could not be done until I was off the Eliquis because of the risk of bleeding. All agreed that the biopsy should wait until my course of Eliquis was completed to avoid the risk of more blood clots. This provided time to go to Telluride for a welcome respite. The biopsy was scheduled for September and went smoothly. The pathologic diagnosis was intermediate-grade prostate cancer. Additional workup with a bone scan showed no evidence of spread. This was all good news. Now the question arose as to how to treat it.

Prostate cancer, in most cases, is very slow-growing. Although it is the second most common cancer in males, most patients die with the cancer rather than from the effects of the cancer. There are multiple effective treatments for prostate cancer, which are all very similar in their effectiveness, making the choice of treatment confusing for patients. For prostate cancer that is confined to the prostate, the two standard choices are surgery and radiation therapy. Both treatments have similar side effects of impotence and incontinence. Although surgery can now be done robotically through small incisions, the removal of the prostate, not the size of the incisions, can cause adverse events and is risky in the elderly. I spent hours reading the literature about these treatments. I noted the emergence of a new treatment strategy for localized prostate cancer—ablation. Ablation of the cancer is performed using varying energy sources, such as heat or cold, to kill cancer cells. It is an outpatient procedure.

Prostate cancer can be multifocal; that is, cancer occurs in different regions of the prostate. This was not the case with my tumor. The only biopsies that showed cancer were from the tumor nodule, while the rest of the prostate was normal. I was a candidate for ablative treatment. Dr. John Ward, who performed the biopsy, was an expert in cryoablation using a probe that maintained a freezing temperature to freeze the entire cancer, thus killing it. Dr. Jonathan Coleman at Memorial Sloan Kettering Cancer Center had a clinical trial using a novel technique called electroporation, where an electric current creates pores in the cancer cells, leading to the cells' death, the advantage being little or no damage to surrounding normal tissues. The location of my cancer made me ineligible for the electroporation trial.

Both Drs. Ward and Coleman thought cryoablation was my best option for controlling the cancer and avoiding treatment side effects.

There were clinical trials associated with the cryoablation procedure. I agreed to participate in these trials to help advance knowledge about the treatment and biology of prostate cancer. Previously, I had participated in randomized trials of the COVID-19 and respiratory syncytial virus vaccines. One study involved submitting a stool sample to characterize my microbiome, which consists of the bacteria that live in the colon. A second clinical trial involved getting a PET-MRI after cryoablation with a novel imaging agent, prostate-specific membrane antigen (PSMA). This has been shown to detect prostate cancer more effectively with CT scans but had not been tested with MRIs.

The cryoablation was performed in December 2022 and went well. There were no adverse events or complications. Six months later, I had the PSMA PET-MRI, which showed no evidence of prostate cancer. Although the use of local ablative treatments for prostate cancer is still investigational, this type of therapy provides an effective treatment that avoids the major side effects of surgery and radiation therapy. Thus, the issue of overtreatment morbidities could be eliminated, and prostate cancer screening in older and higher-risk men may become more acceptable.

My role reversal as a patient was eye-opening. I was fortunate to be able to experience and benefit from outstanding medical care from expert and empathetic physicians and the high level of nursing care as both an inpatient and outpatient at MD Anderson.

While all this was going on, research and clinical trials to bring our cancer immunogene therapy to patients continued. A company I had helped establish, Genprex, was conducting the clinical trials. Our research had shown that TUSC2 immunogene therapy could overcome resistance to targeted drugs (for example, osimertinib) and immunotherapy with anti-PD-1 antibodies. The TUSC2 gene expressed by a plasmid is delivered by a lipid nanovesicle. The special lipid formulation has several advantages. Unlike other liposomes, it is not taken up by just the liver and spleen but is widely distributed to all major organ systems, thus being able to treat widespread metastases. The nanovesicles are selectively taken up by cancer cells to a much higher degree than normal cells, so there is no need to add targeting molecules to the surface of the nanovesicles. Blood vessels supplying the cancer are leaky, which favors more uptake by the cancer than in normal tissues. Reproducibility, the ability of independent laboratories to replicate results in the same experimental system, is a foundation of science. In Chapter 19, I discussed the disappointing and disturbing lack of reproducibility of findings published in prominent journals. Our laboratory has, from the beginning, taken precautions to avoid problems with experimental reproducibility. These include having experiments repeated by multiple different research scientists in the laboratory, carefully validating reagents, and conducting blinded experiments where the individual collecting the data has no knowledge of the treatment groups. Our experiments and findings with TUSC2 have now been reproduced by four independent laboratories at New York University, the University of Texas Health Science Center at Houston, the University of Michigan, and Meharry Medical College. Three clinical trials were designed to test these observations in patients. In the first clinical trial (Acclaim 1), patients with non-small cell lung cancer and an EGFR mutation who had tumor progression on osimertinib would continue on osimertinib combined with the TUSC2 immunogene therapy (Reqorsa®). This indication received a fast-track designation from the FDA. A second clinical trial (Acclaim 2) treated patients with non-small cell lung cancer who had progressed on anti-PD-1 immunotherapy with an anti-PD-1 antibody combined with TUSC2 immunogene therapy. This indication also received fast-track designation from the FDA. A third clinical trial (Acclaim 3) treated patients with a less common but very aggressive form of lung cancer: small-cell lung cancer. Patients first received standard-of-care chemoimmunotherapy. The standard would then be continued maintenance immunotherapy, but in the clinical trial, the standard immunotherapy was combined with TUSC2 immunogene therapy. This indication received an orphan drug designation from the FDA.

The results of the phase 1 portion of the Acclaim 1 clinical trial were presented at the 2023 AACR-NCI-EORTC International Conference on Molecular Targets and Cancer Therapeutics and were very promising. One patient who had previously been treated with carboplatin, pemetrexed, and osimertinib, and then had tumor progression, reported a major tumor regression and continues treatment more than two years later. Another patient whose tumor progressed after treatment with osimertinib had the disease stop growing for close to a year before progression. A third patient, previously treated with cisplatin, pemetrexed, carboplatin, and osimertinib, whose tumor progressed, has had the tumor stop growing for over half a year with TUSC2 immunogene therapy and is continuing treatment. These treatment responses, showing safety and efficacy, were achieved with minimal side effects. I can end this part of my story optimistically, confident that additional data will be obtained that makes this drug available to all the patients who can benefit from it.

The story is not over, and my cancer research continues, supported by the values I have treasured throughout a lifetime—love, compassion, persistence, and integrity.

The author received a commercial research grant from the University of Texas MD Anderson Cancer Center and a sponsored research agreement from Genprex, Inc.; has an ownership interest (including stock, patents, etc.) in Genprex, Inc.; and is a consultant/advisory board member for Genprex, Inc.

All proceeds from the sale of this book will be donated to cancer research.

BIBLIOGRAPHY

1. Ale Ebrahim N, Farhadi H, Salehi H, et al. Does it Matter Which Citation Tool is Used to Compare the H-Index of a Group of Highly Cited Researchers? Aust J Basic Appl Sciences. 06/04 2013;7(7):198-202.
2. Harzing A-W. The Publish or Perish Book 2010. Tarma Software Research Pty Ltd. 1.4.2 H-index. Accessed September 24, 2024, https://harzing.com/popbook/ch1_4_2.htm
3. Nowak JK, Lubarski K, Kowalik LM, Walkowiak J. H-index in medicine is driven by original research. Croat Med J. Feb 2018;59(1):25-32. doi:10.3325/cmj.2018.59.25
4. Meraz IM, Majidi M, Song RD, et al. NPRL2 gene therapy induces effective antitumor immunity in KRAS/STK11 mutant anti-PD-1 resistant metastatic human NSCLC in a humanized mouse model. Cancer Res. Apr 1 2023;83(7)doi:10.1158/1538-7445.Am2023-5120
5. Wikipedia. La Porte, Indiana. Updated October 29, 2024. Accessed September 24, 2024, https://en.wikipedia.org/wiki/La_Porte,_Indiana
6. Wikipedia. Airline Deregulation Act. Accessed September 24, 2024, https://en.wikipedia.org/wiki/Airline_Deregulation_Act
7. Wikipedia. Claudia Goldin. Updated October 18, 2024. Accessed September 24, 2024, https://en.m.wikipedia.org/wiki/Claudia_Goldin
8. Wikipedia. Tractatus Logico-Philosophicus. Updated October 27, 2024. Accessed September 24, 2024, https://en.wikipedia.org/wiki/Tractatus_Logico-Philosophicus
9. Grauer NA. Leading the Way: A History of Johns Hopkins Medicine. Johns Hopkins Unversity Press; 2012.
10. Wikipedia. Flexner Report. Updated October 27, 2024. Accessed September 24, 2024, https://en.wikipedia.org/wiki/Flexner_Report
11. Wikipedia. Baltimore riot of 1968. Updated October 19, 2024. Accessed September 24, 2024, https://en.wikipedia.org/wiki/Baltimore_riot_of_1968
12. Roth JA GA, Kiahara S, Wagner HN, Jr,. Total and regional cerebral blood flow in unanesthetized dogs. Am J Physiol. 1970;219(1):96-101.
13. Roth JA, Rutherford RB. Regional blood flow effects of G-suit application during hemorrhagic shock. Surg Gynecol Obstet. 1971;133:637-643.
14. Williams GM, ter Haar A, Krajewski C, Parks LC, Roth JA. Rejection and repair of endothelium in major vessel transplants. Surgery. 1975;78(6):694-706.
15. Wikipedia. The Immortal Life of Henrietta Lacks. Updated September 7, 2024. Accessed September 24, 2024, https://en.wikipedia.org/wiki/The_Immortal_Life_of_Henrietta_Lacks
16. Eilber FR, Morton DL. Impaired immunologic reactivity and recurrence following cancer surgery. Cancer. 1970;24:362-367.

17. Wikipedia. Donald Morton. Updated January 15, 2023. Accessed September 24, 2024, https://en.wikipedia.org/wiki/Donald_Morton
18. Zhang Y, Zhang Z. The history and advances in cancer immunotherapy: understanding the characteristics of tumor-infiltrating immune cells and their therapeutic implications. Cell Mol Immunol. Aug 2020;17(8):807-821. doi:10.1038/s41423-020-0488-6
19. Wikipedia. Francis Peyton Rous. Updated June 17, 2024. Accessed September 24, 2024, https://en.wikipedia.org/wiki/Francis_Peyton_Rous
20. Chen J, Gao L, Wu X, et al. BCG-induced trained immunity: history, mechanisms and potential applications. J Transl Med. Feb 10 2023;21(1):106. doi:10.1186/s12967-023-03944-8
21. Ishida Y. PD-1: Its Discovery, Involvement in Cancer Immunotherapy, and Beyond. Cells. Jun 1 2020;9(6)doi:10.3390/cells9061376
22. Research S. In Memoriam: Ralph A. Reisfeld, PhD (1926-2020). Updated February 17, 2021. Accessed September 24, 2024, https://www.scripps.edu/news-and-events/press-room/2021/20210217-reisfeld-ralph-in-memoriam.html
23. Roth JA, Slocum HK, Pellegrino MA, Holmes EC, Reisfeld RA. Purification of soluble human melanoma-associated antigens. Cancer Res. Jul 1976;36(7 PT 1):2360-4.
24. Roth JA, Grimm EA, Morton DL. A rapid assay for stimulation of human lymphocytes by tumor-associated antigens. Cancer Res. 1976;36:3001-3010.
25. Roth JA, Holmes EC, Boddie AW, Jr., Morton DL. Lymphocyte responses of lung cancer patients to tumor-associated antigen measured by leucine incorporation. JThoracCardiovascSurg. 1975;70:613-618.
26. Grimm E, Silver HKB, Roth JA, Chee DO, Gupta RK, Morton DL. Detection of tumor-associated antigen in human melanoma cell line supernatants. International Journal of Cancer. 1976;17:559-564.
27. Roth JA, Eilber FR, Nizze JAN, Morton DL. Lack of correlation between skin reactivity to dinitrochlorobenzene and croton oil in patients with cancer. New England Journal of Medicine. 1975;293:388-389.
28. Wikipedia. Nobel Prize Award Process. Updated August 4, 2024. Accessed September 24, 2024, https://en.wikipedia.org/wiki/Nobel_Prize#Award_process
29. Bhattacharya J BP, Goldhaber-Fiebert JD, Holom GH, Packalen M, Studdert DM. Resting on Their Laureates? Research Productivity Among Winners of the Nobel Prize in Physiology or Medicine. NBER. Updated June 2023. Accessed September 24, 2024, https://www.nber.org/papers/w31352#:~:text=Pre%2DNobel%2C%20laureates%27%20publications,winners%20on%20all%20three%20measures. https://www.nber.org/papers/w31352#:~:text=Pre%2DNobel%2C%20laureates%27%20publications,winners%20on%20all%20three%20measures.
30. Andrews TM. 'Biggest scandal' in Swedish medicine touches Nobel Prize with two committee members asked to resign. The Washington Post. Accessed 08/05/2024. https://www.washingtonpost.com/news/morning-mix/wp/2016/09/07/biggest-scandal-in-swedish-medicine-touches-nobel-prize-as-two-committee-members-asked-to-resign/#

31. Montanari S. Nobel Prize winner acknowledges errors in three more papers. The Transmitter. Accessed September 24, 2024, https://www.thetransmitter.org/publishing/nobel-prize-winner-acknowledges-errors-in-three-more-papers/
32. Irving K. Nobel Prize Winner Faces Investigation into Paper Integrity. The Scientist. Updated October 21, 2022. Accessed September 24, 2024, 2024. https://www.the-scientist.com/nobel-prize-winner-faces-investigation-into-paper-integrity-70669
33. Mueller B. Top Cancer Center Seeks to Retract or Correct Dozens of Studies. Accessed October 3, 2024. https://www.nytimes.com/2024/01/22/health/dana-farber-cancer-studies-retractions.html
34. Noorden RV. Exclusive: investigators found plagiarism and data falsification in work from prominent cancer lab. News Feature. Nature. 2022;607(7920):650-652.
35. Saul S. Stanford President Will Resign After Report Found Flaws in His Research. The New York Times. June 19, 2023:18. https://www.nytimes.com/2023/07/19/us/stanford-president-resigns-tessier-lavigne.html#:~:text=Following%20months%20of%20intense%20scrutiny,he%20supervised%20going%20back%20decades
36. Grimes DR. Is biomedical research self-correcting? Modelling insights on the persistence of spurious science. R Soc Open Sci. 01/31/2024 2024;11(1):231056.
37. Landhuis E, Yee D, Claw K, et al. 11 reasons why we've stayed in academia. Nature. Mar 14 2024;627(8003):453-454. doi:10.1038/d41586-024-00724-2
38. Wikipedia. National Cancer Institute. Updated June 6, 2024. Accessed September 24, 2024, https://en.wikipedia.org/wiki/National_Cancer_Institute
39. Roth JA, Wesley RA. Human tumor-associated antigens detected by serological techniques: analysis of autologous humoral immune responses to primary and metastatic human sarcomas by an enzyme-linked immunoabsorbent solid-phase assay (ELISA). Cancer Res. Oct 1982;42(10):3978-86.
40. Roth JA, Grimm EA, Osborne BA, Putnam JB, Jr., Davidson DD, Ames RS. Suppressive immunoregulatory factors produced by tumors. Lymphokine Research. 1983;2(2):67-73.
41. Potter D, Pass HI, Brower S, et al. Prospective randomized study of open lung biopsy versus empirical antibiotic therapy for acute pneumonitis in non-neutropenic cancer patients. AnnThoracSurg. 1985;40:422-428.
42. Pass HI, Potter DA, Macher AM, et al. Thoracic manifestations of the acquired immune deficiency syndrome. JThoracCardiovascSurg. 1984;88:654-658.
43. Schmid S. The discovery of HIV-1,Berlin, Germany. Milestones. Nature Portfolio. 11/28/2018 2018;
44. Roth JA, Putnam JB, Jr., Wesley MN, Rosenberg SA. Differing determinants of prognosis following resection of pulmonary metastases from osteogenic and soft tissue sarcoma patients. Cancer. 1985;55(6):1361-1366.
45. Rizzoni WE, Pass HI, Wesley MN, Rosenberg SA, Roth JA. Resection of recurrent pulmonary metastases in patients with soft-tissue sarcomas. Arch Surg. Nov 1986;121(11):1248-52. doi:10.1001/archsurg.121.11.1248
46. Gomez DR, Blumenschein GR, Jr., Lee JJ, et al. Local consolidative therapy versus maintenance therapy or observation for patients with oligometastatic non-small cell lung cancer without progression after first-line systemic therapy: a multicentre,

randomised, controlled, phase 2 study. Lancet Oncol. Dec 2016;17(12):1672-1682. doi:10.1016/S1470-2045(16)30532-0

47. Roth JA, Pass HI, Flanagan MM, graber gm, Rosenberg JC, Steinberg S. Randomized clinical trial of preoperative and postoperative adjuvant chemotherapy with cisplatin, vindesine, and bleomycin for carcinoma of the esophagus. J Thorac Cardiovas Surg. 1988;96:242-248.
48. Weiss RA, Vogt PK. 100 years of Rous sarcoma virus. J Exp Med. Nov 21 2011;208(12):2351-5. doi:10.1084/jem.20112160
49. Fiala C, Diamandis EP. Mutations in normal tissues-some diagnostic and clinical implications. BMC Med. Oct 29 2020;18(1):283. doi:10.1186/s12916-020-01763-y
50. Rosenberg SA. IL-2: the first effective immunotherapy for human cancer. J Immunol. Jun 15 2014;192(12):5451-8. doi:10.4049/jimmunol.1490019
51. Grimm EA, Mazumder A, Zhang HZ, Rosenberg SA. Lymphokine-activated killer cell phenomenon. Lysis of natural killer-resistant fresh solid tumor cells by interleukin 2-activated autologous human peripheral blood lymphocytes. J Exp Med. Jun 1 1982;155(6):1823-41. doi:10.1084/jem.155.6.1823
52. Cox AD, Der CJ. Ras history: The saga continues. Small GTPases. Jul 2010;1(1):2-27. doi:10.4161/sgtp.1.1.12178
53. Scuderi P, Westin E, Clagett J, et al. Detection of a surface antigen on NIH 3T3 cells transfected with a human leukemia oncogene. Med Oncol Tumor Pharmacother. 1985;2(4):233-242.
54. Roth JA, Ames RS, Byers V, Lee HM, Scannon PJ. Monoclonal antibody 45-2D9 conjugated to the A chain of ricin is specifically toxic to c-Ha-ras transfected NIH 3T3 cells expressing gp74. JImmunol. 1986;136(6):2305-2310.
55. Fu ZW, Li SJ, Han SF, Shi C, Zhang Y. Antibody drug conjugate: the "biological missile" for targeted cancer therapy. Signal Transduct Tar. Mar 22 2022;7(1):93. doi:ARTN 93
10.1038/s41392-022-00947-7
56. Mulshine JL, Ujhazy P, Antman M, et al. From clinical specimens to human cancer preclinical models-a journey the NCI-cell line database-25 years later. J Cell Biochem. Aug 2020;121(8-9):3986-3999. doi:10.1002/jcb.29564
57. Walsh GL, Mehran RJ. A Brief History of Thoracic Surgery at the University of Texas MD Anderson Cancer Center. Elsevier; 2016:719-726.
58. Yang SC, Owen-Schaub LB, Roth JA, Grimm EA. Characterization of OKT3-initiated lymphokine-activated effectors expanded with interleukin 2 and tumor necrosis factor-à. Cancer Res. 1990;50(12):3526-3532.
59. Yang SC, Grimm EA, Parkinson DR, et al. Clinical and immunomodulatory effects of combination immunotherapy with low-dose interleukin 2 and tumor necrosis factor-à in patients with advanced non-small cell lung cancer: a phase I trial. Cancer Res. 1991;51(14):3669-3676.
60. Schneider PM, Hung MC, Ames RS, Putnam EA, Akpakip B, Roth JA. A novel alteration in the epidermal growth factor receptor gene is frequently detected in human non-small cell lung cancer. Lung Cancer. 1990;6:65-72.
61. Schneider PM, Casson AG, Levin B, et al. Mutations of p53 in Barrett's esophagus

and Barrett's cancer: a prospective study of ninety-eight cases. J Thorac Cardiovasc Surg. 1996;111(2):323-333.
62. Wikipedia. Denton Cooley. Updated July 22, 2024. Accessed September 24, 2024, https://en.wikipedia.org/wiki/Denton_Cooley
63. Mendes E. The Study That Helped Spur the U.S. Stop-Smoking Movement. American Cancer Society. Accessed September 24, 2024, 2024. https://www.cancer.org/research/acs-research-news/the-study-that-helped-spur-the-us-stop-smoking-movement.html
64. Key Statistics for Lung Cancer. American Cancer Society. Updated January 29, 2024. Accessed September 24, 2024, https://www.cancer.org/cancer/types/lung-cancer/about/key-statistics.html
65. CDC. Lung Cancer Among People Who Never Smoked. CDC. Updated December 4, 2023. Accessed September 24, 2024, https://www.cdc.gov/lung-cancer/nonsmokers/?CDC_AAref_Val=https://www.cdc.gov/cancer/lung/nonsmokers/index.htm
66. Wosen J. Exodus of life scientists from academia reaches historic levels, new data show. STAT. Updated September 28, 2023. Accessed September 24, 2024, https://www.statnews.com/2023/09/28/scientists-exodus-from-academia-historic-levels/#:~:text=Conversely%2C%2047%25%20of%202022%20life,D
67. Chaudhuri A. The Emerging Physician-Scientist Crisis in America. Commentary. Medscape Oncology. 01/26/2024 2024;
68. Bloom N, Jones CI, Van Reenen J, Webb M. Are Ideas Getting Harder to Find? Am Econ Rev. Apr 2020;110(4):1104-1144. doi:10.1257/aer.20180338
69. Park M, Leahey E, Funk RJ. Papers and patents are becoming less disruptive over time. Nature. Jan 2023;613(7942):138-144. doi:10.1038/s41586-022-05543-x
70. Copeland R. The Billionaires Spending a Fortune to Lure Scientists Away From Universities. The New York Times. January 12, 2024. Accessed September 24, 2024 https://www.nytimes.com/2024/01/12/business/arena-bioworks-scientists-harvard-mit.html?smid=nytcore-ios-share&referringSource=articleShare
71. Kohn DB, Booth C, Shaw KL, et al. Autologous Ex Vivo Lentiviral Gene Therapy for Adenosine Deaminase Deficiency. N Engl J Med. May 27 2021;384(21):2002-2013. doi:10.1056/New England Journal of Medicineoa2027675
72. Mukhopadhyay T, Tainsky M, Cavender AC, Roth JA. Specific inhibition of K-ras expression and tumorigenicity of lung cancer cells by antisense RNA Cancer Res. 1991;51(6):1744-1748.
73. Georges RN, Mukhopadhyay T, Zhang Y, Yen N, Roth JA. Prevention of orthotopic human lung cancer growth by intratracheal instillation of a retroviral antisense K-ras construct. Cancer Res. Apr 1993;53(8):1743-1746.
74. Wikipedia. Li–Fraumeni syndrome. Updated July 29, 2024. Accessed September 24, 2024, https://en.wikipedia.org/wiki/Li%E2%80%93Fraumeni_syndrome
75. Casson AG, Mukhopadhyay T, Cleary KR, Ro JY, Levin B, Roth JA. p53 gene mutations in Barrett's epithelium and esophageal cancer. Cancer Res. 1991;51(16):4495-4499.
76. Chung KY, Mukhopadhyay T, Kim J, et al. Discordant p53 gene mutations in primary

head and neck cancers and corresponding second primary cancers of the upper aerodigestive tract. Cancer Res. Apr 1993;53(7):1676-1683.

77. Fujiwara T, Grimm EA, Mukhopadhyay T, Cai DW, Owen-Schaub LB, Roth JA. A retroviral wild-type p53 expression vector penetrates human lung cancer spheroids and inhibits growth by inducing apoptosis. Cancer Res. 1993;53(18):4129-4133.
78. Cai DW, Mukhopadhyay T, Liu Y, Fujiwara T, Roth JA. Stable expression of the wild-type p53 gene in human lung cancer cells after retrovirus-mediated gene transfer. Hum Gene Ther. Oct 1993;4(5):617-624.
79. Ji L, Nishizaki M, Gao B, et al. Expression of several genes in the human chromosome 3p21.3 homozygous deletion region by an adenovirus vector results in tumor suppressor activities in vitro and in vivo Cancer Res. 2002;62(9):2715-2720.
80. Ito I, Ji L, Tanaka F, et al. Liposomal vector mediated delivery of the 3p FUS1 gene demonstrates potent antitumor activity against human lung cancer in vivo. Cancer Gene Therapy. 2004;11(11):733-739.
81. Lu C, Stewart DJ, Lee JJ, et al. Phase I clinical trial of systemically administered TUSC2(FUS1)-nanoparticles mediating functional gene transfer in humans. Clinical Trial, Phase I

Research Support, N.I.H., Extramural

Research Support, Non-U.S. Gov't. PloS one. 2012;7(4):e34833. doi:10.1371/journal.pone.0034833

82. Pu X, Zhang R, Wang L, et al. Patient-derived tumor immune microenvironments in patient-derived xenografts of lung cancer. J Transl Med. Nov 26 2018;16(1):328. doi:10.1186/s12967-018-1704-3
83. Meraz IM, Majidi M, Meng F, et al. An Improved Patient-Derived Xenograft Humanized Mouse Model for Evaluation of Lung Cancer Immune Responses. Cancer Immunol Res. Aug 2019;7(8):1267-1279. doi:10.1158/2326-6066.CIR-18-0874
84. Meraz IM, Majidi M, Cao X, et al. TUSC2 Immunogene Therapy Synergizes with Anti-PD-1 through Enhanced Proliferation and Infiltration of Natural Killer Cells in Syngeneic Kras-Mutant Mouse Lung Cancer Models. Cancer Immunol Res. Feb 2018;6(2):163-177. doi:10.1158/2326-6066.CIR-17-0273
85. Skoufalos MN. Finding Peace from Hiroshima. IAEA Bulletin2006.
86. Fujiwara T, Grimm EA, Mukhopadhyay T, Zhang WW, Owen-Schaub LB, Roth JA. Induction of chemosensitivity in human lung cancer cells in vivo by adenoviral-mediated transfer of the wild-type p53 gene. Cancer Res. 1994;54(9):2287-2291.
87. Roth JA, Nguyen D, Lawrence DD, et al. Retrovirus-mediated wild-type p53 gene transfer to tumors of patients with lung cancer. Nature Medicine. 1996;2(9):985-991.
88. Fiore K. New England Journal of Medicine Begins Limiting Access for Certain News Organizations. MedPage Today. Updated April 19, 2024. Accessed September 24, 2024, https://www.medpagetoday.com/special-reports/exclusives/109756
89. WHO. Cancer. World Health Organization. Updated February 3, 2022. Accessed September 24, 2024, https://www.who.int/news-room/fact-sheets/detail/cancer
90. Amin MB, Edge S, Greene F, et al. AJCC Cancer Staging Manual. 8th ed. Springer International Publishing: American Joint Commission on Cancer; 2017.

91. Wozniak AJ. Cisplatin Alone vs Cisplatin Plus Vinorelbine in Stage IV NSCLC. Oncology. 1997;11(10)
92. Roth JA, Fossella F, Komaki R, et al. A randomized trial comparing perioperative chemotherapy and surgery with surgery alone in resectable stage IIIA non-small cell lung cancer. J Natl Cancer Inst. 1994;86(9):673-680.
93. Rosell R, Gomez-Condina J, Camps C, et al. A randomized trial comparing preoperative chemotherapy plus surgery with surgery alone in patients with non- small-cell lung cancer. New England Journal of Medicine. 1994;330(3):153-158.
94. Arriagada R, Bergman B, Dunant A, et al. Cisplatin-based adjuvant chemotherapy in patients with completely resected non-small cell lung cancer. N Engl J Med. 2004;350(4):351-360.
95. Brandt WS, Yan W, Zhou J, et al. Outcomes after neoadjuvant or adjuvant chemotherapy for cT2-4N0-1 non-small cell lung cancer: A propensity - matched analysis. J Thorac Cardiovasc Surg. Feb 2019;157 (2): 743 - 753 e3. doi: 10.1016 / j.jtcvs.2018.09.098
96. Felip E, Rosell R, Maestre JA, et al. Preoperative chemotherapy plus surgery versus surgery plus adjuvant chemotherapy versus surgery alone in early-stage non-small cell lung cancer. J Clin Oncol. Jul 1 2010;28 (19): 3138-45. doi:10.1200 / JCO.2009.27.6204
97. Rabatic BM, Kong FM. Pros: concurrent chemo-radiotherapy remains the ideal treatment in fit patients with large volume unresectable stage III non-small cell lung cancer. Transl Lung Cancer Res. Apr 2016;5(2):190-4. doi:10.21037/tlcr.2016.04.08
98. Albain KS, Swann RS, Rusch VW, et al. Radiotherapy plus chemotherapy with or without surgical resection for stage III non-small cell lung cancer: a phase III randomised controlled trial. Lancet. Aug 1 2009;374(9687):379-386. doi:10.1016/S0140-6736(09)60737-6
99. Eberhardt WE, Pottgen C, Gauler TC, et al. Phase III Study of Surgery Versus Definitive Concurrent Chemoradiotherapy Boost in Patients With Resectable Stage IIIA(N2) and Selected IIIB non-small cell Lung Cancer After Induction Chemotherapy and Concurrent Chemoradiotherapy (ESPATUE). J Clin Oncol. Dec 10 2015;33(35):4194-201. doi:10.1200/JCO.2015.62.6812
100. van Meerbeeck JP, Kramer GW, Van Schil PE, et al. Randomized controlled trial of resection versus radiotherapy after induction chemotherapy in stage IIIA-N2 non-small cell lung cancer. J Natl Cancer Inst. Mar 21 2007;99(6):442-50. doi:10.1093/jnci/djk093
101. Shewale JB, Corsini EM, Correa AM, et al. Time trends and predictors of survival in surgically resected early-stage non-small cell lung cancer patients. J Surg Oncol. Sep 2020;122(3):495-505. doi:10.1002/jso.25966
102. Pless M, Stupp R, Ris HB, et al. Induction chemoradiation in stage IIIA/N2 non-small cell lung cancer: a phase 3 randomised trial. Lancet. Sep 12 2015;386(9998):1049-56. doi:10.1016/S0140-6736(15)60294-X
103. Thomas M, Rube C, Hoffknecht P, et al. Effect of preoperative chemoradiation in addition to preoperative chemotherapy: a randomised trial in stage III non-small cell

lung cancer. Lancet Oncol. Jul 2008;9(7):636-48. doi:10.1016/S1470-2045(08)70156-6

104. Van Schil PE, Berzenji L, Yogeswaran SK, Hendriks JM, Lauwers P. Surgical Management of Stage IIIA Non-Small Cell Lung Cancer. Front Oncol. 2017;7:249. doi:10.3389/fonc.2017.00249

105. Antonia SJ, Villegas A, Daniel D, et al. Durvalumab after Chemoradiotherapy in Stage III non-small cell Lung Cancer. New England Journal of Medicine. Nov 16 2017;377(20):1919-1929. doi:10.1056/New England Journal of Medicineoa1709937

106. Forde PM, Spicer J, Lu S, et al. Neoadjuvant Nivolumab plus Chemotherapy in Resectable Lung Cancer. N Engl J Med. May 26 2022;386(21):1973-1985. doi:10.1056/New England Journal of Medicineoa2202170

107. Cascone T, William WN, Weissferdt A, et al. Neoadjuvant nivolumab or nivolumab plus ipilimumab in operable non-small cell lung cancer: the phase 2 randomized NEOSTAR trial. Nature Medicine. Mar 2021;27(3):504-514. doi:10.1038/s41591-020-01224-2

108. Provencio M, Nadal E, González-Larriba JL, et al. Perioperative Nivolumab and Chemotherapy in Stage III non-small cell Lung Cancer. New England Journal of Medicine. Aug 10 2023;389(6):504-513. doi:10.1056/New England Journal of Medicineoa2215530

109. Cascone T, Awad MM, Spicer JD, et al. Perioperative Nivolumab in Resectable Lung Cancer. N Engl J Med. May 16 2024;390 (19):1756-1769. doi:10.1056 / New England Journal of Medicineoa2311926

110. Wikipedia. Nature (journal). Updated July 21, 2024. Accessed September 24, 2024, https://en.wikipedia.org/wiki/Nature_(journal)#:~:text=Founded%20in%20autumn%201869%2C%20Nature,in%20explanatory%20and%20scientific%20journalism

111. Mastroianni A. The rise and fall of peer review. Experimental History. Updated December 13, 2022. Accessed September 24, 2024, https://www.experimental-history.com/p/the-rise-and-fall-of-peer-review

112. Fried E. Antidotes to cynicism creep in academia. Updated March 4, 2024. Accessed September 24, 2024, https://eiko-fried.com/antidotes-to-cynicism-creep/

113. Peir EL, Brauer M, Filut A, et al. Low agreement among reviewers evaluating the same NIH grant applications. PNAS. 03/05/2018 2018;115(12):2952-2957.

114. Baxt WG, Waeckerle JF, Berlin JA, Callaham ML. Who reviews the reviewers? Feasibility of using a fictitious manuscript to evaluate peer reviewer performance. Ann Emerg Med. Sep 1998;32(3 Pt 1):310-7. doi:10.1016/s0196-0644(98)70006-x

115. COS. Reproductibility Project Cancer Biology. COS. Accessed September 24, 2024, https://www.cos.io/rpcb

116. Van Noorden R. More Than 10,000 Research Papers Were Retracted in 2023-a New Record. Nature. Dec 21 2023;624(7992):479-481. doi:10.1038/d41586-023-03974-8

117. Freyer FJ, Ryan A. How does bad data slip through? Allegations of research fraud raise questions about 'peer review. Boston Globe. January 28, 2024. Accessed 8/5/2024. https://www.bostonglobe.com/2024/01/28/metro/dana-farber-cancer-institute-retractions/

118. Wikipedia. bioRxiv. Updated June 6, 2024. Accessed September 24, 2024, https://en.wikipedia.org/wiki/BioRxiv#References

119. McGill B. The state of academic publishing in 3 graphs, 6 trends, and 4 thoughts. Dynamic Ecology/WordPress. Updated April 29, 2024. Accessed September 24, 2024, https://dynamicecology.wordpress.com/2024/04/29/the-state-of-academic-publishing-in-3-graphs-5-trends-and-4-thoughts/

120. Sanderson K. Journal Editors Are Resigning En Masse: What Do These Group Exits Achieve? Nature. Apr 11 2024;628(8007):244-245. doi:10.1038/d41586-024-00887-y

121. New ways to pay for research could boost scientific progress. The Economist. Accessed 10/18/2024. https://www.economist.com/science-and-technology/2023/11/15/new-ways-to-pay-for-research-could-boost-scientific-progress

122. Young M. What is "Read-and-Publish?". The University of Texs at Dallas Eugene McDermott Library. Updated August 9, 2023. Accessed September 24, 2024, https://utdallas.libanswers.com/faq/340748#:~:text=Read%2Dand%2DPublish%20agreements%20vary,retains%20copyright%20of%20their%20work

123. Wikipedia. The Crucible. Updated June 9, 2024. Accessed September 24, 2024, https://en.wikipedia.org/wiki/The_Crucible

124. Wikipedia. Memorial Sloan Kettering Cancer Center. Updated August 5, 2024. Accessed September 24, 2024, https://en.wikipedia.org/wiki/Memorial_Sloan_Kettering_Cancer_Center

125. Jin X, Nguyen D, Zhang WW, Kyritsis AP, Roth JA. Cell cycle arrest and inhibition of tumor cell proliferation by the p16 INK4 gene mediated by an adenovirus vector. Cancer Res. 1995;55(15):3250-3253.

126. Nguyen DM, Wiehle SA, Koch PE, et al. Delivery of the p53 tumor suppressor gene into lung cancer cells by an adenovirus/DNA complex. Cancer Gene Therapy. 1997;4(3):191-198.

127. Roth JA, Cristiano RJ. Gene therapy for cancer: what have we done and where are we going? J Natl Cancer Inst. 1997;89(1):21-39.

128. Wikipedia. Wieskirche. Updated September 9, 2023. Accessed September 24, 2024, https://en.wikipedia.org/wiki/Wieskirche

129. Dornberg J. Augsburg Marks 20 Centuries. The New York Times. June 6, 1985:9. Accessed 08/06/2024. https://www.nytimes.com/1985/06/30/travel/augsburg-marks-20-centuries.html

130. Spitz FR, Nguyen D, Skibber JM, Meyn RE, Cristiano RJ, Roth JA. Adenoviral-mediated wild-type p53 gene expression sensitizes colorectal cancer cells to ionizing radiation. Clin Cancer Res. 1996;2(10):1665-1671.

131. Wikipedia. Jesse Gelsinger. Updated August 25, 2023. Accessed September 24, 2024, https://en.wikipedia.org/wiki/Jesse_Gelsinger

132. Rosenberg SA, Blaese RM, Brenner MK, et al. Human gene marker/therapy clinical protocols. Hum Gene Ther. 1999;10 (18):3067-3123.

133. Weinberg RA. How TP53 (almost) became an oncogene. J Mol Cell Biol. Jul 2019;11(7):531-533. doi:10.1093/jmcb/mjz061

134. Swisher SG, Roth JA, Nemunaitis J, et al. Adenovirus-mediated p53 gene transfer in advanced non-small cell lung cancer J Natl Cancer Inst. 1999;91(9):763-771.

135. Nemunaitis J, Swisher SG, Timmons T, et al. Adenovirus-mediated p53 gene transfer in sequence with cisplatin to tumors of patients with non-small cell lung cancer. J Clin Oncol. 2000;18(3):609-622.

136. Clayman GL, El-Naggar AK, Lippman SM, et al. Adenovirus-mediated p53 gene transfer in patients with advanced recurrent head and neck squamous cell carcinoma. Journal of Clinical Oncology. 1998;16(6):2221-2232.

137. Swisher SG, Roth JA, Komaki R, et al. Induction of p53-regulated genes and tumor regression in lung cancer patients after intratumoral delivery of adenoviral p53 (INGN 201) and radiation therapy. Clinical Trial

Clinical Trial, Phase II

Research Support, Non-U.S. Gov't

Research Support, U.S. Gov't, P.H.S. Clin Cancer Res. Jan 2003;9(1):93-101.

138. Prudkin L, Behrens C, Liu DD, et al. Loss and reduction of FUS1 protein expression is a frequent phenomenon in the pathogenesis of lung cancer. Clinical Cancer Research. 2008;14 (1):41-47.

139. Uno F, Sasaki J, Nishizaki M, et al. Myristoylation of the FUS1 protein is required for tumor suppression in human lung cancer cells. Cancer Res. 2004;64 (9):2969-2976.

140. Lin J, Xu K, Gitanjali J, Roth JA, Ji L. Regulation of tumor suppressor gene FUS1 expression by the untranslated regions of mRNA in human lung cancer cells. Biochem Biophys Res Commun. Jul 1 2011;410(2):235-41. doi:10.1016/j.bbrc.2011.05.122

141. Ji L, Roth JA. Tumor suppressor FUS1 signaling pathway. J Thorac Oncol. 2008;3(4):327-330.

142. Templeton NS, Lasic DD, Frederik PM, Strey HH, Roberts DD, Pavlakis GN. Improved DNA: liposome complexes for increased systemic delivery and gene expression. Nat Biotechnol. 1997;15(7):647-652.

143. Ito I, Ji L, Tanaka F, et al. Liposomal vector mediated delivery of the 3p FUS1 gene demonstrates potent antitumor activity against human lung cancer i n vivo Cancer Gene Therapy. 2004;11:733-739.

144. Zandi R, Xu K, Poulsen H, Roth J, Ji L. Overexpression of the Novel Tumor Suppressor Gene FUS1 Suppresses the Growth of Small Cell Lung Cancer Cells. J Clinic Experiment Pathol. 2011;S5.001

145. Ramesh R, Saeki T, Templeto N, et al. Inhibition of primary and disseminated human lung cancers by systemic delivery of p53 tumor suppressor gene using DOTAP: Cholesterol liposome. Mol Ther. 2000;1:324.

146. Walker's Cay. Accessed September 24, 2024, 2024. https://www.walkerscay.com

147. Thomas J, Abelson R. How a Top Medical Researcher Became Entangled With Enron. The New York Times. January 28, 2002:1. Accessed 8/6/2024. https://www.nytimes.com/2002/01/28/business/how-a-top-medical-researcher-became-entangled-with-enron.html

148. Pollack A. Business; A Drug's Royalties May Ease Hunger. The New York Times.

March 7, 2004:5. https://www.nytimes.com/2004/03/07/business/business-a-drugs-royalties-may-ease-hunger.html

149. Gillison ML, Trotti AM, Harris J, et al. Radiotherapy plus cetuximab or cisplatin in human papillomavirus-positive oropharyngeal cancer (NRG Oncology RTOG 1016): a randomised, multicentre, non-inferiority trial. Lancet. Jan 5 2019;393(10166):40-50. doi:10.1016/S0140-6736(18)32779-X
150. Prud'Homme A. Investigating ImClone. Vanity Fair2013.
151. Pearson S, Jia HP, Kandachi K. China approves first gene therapy. Nature Biotechnology. Jan 2004;22(1):3-4. doi:10.1038/nbt0104-3
152. Zhang WW, Li L, Li D, et al. The First Approved Gene Therapy Product for Cancer Ad-p53 (Gendicine): 12 Years in the Clinic. Hum Gene Ther. Feb 2018;29(2):160-179. doi:10.1089/hum.2017.218
153. Qi L, Li G, Li P, et al. Twenty years of Gendicine(R) rAd-p53 cancer gene therapy: The first-in-class human cancer gene therapy in the era of personalized oncology. Genes Dis. Jul 2024;11(4):101155. doi:10.1016/j.gendis.2023.101155
154. Chen S, Chen J, Xi W, Xu W, Yin G. Clinical therapeutic effect and biological monitoring of p53 gene in advanced hepatocellular carcinoma. Am J Clin Oncol. Feb 2014;37(1):24-9. doi:10.1097/COC.0b013e3181fe4688
155. Li Y, Li LJ, Wang LJ, et al. Selective intra-arterial infusion of rAd-p53 with chemotherapy for advanced oral cancer: a randomized clinical trial. BMC Med. Jan 30 2014;12:16. doi:10.1186/1741-7015-12-16
156. Ma WS, Ma JG, Xing LN. Efficacy and safety of recombinant human adenovirus p53 combined with chemoradiotherapy in the treatment of recurrent nasopharyngeal carcinoma. Anti-Cancer Drug. Feb 2017;28(2):230-236. doi:10.1097/Cad.0000000000000448
157. Nemunaitis J, Clayman G, Agarwala SS, et al. Biomarkers Predict p53 Gene Therapy Efficacy in Recurrent Squamous Cell Carcinoma of the Head and Neck. Clin Cancer Res. Dec 15 2009;15(24):7719-7725. doi:10.1158/1078-0432.CCR-09-1044
158. Introgen Receives Notice ADVEXIN(R) U.S. BLA Not Sufficiently Complete to File. Business Wire, Inc. Accessed September 24, 2024, https://go.gale.com/ps/i.do?id=GALE%7CA184321947&sid=sitemap&v=2.1&it=r&p=HRCA&sw=w&userGroupName=anon%7Ef36dcfe6&aty=open-web-entry
159. Hashimoto M, Kuroda S, Kanaya N, et al. Long-term activation of anti-tumor immunity in pancreatic cancer by a p53-expressing telomerase-specific oncolytic adenovirus. Br J Cancer. Apr 2024;130(7):1187-1195. doi:10.1038/s41416-024-02583-0
160. Li Y, Guo W, Li X, et al. Expert consensus on the clinical application of recombinant adenovirus human p53 for head and neck cancers. Int J Oral Sci. Nov 16 2021;13(1):38. doi:10.1038/s41368-021-00145-1
161. Wikipedia. Chulabhorn. Updated July 22, 2024. Accessed September 24, 2024, https://en.wikipedia.org/wiki/Chulabhorn
162. Wikipedia. Angkor Wat. Updated August 1, 2024. Accessed September 24, 2024, https://en.wikipedia.org/wiki/Angkor_Wat
163. Shirvani SM, Chang JY, Roth JA. Can Stereotactic Ablative Radiotherapy in Early

Stage Lung Cancers Produce Comparable Success as Surgery? Thoracic Surgery Clinics. 08/2013 2013;23(3)(Lung Cancer, Part II):369-381.

164. Ito I, Began G, Mohiuddin I, et al. Increased uptake of liposomal-DNA complex by lung metastasis following intravenous administration. Mol Ther. 2003;7(3):409-418.

165. Huschka R, Barhoumi A, Liu Q, Roth JA, Ji L, Halas NJ. Gene silencing by gold nanoshell-mediated delivery and laser-triggered release of antisense oligonucleotide and siRNA. ACS Nano. Sep 25 2012;6(9):7681-91. doi:10.1021/nn301135w

166. Kim MP, Chen Y, Bekele BN, et al. Activating enhancer-binding protein-2β nucleolar localization predicts poor survival after stage I non-small cell lung cancer resection. Ann Thorac Surg. Sep 2011;92 (3): 1044-50. doi:10.1016 / j.athoracsur.2011.04.029

167. Bonnet House Museum & Gardens. Accessed September 24, 2024, https://www.bonnethouse.org/

168. Meng J, Dai B, Fang B, et al. Combination treatment with MEK and AKT inhibitors is more effective than each drug alone in human non-small cell lung cancer in vitro and in vivo. PloS one. Nov 29 2010;5(11):e14124. doi:10.1371/journal.pone.0014124

169. Wikipedia. Ronald DePinho. Updated December 5, 2023. Accessed September 24, 2024, https://en.wikipedia.org/wiki/Ronald_DePinho

170. Slamming the Door: How Al Gilman Taught Texas a Lesson in Science. Cancer History Project. Accessed September 24, 2024, https://cancerhistoryproject.com/article/slamming-the-door-how-al-gilman-taught-texas-a-lesson-in-science/

171. Dai B, Yan S, Lara-Guerra H, et al. Exogenous restoration of TUSC2 expression induces responsiveness to Erlotinib in Wildtype Epidermal Growth Factor Receptor (EGFR) lung cancer cells through context specific pathways resulting in enhanced therapeutic efficacy. PloS one. 2015;10(6):e0123967.

172. Group NM-aC. Preoperative chemotherapy for non-small cell lung cancer: a systematic review and meta-analysis of individual participant data. Lancet. May 3 2014;383(9928):1561-71. doi:10.1016/S0140-6736(13)62159-5

173. Wikipedia. Endurance (1912 ship). Updated July 10, 2024. Accessed September 24, 2024, https://en.wikipedia.org/wiki/Endurance_(1912_ship)

174. Chang JY, Senan S, Paul MA, et al. Stereotactic ablative radiotherapy versus lobectomy for operable stage I non-small cell lung cancer: a pooled analysis of two randomised trials. Lancet Oncol. 2015;16(6):630-637.

175. Wikipedia. Masada. Updated July 22, 2024. Accessed September 24, 2024, https://en.wikipedia.org/wiki/Masada

176. Xiaobo C, Majidi M, Feng M, et al. TUSC2 (FUS1)-erlotinib induced vulnerabilities in epidermal growth factor receptor (EGFR) wildtype non-small cell lung cancer (NSCLC) targeted by the repurposed drug auranofin. Scientific reports. 2016;6:35741.

177. Hao C, Wang L, Peng S, et al. Gene mutations in primary tumors and corresponding patient-derived xenografts derived from non-small cell lung cancer. Cancer letters. 2015;357(1):179-185.

178. Harder B. America's Best Hospitals: the 2024-2025 Honor Roll and Overview. US

News Health. Updated July 16, 2024. Accessed September 24, 2024, https://health.usnews.com/health-care/best-hospitals/articles/best-hospitals-honor-roll-and-overview

179. Chang J, Mehran R, Feng L, et al. Stereotactic ablative radiotherapy for operable stage I non-small cell lung cancer (revised STARS): long-term results of a single-arm, prospective trial with prespecified comparison to surgery. Lancet Oncol. 09/01 2021;22(10):1448-1457. doi:10.1016/S1470-2045(21)00401-0
180. Meraz IM, Majidi M, Shao R, et al. TUSC2 immunogene enhances efficacy of chemo-immuno combination on KRAS/LKB1 mutant NSCLC in humanized mouse model. Commun Biol. Feb 24 2022;5(1):167. doi:10.1038/s42003-022-03103-7
181. Meraz IM, Majidi M, Fang B, et al. 3-Phosphoinositide-dependent kinase 1 drives acquired resistance to osimertinib. Commun Biol. May 11 2023;6(1):509. doi:10.1038/s42003-023-04889-w

INDEX

INDEX

Italics indicate the page number of a photograph.

O

P

R

S

www.ingramcontent.com/pod-product-compliance
Lightning Source LLC
LaVergne TN
LVHW050527160826
845677LV00011B/1970

* 9 7 9 8 8 9 6 9 1 1 5 3 1 *